Also by Robert Calder

W. Somerset Maugham and the Quest for Freedom

Willie: The Life of W. Somerset Maugham

A RICHER DUST

Family, Memory and the Second World War

ROBERT CALDER

VIKING
CANADA

VIKING CANADA

Penguin Group (Canada), a division of Pearson Penguin Canada Inc.,
10 Alcorn Avenue, Toronto, Ontario M4V 3B2

Penguin Group (U.K.), 80 Strand, London WC2R 0RL, England
Penguin Group (U.S.), 375 Hudson Street, New York, New York 10014, U.S.A.
Penguin Group (Australia) Inc., 250 Camberwell Road, Camberwell, Victoria 3124, Australia
Penguin Group (Ireland), 25 St. Stephen's Green, Dublin 2, Ireland
Penguin Books India (P) Ltd, 11, Community Centre, Panchsheel Park,
New Delhi – 110 017, India
Penguin Group (New Zealand), cnr Rosedale and Airborne Roads, Albany, Auckland 1310,
New Zealand
Penguin Books (South Africa) (Pty) Ltd, 24 Sturdee Avenue, Rosebank 2196, South Africa

Penguin Group, Registered Offices: 80 Strand, London WC2R 0RL, England

First published 2004

1 2 3 4 5 6 7 8 9 10 (FR)

NATIONAL LIBRARY OF CANADA CATALOGUING IN PUBLICATION

Calder, Robert Lorin, 1941–
A richer dust : family, memory and the Second World War / Robert Calder.

ISBN 0-670-04313-3

1. Calder, Kenneth. 2. Soldiers—Saskatchewan—Biography.
3. Post-traumatic stress disorder—Patients—Saskatchewan—Biography.
4. Suicide victims—Saskatchewan—Biography.
5. World War, 1939-1945—Psychological aspects. I. Title.

FC3525.1.C44C44 2004   940.53'1   C2003-905836-0

Visit the Penguin Group (Canada) website at **www.penguin.ca**

To the memory of
Captain Kenneth Alexander Calder RCA
and to
Lieutenant John C. Gardiner RCA

You smug-faced crowds with kindling eye
Who cheer when soldier lads march by,
Sneak home and pray you'll never know
The hell where youth and laughter go.

—SIEGFRIED SASSOON,
"SUICIDE IN THE TRENCHES"

ACKNOWLEDGEMENTS

This is the most personal book I have written, but it would not have happened without the generous assistance of many people. My greatest debt is to John Gardiner, whose fierce loyalty to a friend's memory kept my uncle's final thoughts alive for so many years and delivered them to my brother and me. For that, for the long conversations about Ken, Italy and so many other matters, and for his encouragement of this project I am deeply grateful. His enthusiasm has been shared by his daughter, Suzanne, who has offered unqualified support and assistance.

I am also grateful to Ronald MacFarlane, who spent many hours recounting his experiences in the Italian campaign, responding to my queries and introducing me to other veterans of the Second Light Anti-Aircraft Battery. Michael and Jeffrey Stephaniuk and Dolores Zelinski welcomed me to two of their Italian Campaign Veterans Reunions in Yorkton, Saskatchewan, where I was able to meet and learn from a number of remarkable veterans.

Others who generously talked to me about Ken's military experiences were the late Roger Jean-Marie, Stan Ingleby, Ron Jones, Harold "Eddie" Shore, the late Garnet Matchett, the late Ernie Barshel, Chester Fannon, Gordon Irvine, Doug Lumb, Arthur Hoole, Al Affleck, Joe Yurkoski and Calvin Smith. Others who responded to inquiries were Frank Brazier, Jack Anderson, Lou Pickett, Sid Johnston, Harold Fretwell, Mariette Jean-Marie, Henk Hulshof, John Archer, Charles and Phyllis Bassingthwaite, and Farley Mowat.

My knowledge of Ken's civilian life and relationships was enriched by my conversations with a number of people who knew him or his story: the late Helena Nichols, the late Evelyn Lett, the late Hilda

Evans, David Story, the late Jack Fenwick and his wife Norah, Phyllis Burton, George Fenwick, Mona Jones, Lillian and Melvin McGillivray, Dr. Peggy Quinney and Dr. Art Quinney.

Warrant Officer Daryl Bazin, Colonel A.H. Carington Smith, Lieutenant-Colonel Robert Buckley, Angela Arnone, Gordon Barnhart, the *Legion Magazine* and the *Gunner's Newsletter* offered advice and provided direction to my research. My reading of the wartime issues of the Moose Jaw *Times-Herald* and Regina *Leader-Post* was made so much easier by the long hours Pat Borgerson spent poring over microfilms. The following institutions provided essential archival material: the National Archives of Canada (Tony Bonacci), the Saskatchewan Archives Board, the Directorate of History and Heritage, Department of National Defence (Isabel Campbell), the British Columbia Government Archives, the Special Collections Department of the University of British Columbia, the Court Registry of the Ministry of the Attorney General of British Columbia, the British Columbia Information Management Services, the Selkirk Mental Health Centre (Phyllis Bergmann), the Winnipeg Health Services Centre, the Saskatchewan Registered Nurses Association, the College of Physicians and Surgeons of Saskatchewan, the College of Physicians and Surgeons of British Columbia, the University of Saskatchewan Library, the Vancouver Public Library, the City of Vancouver Archives and the Moose Jaw Public Library.

In trying to understand the history of the Second World War and the experiences of the men who fought it, I have found the following books especially useful: Farley Mowat's *The Regiment, And No Birds Sang* and *My Father's Son,* David Bercuson's *Maple Leaf against the Axis,* Peter Stursberg's *The Sound of War,* Terry Copp and Bill McAndrew's *Battle Exhaustion,* Bill McAndrew's *The Italian Campaign,* Daniel Dancock's *The D-Day Dodgers,* Mark Zuehlke's *The Liri Valley,* John Ellis's *The Sharp End,* George Blackburn's *The Guns of Victory* and *Where the Hell Are the Guns,* Reginald Roy's *Sherwood Lett,* G.W.L. Nicholson's *The Gunners of Canada* and *The Canadians in Italy,* Howard Mitchell's

My War, Jack Donoghue's *The Edge of War,* Desmond Morton's *A Military History of Canada,* C. Sydney Frost's *Once a Patricia,* Strome Galloway's *Bravely into Battle,* Richard Malone's *A Portrait of War 1939–1945,* Fred Madjany's *The Battle of Cassino,* W.A.B. Douglas's and Brereton Greenhous's *Out of the Shadows,* Colin Duquemin's *Stick to the Guns,* Robert McDougall's *A Narrative of War,* Bill McNeil's *Voices of a War Remembered,* Paul Fussell's *Doing Battle,* Richard Turner's *Reminiscences of an Artillery Officer's Service,* Mary Jo Leddy's *Memories of War, Promises of Peace,* Fred and Norah Egener's *A Time Apart,* Mark Maclay's *Aldershot's Canadians,* Alex Bowlby's *Recollections of Rifleman Bowlby,* John Guest's *Broken Images: A Journal* and Bill McNeil's *Voices of a War Remembered.* The lines from "Suicide in the Trenches" are copyright Siegfried Sassoon and are reprinted by kind permission of George Sassoon.

At various stages of its writing, this book has been made better by the critical eyes of other writers: Warren Cariou, David Carpenter and my daughter, Alison, provided thoughtful critiques of the early chapters and set me in the right direction. Odile Calder read the completed typescript and offered shrewd advice about both style and content. Military historian Bill McAndrew's reading of the war chapters contributed substantially to the accuracy of my account of the campaigns in Italy and Holland. Any errors remaining in the book are mine. I am grateful to Diane Turbide, at Penguin Canada, for her encouragement and advice, and to John Sweet, whose meticulous editing improved the final text.

In the end, two people have been especially supportive and helpful. It was my brother, Kenneth, who so many years ago recognized the importance of preserving the family papers and memorabilia that had been handed down to us. Had it not been for him, these documents would have been lost. And as I began to collect material, he provided not only a keen memory of family history but a professional historian's practical knowledge of research sources and strategies. Finally, his careful critiques of various drafts, his insistence on both accuracy of detail and precision of language, have contributed immeasurably to whatever strengths the book might have.

No one, however, has lived with my writing of *A Richer Dust* as intensely as my wife, Holly. She has done so much more than merely tolerate my long absences in my study or at our lake retreat, my chronic irritability at deadlines missed and the pattern of our lives being built around the production of words. She has collaborated in so many important ways: scanning newspaper microfilms, reading drafts, accompanying me on field trips and interviews, and giving me a more objective perspective on the delicate issues of a complex story. I am extraordinarily lucky to have such a partner.

I am grateful to the University of Saskatchewan, which granted me a sabbatical leave in order to write the book, and which gave me a President's Social Science and Humanities Research Grant to enable me to tour the significant battle sites in Italy.

A RICHER
DUST

CHAPTER ONE

On an afternoon in the middle of July 1945, Lieutenant John Gardiner of the Royal Canadian Artillery was sitting in the back of an army supply truck bouncing along a narrow road near Utrecht, in the middle of Holland. The ride was no more comfortable than usual—it never could be in a military vehicle—but Gardiner was in good spirits. How could he not be? The sun was shining, there were patches of blue sky and the weather was warm; one could only rejoice at that after the rains, the floods and the mud of the Dutch spring. Moreover, except for the monotonous droning of the truck engine, the countryside was still. For nearly three months now, there had been no sounds of machine-gun fire, mortar assaults or artillery bombardments. For the first summer in three years, nobody was trying to kill John Gardiner.

On July 10, 1943, Gardiner had landed in southern Sicily with the First Canadian Infantry Division, and as an officer in the Second Light Anti-Aircraft Battery he had fought his way across Sicily, up the boot of Italy to Ortona, through the bloody battlefield of the Liri Valley, and over the seemingly endless rivers and marshes of the Gothic line in northern Italy. In March 1945 he had come to Holland with the First Division to clean out pockets of German resistance and to help provide food and supplies to a starving Dutch populace.

Now, with the European war over, Gardiner was impatient to get back to Canada—to his home, his family and especially his fiancée. His battery had turned in all its guns to the Demobilization Dump at Nijmegen in late June, and the army was now trying to fill up the days of thousands of idle men by providing sports activities: softball, volleyball, swimming, even horseshoe tossing. Those less athletically inclined were offered hastily arranged academic courses, taught by whatever officer had some expertise, in agriculture, welding, mathematics, English or typing. This was of little interest to Gardiner, however; before the war, he had completed several years of university study, and now he wanted only to get back to Montreal so he could complete his degree, get married and get on with the life that had been suspended in 1939.

Only a week before, Gardiner had taken an important step toward that future when, anticipating his repatriation, the army transferred him to the Fifth LAA Battery, a unit based in Montreal, his own military district and close to his home in St-Lambert. This meant, though, that for some weeks he would have to make a twice-weekly trip to the Second LAA headquarters to pick up his mail, and so on this day he had hitched a ride on the supply truck.

"You've struck it rich again, Lieutenant," said the sergeant in the mailroom as he handed him a bundle. "Somebody over there sure thinks a lot about you." Not bad indeed, thought Gardiner, as he sifted through the letters: a couple from his parents, one from a sister and of course several from Juliette, his fiancée. One letter, though, particularly caught his eye, and as he shoved the rest in his pocket to read on the bumpy return journey, he began to open it. It was from Ken Calder, a man he had come to know well on the battlefields of Italy and in the mud of Holland.

Calder was a '39er, one of the Canadians who had sailed to Great Britain in December 1939, and he had served in Europe until the day the Germans surrendered, in May 1945. Then he had left for England and for home, to be reunited with the wife he had married eight days before he boarded the troop train for overseas duty. He had not seen her for five and a half years, and Gardiner knew that his friend was worried. Her letters in the last year, while not explicitly negative, troubled Calder, and he had no way of knowing what he would find when he saw her again. By now, thought Gardiner, they would have been reunited in Vancouver, where she was working as a nurse, and he was curious about how that had gone.

Sitting in the back of the truck with several other men, waiting for the driver to return, Gardiner began to read Calder's meticulous, controlled handwriting:

6 July, 1945
Vancouver

My dear John:

Wish I weren't writing this tonight but you dared me to tell you how things are back here. You being, in my opinion, the best friend I've got, here it is: the whole shot with nothing held back. By the time this gets to you I will already be rotting in my grave but, then, what does it matter after all? . . .

Gardiner had scarcely begun to read when his eyes welled up and he could barely make out the words on the page. Embarrassed by the stares of the others, he mumbled an apology, stumbled out of the truck and made his way through the encampment to the forest beyond. Sitting on an old log, he finished the letter. There on its pages a man was pouring out the pain of his life, and Gardiner found it nearly unbearable. Flooded with grief and anger, he began to pound his fist into the gnarled wood beside him, oblivious to the blood smearing his knuckles. Nothing he would read in a long lifetime would ever affect him so profoundly.

In that summer of 1945, I was four years old and living in Moose Jaw, Saskatchewan, in a small house on Hochelaga Street with my mother and my seventeen-month-old brother, Kenneth. My father, a captain in the Canadian Army, had spent most of the war years as a training officer at various military bases in western Canada, and was home only rarely and for short visits. In my memory he is only an alien presence, an unfamiliar smell, someone who disturbed the comfortable, predictable, maternal warmth of the house.

Like all small children, my world was centred on my own immediate surroundings, bounded almost exclusively by the corners at each end of the block, and I happily patrolled the cracked and pitted sidewalk between them on my tricycle. I had a small band of friends: the older girl in the next house who kept a protective eye on me and a boy across the street with whom I would explore the wilderness of the vacant lot two doors away. My other companion was Spunky, an excitable offspring of a long line of black-and-white Boston terriers owned by the Calder family.

My little world nonetheless had its perils. The honey bees in the neighbours' yard, I learned, could exact a painful vengeance on a small boy attempting to block the entrance to their hive. Two slightly older boys who lived at the far end of the street flaunted their status as the local bullies, and my forays into their territory were always undertaken with an eye to how quickly I could retreat to the safety of my yard and my mother's protection. Even my friends, my allies, liked to torment me by pointing to the uniformed motorcycle cop, Mickey Mackie, parked in an alley across the street watching for speeders. If I did not behave myself, they warned me gravely, "he'll come and get you."

My only knowledge of the world beyond my street had been gained under the watchful eye of my mother, as I accompanied her shopping or on visits to friends and relatives. The morning of June 19, however, was to be different. There was an air of excitement in the house. My father was home on leave from Camp Shilo, in Manitoba, but I did not see much of him because he left the house that day soon after breakfast. I was then cleaned up, dressed up, brushed up and combed, and told that I was going to do something I had never done before: I was going to walk to my grandparents' house over on Alder Avenue all by myself. To get there, I would have to venture four blocks beyond the farthest point of my tricycle patrols, a stroll through a seeming no man's land of unfamiliar territory before I reached the safety of the Calder home. I was thrilled by the urgency with which my mother got me ready and by the importance she attached to my expedition.

The reason for this walk, and for the excitement in the house, was a man I had never seen before: my uncle Ken, my father's only brother, who was returning to Moose Jaw for the first time in nearly six years. I knew him only as the person who had sent me a birthday present of a stuffed tartan Scottie dog, with the word "CANADA" and red patches that he had sewn on each side of it and a collar with a band that said: "Second LAA RCA." The night before, he had arrived, along with 154 other returning soldiers, to a tumultuous crowd of relatives and friends waiting expectantly in the Regina railway station. My grandparents and my father had driven the forty-five miles across the flat southern prairie to pick him up, and now, in the light of a warm Saskatchewan June morning, I was going to see him for the first time. One young man was being sent off on the most adventurous mission of his life to meet another man who had travelled far beyond the wildest imaginings of his own youth.

My mother walked with me down to the end of our block and watched while I made my way around the corner, down the avenue and across Caribou Street. Even with motor traffic diminished by wartime restrictions on gasoline and tires, this seemed a risky venture to a small boy. From there, Grandma Calder, strategically placed on a corner near her house, was able to watch me make my way along the Technical Collegiate playing field, down First Avenue and across a vacant corner lot into her domain. On any other day the profusion of lamb's quarters, plantain, milkweed and scrub grass would have been too appealing, and I would have foraged along the dirt path for some dandelion flowers to take to my grandmother. On this morning, however, with Mother's firm command "Don't dawdle" still fresh in my mind, I understood that I had more serious matters to attend to.

With my grandmother at my side, I walked the remaining half-block to 923 Alder Avenue, a well-kept two-storey yellow wooden house built early in the century. As I tentatively made my way up the sidewalk, through the gap in the lilac hedge, its few remaining blossoms still fragrant in the morning air, I saw my father sitting on the wooden porch steps, a cigarette dangling between his fingers and a smile on his face. As I approached, he said, "Bobby, say hello to your uncle Ken." Beside him sat a man with a shock of thick dark hair, dark eyes and a full moustache. His broad grin, twisted slightly to one side, did much to dissolve my natural shyness, and I was won over completely when he gave me a little tin of English toffees brought from so far away.

I was aware of being the centre of attention, on show, so to speak, as my father's—and my grandparents'—trophy put before the returning soldier. Look what I produced, younger brother, while you were fighting the Germans, my father's smile suggested. And I seemed to pass inspection, if Uncle Ken's affable questions and kindly interest in my toys and my doings were any indication.

As the morning wore on and the novelty of our meeting faded, I busied myself with my building blocks on the kitchen floor while the brothers sat at the table drinking coffee and catching up on six years lived apart. From time to time I stole a glance at my uncle, so unfamiliar to me yet so important to my father and grandparents. I sensed that something significant had changed in my family life and that nothing would ever be quite the same again. This man seemed so different from my father and grandfather, but I liked him already and wanted to see him again.

I never did see my uncle Ken again. Or, rather, I did see him one more time, though I did not then know it. About three weeks after our meeting there was more unexpected activity in our house. I was surprised to see my father back home so soon, but this time there were no smiles. Instead, there were sombre conversations, and he and my mother were more than usually occupied with matters at my Calder grandparents' home. These were not, it seemed, things to concern a little boy, and so I was not included in the trips to Alder Avenue.

One afternoon a few days later my parents left me in the company of my other grandmother and departed the house. At a certain point Grandma Remey walked me down to Main Street, Moose Jaw's central thoroughfare, and we stood in front of Johnstone Dairies, a large old brown brick building pleasantly familiar to me because it was where my mother would buy me an ice cream cone on the way home from shopping. But there were no ice cream cones on this day.

Before long, a procession came very slowly down the street: a gun carriage covered with a flag and lots of flowers, a group of soldiers marching in slow and measured step, and then a military band playing sombre music. Following it was a line of cars moving more slowly than I had ever seen cars move. My grandmother told me I should watch closely because this procession had something important to do with my uncle. I stood, I think, as dutifully observant as a four-year-old boy can be, but I wondered why my grandparents and mother and father were riding in cars in this parade, and I resented being left on the sidewalk in the crowd of people who had gathered to watch. With drums muffled, the procession turned off Main Street onto Caribou and made its way slowly out to the prairie grassland west of town, to Rosedale Cemetery. As the groups of people left the sidewalks to return to their affairs and the traffic began to come to life again along Main Street, my grandmother and I walked the two blocks back to the little house to wait for my parents to come home. Grandma Remey, by nature stern and taciturn, was even quieter than usual. I wanted to know more about this parade, but all she would say was, "Someday, when you're much older, your mother will tell you all about it."

I was indeed much older before I understood what a funeral cortège was, and at least a dozen years went by before I began to learn what had led to my uncle being carried through the streets of Moose Jaw on a sunny July afternoon in 1945. Nearly sixty years later, I am still trying to understand what happened to him in that last wartime summer.

A few days after I had met him on my grandparents' front steps, Ken left for Vancouver to be reunited with the wife whom he had married a week before he left for England and whom he had not seen for five and a half years. Eight days after he had arrived in Vancouver, on an afternoon when she was away from the apartment, Captain Kenneth Alexander Calder, Royal Canadian Artillery, put on his uniform, turned on the gas of the kitchenette stove and killed himself. He was thirty-four years old.

Within a year of Ken's death, my father too disappeared from our lives. Though I was unaware of it, my parents' marriage had been deteriorating for some time, a process undoubtedly exacerbated by my father's long absences in various training centres, and my mother was already contemplating divorce when Ken passed through Moose Jaw. She began proceedings early in 1946, and her divorce was granted a year later.

When we were young and asked her why she had sought a divorce, Mother replied somewhat vaguely that she had come to the conclusion that "you boys would be better off without your father." Much later, after some of our strategic grilling, she admitted that the grounds were adultery, that she had begun to hear stories of affairs with various women in the military centres in which her husband had been serving. His own father, a Canadian Pacific Railway brakeman, learned painfully of some of this from the gossip of fellow trainmen working the Western routes.

Three years after my mother's death in 1994, I travelled to Moose Jaw, and in some dusty and brittle divorce documents contained in its stately old courthouse found the immediate cause of the end of the marriage. On the twenty-eighth of September, 1945, a man in Kingston had returned to his home, gone upstairs and found two people asleep in his bed; one was his wife and the other was Earle Fenwick Calder—my father. After calling a police constable, who arrived too late to witness the adultery but was able to evict the intruder, the man began divorce proceedings, and in April 1946 the sheriff of Moose Jaw called at our house to serve a writ of summons on Earle as co-respondent. Three months later, my mother filed for divorce.

In 1946, divorces were not easily obtained in Canada. There had to be strong, incontrovertible grounds established after a lengthy hearing, and the decision had to be approved by the Senate of Canada. These laws meant that, ironically, the man in Kingston never got his divorce; he was the only one who had actually seen the offending couple in bed and the law did not permit divorces to be granted solely on the testimony of the complainant. His testimony was, however, admissible in other divorce cases, and so he found himself trapped in his own deteriorating marriage but providing the evidence that gave my mother her divorce.

Throughout the difficult divorce process, my Calder grandparents encouraged and supported my mother rather than their own son. So enraged was my father by what he saw as an act of betrayal that he threatened violence against even his own parents, an alarming possibility in a man who still had his service revolver. Those who knew him and his hot temper were concerned enough that in the end the sheriff of Moose Jaw resorted to a traditional Western form of law enforcement: he ran Earle out of town, discreetly but firmly telling him to leave or risk being arrested for issuing threats.

Shortly afterward, Earle moved to Winnipeg, and he effectively vanished from our lives. We saw him only twice thereafter—brief and awkward visits when he returned for the funerals of his parents in 1954 and 1956—and we never in our lives received a single letter, card, telephone call or visit. No relative or friend ever reported hearing him ask about his sons.

As traumatic as it might have been for my parents and my Calder grandparents, the divorce had no immediate impact on Kenneth and me and caused little perceptible change in our lives. I had known my father only on his occasional trips home, and I doubt that he paid very much attention to me when he was there. My only recollection of his doing anything with me was on a summer day on a relative's farm south of Moose Jaw when, against the wishes of my mother, he grabbed his twelve-gauge shotgun, filled his pocket with shells and took me—then no more than four years old—with him down the hill to a poplar grove. He was out to shoot crows, and after warning me to stay well behind him, he fired explosively at the black silhouettes darting among the green branches.

My father's remoteness in my early years meant that when the divorce came, I suffered none of the trauma of the child who sees a beloved or even familiar parent leave the family home, and it was only later that I realized something essential was missing from my life. For my mother, of course, things were much different. Her pride prevented her from seeking alimony, but the divorce decree required Earle to provide $30 a month for the maintenance of his sons. Once in Winnipeg, however, he never paid a dime, and the laws of the day precluded a woman securing payment from an out-of-province defaulter. Having left high school after grade ten and with no job qualifications, Mother had only a salary of $18.50 a week as a doctor's receptionist and Mackenzie King's newly created but modest family allowance cheques with which to support herself and us.

It did not take long for our financial straits to force big changes to our lives. First we moved across town into Grandma Remey's two-bedroom house on South Hill, the working-class neighbourhood in which Mother had grown up. Then we left Moose Jaw entirely.

Mother's older sister, Dora, had married a young medical student, Arthur Scharf, in the late twenties, and now he was a well-established eye, ear, nose and throat specialist with a thriving practice, a growing family and a social prominence in Saskatoon. He proposed that Mother become his receptionist, for a better salary than someone with her qualifications could normally expect to get, with part of the arrangement being that my grandmother would also move and live with us in the upper floor of a rental house the Scharfs owned across the lane from their own home. For economic reasons, and with ambitions for her sons to attend the University of Saskatchewan located directly across the street, Mother accepted the offer, and we moved to Saskatoon in the late summer of 1948.

This arrangement meant that in only three years the dynamics in our family had dramatically altered. Uncle Ken's suicide and our father's departure meant that we had no immediate Calder relatives except our grandparents, and with their deaths in 1954 and 1956 we lost almost all contact with our father's family. As a result, we developed a much closer relationship with the Scharf family than is customary, even for people living in close proximity. With my cousin Jack, five years older than me, I formed a bond more akin to that of brothers, one that has lasted more than fifty years. Linda, born two years after me, has always been more like a sister than a cousin. A third Scharf cousin, Alan, older than I was by eleven years, left for graduate study at the University of Toronto when I was eleven, and this has made our relationship more distant.

Kenneth and I did not, however, find a surrogate father in Uncle Art, a man distant even to his own children. He was generous, but he hid his emotional life behind a wall of good humour and middle-class urbanity; and, like most men of his generation, he did not know how to communicate intimately with his children. He would give his daughter five dollars to buy milkshakes for the neighbourhood children, but he would never throw a ball around with her or watch his son play hockey. To my brother and me, at a further remove, he was a benign patriarch, someone on whom we were economically dependent. He was not a father, and we would never have thought of seeking his advice or confiding in him if we had a problem. Even so, he seemed to me to have an enviable life of wealth and freedom, and from my early teens on I was determined to become a medical doctor.

Having only briefly lived in a home with a father whom we could remember, Kenneth and I did not miss a family life we had not known. Outside the house, however, with our friends, we were conscious of being different. Several other children at our school were fatherless—the men lost in the war or in accidents—but we were the only offspring of divorced parents that we knew. The social stigma then so strongly associated with divorce, which my mother certainly felt, was never really apparent to us, but we occasionally had to find an answer to the awkward question, "Where's your dad?"

The only time I ever envied other children was when I saw fathers showing their sons how to hit a ball, throw a pass or shoot a puck, or when they took them to buy the proper skates or shoulder pads. I didn't play an organized sport until I took up softball at the age of thirty-five, and then the sense of being part of a team was so intoxicating that I continued playing into my fifties. As a child, my brother was even less athletic, and to this day he has less interest in sports, even as a spectator, than any man I know.

Though Kenneth and I grew into adolescence and young adulthood in Saskatoon, we kept in touch with our Moose Jaw roots until the deaths of our paternal grandparents. No one could have been more devoted to their grandchildren than the Calders, and we were much photographed, fussed over and shown off. At every birthday and on other special occasions we knew there would be a parcel from Moose Jaw, wrapped in sturdy brown paper, tied securely with heavy string and addressed with an indelible pencil on both sides. On the first occasion that Grandma Calder had sent a package of books and chocolate overseas to Ken, she was dismayed to learn that it had fallen apart in the mail. After that, only bombs or fire could wreck one of her parcels. (Even now I address both sides of my packages.)

Kenneth and I took our grandparents' adoration as our due. Had we thought about it, we would have recognized that we were all they had left of their family in old age. Their first-born, a daughter named Edna Muriel, had died of what was then called "summer complaint" in 1908 at the age of fifteen months, Ken had taken his own life and Earle had cut himself off from them in anger and disgrace. If they were bitter and disillusioned by the destruction of their family, they hid it behind a wall of affection and absolute devotion to their grandsons.

Mother took us frequently to Moose Jaw, but I was luckier than Kenneth because every July from 1949 to 1955 I was put on the bus to spend the summer months with my grandparents. Since two boys might be more than an elderly couple could handle, Kenneth had to stay in Saskatoon, though he often made shorter visits with me. It may have been an illusion, but I felt a sense of absolute freedom during those summers that I have never experienced since, nor expect to ever again, even in retirement. I always had a season's pass to Moose Jaw's famous Natatorium swimming pool and there began a lifelong habit of swimming every day, and on the way home through Crescent Park I would stop at the public library to find a book in which to lose myself on my grandparents' verandah. I had a friend, George McCarthy, who lived across the street, and for the summer we were inseparable pals. We would sneak into the local ballpark, look for adventure at the Moose Jaw Exhibition and try to jam the Coke machine at the service station around the corner with a slug. In my final year there, we began to find it more interesting to spy on the Girl Guide camp south of town.

One of the reasons I was at such liberty in those golden summer months in Moose Jaw was the absence of my grandfather during the week. He had retired from the CPR, but, though he was then in his seventies, he took another job travelling the gravel roads through southwestern Saskatchewan as a salesman for the Co-operative Creamery. In Shaunavan, Assiniboia, Ponteix and dozens of other dusty little prairie towns, the Chinese café owners placed their orders for milk, cheese and ice cream with him, and paid their bills—always in cash, never by cheque. So respected was Grandpa Calder that, when he retired several years later, the earnest young man who replaced him returned to Moose Jaw from his first southern road trip empty-handed and nearly in tears of frustration: the café owners wouldn't pay him, they would give their money only to "Mr. Calder." For them, Mr. Calder *was* the Co-operative Creamery. So my grandfather had to take to the road one last time, to explain to each customer that the young man with him indeed worked for the Creamery and could be trusted.

Grandpa Calder was always home for the weekend, and we observed a Sunday ritual that never changed in all the years I was there. After the morning service at St. Andrew's United Church we would have lunch at home, and then drive to the cemetery several miles to the west of the city so that my grandmother could tend to Uncle Ken's grave. Marked by a standard Canadian military tombstone erected in 1948, it lay beside the burial plots of Grandma Calder's father and of the baby Edna Muriel, taken so young and so long ago. While I would amuse myself looking at names and headstones, watching a gopher bound across the sparse prairie grass or perhaps finding the occasional wildflower along the fence, my grandmother picked weeds and arranged before Ken's tombstone the pansies, snapdragons or lilies freshly cut from her garden. As if he could do no more than deliver his wife to this shrine, Grandpa Calder stood mute in the shade of a nearby tree or went back to putter with his car. What silent conversations they carried on with the memory of their dead son I can only guess at. I do know that the drive back into town, along the same road on which the cortège had carried Ken only a few years earlier, was always quiet. And it always ended with an ice cream cone for me.

CHAPTER TWO

Our grandparents never spoke to us of our father and rarely of Uncle Ken, though whenever we drove by a marshy area of Moose Jaw's little creek, my grandmother invariably commented that Ken had said its smell reminded him of Italy. The house was nonetheless full of silent reminders of him and of a war still fresh in the minds of those who had so recently lived through it. On a table in the living room was a portrait of him, and across the room a second picture showed him standing in front of an eighteen-pound howitzer. On another table sat a nickel-plated lighter in the shape of an artillery piece. In the dining room hung an impressive framed document that I now realize was his King's Commission, George VI's appointment of him as an officer in the Royal Canadian Army. Sitting on a large old upright radio was a styl-ized British lion carved from oak taken from the bomb-damaged St. George's Chapel, and on the wall was a Windsor oak plaque that said "X Battery Super Heavy Group" on it. There was nothing in the house to suggest that our father had ever lived there—unless you counted a twenty-pound pike he had caught in Last Mountain Lake, mounted on a handsome wooden plaque and hanging in a dark and dusty corner of the back porch.

In our bedroom upstairs, which had been Ken and Earle's own room when they were growing up, was another photograph of Ken, dapper and handsome in his officer's uniform, leaning against a mili-tary biplane. There was a metal trunk with Uncle Ken's name and that of his unit stamped on the side, and at the foot of the bed was a khaki army blanket then employed to keep little boys warm on chilly autumn evenings. On the bedside table was a lamp fashioned from a large and gleaming artillery shell. Tucked under some clothing in the chest of drawers, we once discovered to our delight two automatic pistols in leather cases—an Italian Beretta and a German Luger. Later, in cleaning out the house after my grandmother's death, we found bayonets, a commando dagger, a Gurkha kukri with its deadly curved blade, a package of aircraft recognition cards, some army mess tins, and various cartridges, shells and other military paraphernalia.

Though we knew little about Uncle Ken and our father, and indeed asked few questions about them, the military relics made a great impression on young minds already attracted to the war films we saw regularly in Saturday morning double features. The Canadian historian David Bercuson, younger than me by four years, recalls that in the post-war years "war books, war comics, and war movies were the fare of every boy. We refought the war with our toy guns, trying to emulate the scruffy infantrymen we saw shuffling in the newsreels. We were acutely conscious that there had been a war, that it had been very important, and that most of our fathers, uncles, teachers, and friends' fathers had been in it."

For Kenneth and me, an awareness of the recent war was further intensified one day when we discovered a giant stack of *Star Weekly*s faithfully saved throughout the war and stored in our grandparents' back porch. As we happily plundered their pages for pictures of fighter planes, tanks and cannons to paste in a mammoth scrapbook, the martial propaganda that had been aimed at our elders only a few years earlier struck home with us, and we became gripped by a passion for guns, things military and anything in khaki. We took to haunting the war surplus section of the Moose Jaw Army and Navy Store, still amply supplied with an exotic variety of canteens, folding camp shovels and mess kits in 1950; and at the age of fourteen I was even able to harass my mother into letting me buy a surplus .303 Lee-Enfield rifle. It would be two years before I was old enough legally to fire it, but it was thrilling merely to hold a weapon in my hands.

As Kenneth and I grew into adolescence, we became increasingly aware that our uncle and our father had been skilled hunters and fishermen, and champion marksmen. There was that huge pike on the porch wall, and some faded photographs of men leaning against automobiles with rows of mallards arrayed on the ground in front of them. In a little wooden box in a bedroom of my grandparents' house we found a number of gold, silver and bronze Dominion Marksmen medals, and another awarded to Ken for being on the provincial champion small-bore rifle team in 1939–40. In fact, as we learned from some yellowed newspaper clippings, Ken and Earle had both been on the winning team in 1938 as well as 1939. In one of those years their team had placed sixth in a national competition. Sparked by these discoveries, Kenneth and I developed an interest in outdoorsmanship, and I even joined a small-bore rifle club in Saskatoon.

Our fascination with things military had another, and much more profound, effect on Kenneth. As a young child he had shown no interest in reading, to the point that my mother began to be concerned. Then he discovered my "Biggles" books, W.E. Johns's romantic, jingoistic tales of a dashing British Second World War fighter pilot and his heroic pals. Before long he had devoured my collection and was seeking out the rest of the series. This soon broadened into an interest in the Second World War in general and German history in particular. By high school he knew he wanted to become a student of modern history.

Perhaps because he was named after him, Kenneth at a very early age became inordinately attached to the memory of Uncle Ken—not his own memory, because he could not possibly remember a man who died when he was only eighteen months old, but his own *idea* of Captain Kenneth Calder, RCA. When we had asked about the absence of this man, so strongly present in the various relics in our grandparents' home, Mother explained ambiguously that he had died "as a result of the war." In young boys' imaginations this assuredly meant that he had been killed in battle.

My brother's interest in Ken led first to his putting an enlarged 1939 photograph of him—one of many that had come from the house in Moose Jaw—on his bedroom wall. It was a picture of a young man in a Canadian Army officer's uniform: neatly knotted tie, close-fitting tunic with Sam Browne belt across the shoulder, and a peaked cap with the badge of the Royal Canadian Artillery. His shoulders at an angle to the camera, his look is intent though the eyes are soft. Together with the fine features, strong jawline and thin Ronald Colman moustache, he is every inch the heroic soldier of a young boy's imagination.

Before long, Kenneth hung a second photograph of Ken, and years later he was able to add a framed certificate naming a lake in northern Saskatchewan after him. Recently, his wife, Odile, said to me, "In the thirty years I've known your brother, he's always had a picture of your uncle on his wall. Not always one of you or even your mother, but always one of Ken." Then she added shrewdly, "I think that he's built an image of his uncle in his mind: the good officer, who served his country responsibly and courageously. It's what he's wanted to be."

This fascination with Uncle Ken led to an odd incident when Kenneth was eight or nine years old. One early November afternoon I was hanging around with some friends outside the confectionery store near our school when Kenneth came up with a grin on his face.

"Guess what," he said.

"What?"

"You know the Remembrance Day ceremony next week?"

"Yeah."

"Well, Miss Chase asked if anyone in the class had a father who died in the war, and I told her that I did. So I get to carry the flag in the ceremony. In front of the whole school!"

"You moron!" I replied. "It wasn't our father who was killed in the war, it was Uncle Ken."

"Was not!"

"Was so! Everybody knows that. Ask Mom."

It wasn't until Mother patiently explained things to Kenneth that he believed me. And he did not carry the flag on Remembrance Day.

The confusion of the two men in Kenneth's mind had as much to do with our lack of knowledge of our father as it did with our awareness of the death of our uncle. As loving as she was, my mother was never effusive, and she believed much more in doing things than in talking about them. Her strategy in dealing with her sons and their departed father was to say little and wait to respond to whatever questions they might ask. We, however, took our lead from her and, in our early years, avoided raising the subject.

The silence about this part of our family history was so pronounced that when I was thirteen a well-meaning and normally unintrusive cousin of our father felt compelled to write to offer my mother some advice:

> *Even though [the boys] have not mentioned their father, that is no sign that they are not wondering about many things. It might be better for you to open the subject with them, either each one alone or both together, and encourage them to talk to you about it. They are bright boys, and it is not good for them mentally to get the idea that there is something shameful, which they cannot mention even to you. Of course they would not want to talk about it outside the family, but they will feel more secure and satisfied if they know that you have accepted it as one of those things which sometimes happens in life but which you are not letting spoil your life or theirs. Tell them any good things you can remember about Earle, and tell them he became sick in his mind some years ago. Perhaps like a sickness of the body, he may recover some time . . . When they grow older you can tell them more if they seem to want to hear it.*

This letter was occasioned by the death of my grandfather in 1954, when the subject was made more relevant by the return of my father for the funeral. Recalling the threats he had made eight years earlier, and having had no contact with him since, my grandmother was apprehensive about his reappearance. She was concerned, moreover, that he would demand part of the estate, though my grandfather had emphatically left everything to her.

My mother nevertheless believed that Earle should be at his father's funeral and, without my grandmother's knowledge and with the help of the Salvation Army, located him in Winnipeg, where he was working for a moving and storage company. Neither Mother nor Grandma Calder felt comfortable being alone with him in the family home, however, so he stayed for the duration with a cousin.

If the two women were apprehensive on the morning Earle was to arrive, Kenneth and I were excited. We tried to busy ourselves with our Superman and Blackhawk comics, but we were listening for a knock from the front porch. Then, glancing out the kitchen window while she was mixing some cookie dough, Grandma Calder suddenly exclaimed, "Oh!" There was a man standing in the backyard, and the man was Earle. He had slipped down the narrow gravel driveway running beside the house and seemed to be gathering his courage to knock on the back door.

It was clear to the adult members of the family that Earle had fallen on hard times in the eight years since he had left Moose Jaw, and even to my young eye he looked shabby. His return bus ticket had been paid for by the Salvation Army, and since the only clothes he owned were the threadbare ones he was wearing, he went through my grandfather's closet for something that, however outdated, might be suitable for a funeral. When it was learned that he did not own a watch, Kenneth was cajoled by Mother and Grandma Calder into surrendering his grandfather's gold pocket watch, which had made him the envy of the rest of us in the few days since his grandmother had decided he should have it. It was a relic of a man we loved and respected, a handsome watch he'd always kept in his vest pocket, where it was attached by a chain. The cheap replacement hastily purchased from Woolworth's had no such cachet and did nothing to lessen my brother's indignation.

Though he might not cut an impressive figure, Kenneth and I were nonetheless intensely curious to see this man who was our father. Initially, he was awkward with us, partly I suppose because of the situation and partly because he never had much experience with children. We, of course, were uncertain how we should behave, especially when my mother, for whom it must have been an ordeal, was present. After a while, though, we all became more relaxed, and we showed him our collection of balsa wood gliders and toy guns, which, though made of tin, fired only harmless rubber darts.

Our treasures quickly paled to childish playthings when we learned that Earle had been a small-arms instructor during the war and had taught self-defence. He even knew jiu-jitsu! Before long we were slipping, expertly we thought, out of full nelsons and taking each other down on the lawn in front of my grandparents' house. I recall being pleased that my summer friend, George McCarthy, was there to see how much my father knew about such combat manoeuvres. Armed with the secret of these exotic martial skills, I knew we would be able to lick a legion of Moose Jaw toughs.

When Earle returned to Winnipeg after the funeral, it was with no promises of seeing us again, but Kenneth and I quietly hoped that the renewed contact might in some way continue. However, as if the meeting had never occurred, we heard nothing from our father, and we made no attempt to approach him. Eighteen months later, in the days following my grandmother's funeral, we met him for a second, briefer time, an occasion lacking the curiosity value of the first and certainly without any deepening of a relationship with him. His detachment from us is reflected in a brief letter he wrote to his American cousin a few weeks later, which, when I discovered it forty-one years later, still had the power to pain me: "I was very happy to see you in Moose Jaw. You were one of two people I hoped most to see. Uncle Frank was the other."

My grandmother left the bulk of her estate to Mother, with a thousand dollars going to a bachelor brother in Maple Creek and a thousand dollars being held in trust for each of Kenneth and me. In an attempt to forestall any challenge by my father, she left him eight hundred dollars. He took the money and returned to Winnipeg. We never saw him again.

⌒

Grandma Calder's death cut our last meaningful link with Moose Jaw, and we got on with our young lives in Saskatoon. As our mother had hoped, Kenneth and I both went to the university and both earned master's degrees—his in History and mine in English. In 1965, I was married and began to teach as an instructor in the Department of English. By the summer of 1967, we had both been admitted to Ph.D. programs in Britain and had won fellowships—mine a Canada Council Doctoral Fellowship and his a Commonwealth Scholarship.

Several months before we were to leave for Britain, Uncle Art received a letter from the Hospital for Mental Diseases in Selkirk, Manitoba. It was from Dr. H.U. Penner, of the hospital's Division of Psychiatry:

> This letter is to request some information and help. Mr. Earle Calder has been a patient for some 3 ½ years at the hospital here. We are interested in having Earle re-establish some of the contacts which he formerly had. We are requesting your assistance in tracing his family and to help us in contacting the family. My understanding is that he has two sons in Saskatoon.

After discussing the matter with Mother, Uncle Art replied to Dr. Penner:

> I was disappointed but not too surprised to hear about Earle Calder. When I last saw him many years ago he was not a very

responsible person. However, as a physician & former brother-in-law (his wife of many years has recently re-married), I hope you will feel free to give me any pertinent history, as well as his mental & physical history and prognosis. When I hear from you I shall write you again.

After Dr. Penner wrote to say that Earle was being treated for the effects of chronic alcoholism and repeated his suggestion that he would benefit from contact with his sons, Mother decided that Kenneth and I should be told. We were no longer young boys entranced by jiu-jitsu moves, but young men capable of making responsible decisions.

Kenneth and I discussed the matter at some length. We were disconcerted. On the one hand, our curiosity made us interested in seeing our father again; on the other, we knew instinctively that this would disturb Mother. As well, any contact with our father invited future obligations—Mother feared that he would begin to ask us for money—and perhaps more involvement than we wanted. He might, we speculated, move to Saskatoon, and he could then become our responsibility or an interference. We were about to embark on an adventure beyond anything we could have imagined as children, and we were not prepared to jeopardize it for a man to whom we owed nothing. And so we did nothing.

Three years later, I completed my Ph.D. in English Literature at Leeds University, and with our six-month-old daughter, Alison, my wife and I returned to Saskatoon, where I was granted tenure at the University of Saskatchewan. We bought a house in my old neighbourhood, and within a few years had added two sons, Kevin and Lorin, to our family.

Even before Kenneth finished his Ph.D. in History at the London School of Economics, he was recruited by the Department of National Defence for its Defence Research Board. During his last year in Britain, while serving as best man at a friend's wedding in Argentonsur-Creuse, he fell in love with the bride's sister, Odile Gravereaux, and in 1972 they were married. When their son was born in 1981, he was christened Robert—after me—Alexandre, a rendering of Uncle Ken's middle name that also honoured the French side of Robert's parentage.

There was an inevitability about Kenneth's ending up connected to the Canadian military. Conscious that both Uncle Ken and our father had been soldiers—indeed, we knew little else about them—Kenneth had joined the militia at the age of sixteen. Quite deliberately, he chose an artillery unit: the Twenty-first Medium Battery in Saskatoon. This was the era when the Diefenbaker government focused the militia on national survival in the aftermath of a nuclear attack, and when after two years Kenneth had not touched a single artillery piece, he quit.

In his first year of university Kenneth joined the Canadian Officers' Training Corps. As an officer cadet for two summers, he endured the heat, sand and poison ivy of the Royal Canadian Armoured Corps School at Camp Borden, Ontario. Kenneth felt at home in the army—as Colonel Charlie Simonds, son of Ken's commander in Italy, General Guy Simonds, once said, "a member of the family"—and did well. The course report after his first summer said: "Ordinarily he is a quiet withdrawn person but when placed in command of men, his personality changes to that of a self-assured, imaginative and decisive leader. He organizes and controls those under his command with ease, by means of logical, easily understood orders which he ensures are carried out."

Now, in 1971, perhaps predictably, Kenneth was back with the military—not as a soldier like those two uniformed men in the family photograph album, but nonetheless a part of National Defence.

CHAPTER THREE

One day in January 1975 my mother asked me to drop in to see her in her Saskatoon home; she had, she said tersely, something to show me. It was a short obituary from the *Winnipeg Tribune* that a friend had sent her:

EARLE CALDER

> On December 28, 1974 at Selkirk, Mr. Earle Calder, aged 64 years formerly of Moose Jaw, Sask. Graveside burial services will be held in the military section of St. Clements Churchyard Cemetery on Tuesday December 31 at 10.30 a.m. with Rev. Daniel Ash officiating. Gilbart Funeral Home, Selkirk, in care of arrangements.

Mother said very little. For my part, I read the clipping with interest but no more emotion than if it had announced the death of some noted but distant public figure—a politician, a film star or an athlete. I thought only abstractly of what he had denied himself: the sons he barely knew, their achievements that he could not share, and the grandchildren he had never seen and probably never knew existed. I wondered how he had died, how he had lived out his final years, but I felt no grief. It was, I thought, the end of a story that had lost its impact for me—if, indeed, there had ever been any impact—many years earlier.

After that, life went on. In the mid-seventies, my marriage broke down and I was divorced. Painfully aware that I was then nearly the same age as my father was when he left Moose Jaw, I worked very hard to maintain a close contact with my children and to preserve some semblance, at least, of a fatherly relationship with them. For ten years I lived with a stylish young woman, whose ambitions would later make her one of Saskatchewan's most recognizable political figures. But this relationship too broke down. Then, in the summer of 1991, I fell in love with Holly, a beautiful and bright student who had been in my British Novel class, and in September 1994, two months before my mother died, we were married.

At the age of fifty-three, I was where I wanted to be—in a calm and secure bay, as I characterized it in the poem I gave Holly on the morning of our wedding. I had carved a respectable academic career, I had earned a modest reputation as a writer, and I had (I think) preserved as good a relationship with my children as a divorced parent can have. My mother's dying was distressing—she had always been so strong and seemingly immutable—but it was a nightmare that Kenneth and I always knew we would face, and now it was over. With the silencing of her voice, there seemed to be nothing more to be said about Moose Jaw, Ken, Earle, and our family's past.

Kenneth in the meantime had enjoyed a successful career in Ottawa, moving up in the Department of National Defence so that by August 1991 he had become the Assistant Deputy Minister for Policy and Communications. Until 1996 he had, as a good bureaucrat would say, succeeded in having no public profile, but that changed when the Somalia Inquiry into the beating death of Sidane Arone began to hear testimony from high-ranking military officers and civilian administrators in the department. Kenneth's name started to appear in testimony and newspaper articles.

The media, responding to the Canadian public's disgust with the brutal murder, went into a feeding frenzy. They looked for a story more sensational than the killing of a Somalian teenager: cover-ups in the highest echelons of the Department of National Defence. Opposition parties sought to embarrass the government and force some department resignations. The atmosphere of the time was well caught by the late Brian Dickson, former Chief Justice of the Supreme Court of Canada, in his 1997 Vimy Award address, when he "observed the careers of several individuals destroyed and their characters savagely attacked, without their having been given a real chance to answer the charges made against them." He also wondered "whether all those called to account for the regrettable events really enjoyed rights of due process during the very public ordeal they had to endure. Why, in such circumstances, presume guilt rather than innocence before making what amounts to public judgements on such weighty issues?" Kenneth had built an impeccable career over twenty-five years, but who could say what might be the consequences for him or for his friends and colleagues of a false witness, an unfortunate phrase or even an unfavourable television performance?

At this point, something remarkable happened.

As if summoned from the shadows of the remote and little-known past by his nephew's long-standing veneration and by his current crisis, Uncle Ken came dramatically back into our lives.

The uncomfortable publicity that surrounded the inquiry had broadcast the name "Ken Calder" across the country, and it had presented the name in a military context. For one man, a Second World War veteran, this linking reawakened painful and troubling memories, and so I received a telephone call from Kenneth one June evening in 1996. "You're not going to believe this," he told me. "I can hardly believe it myself. Let me read you a letter I just got in the mail from a man in Quebec." This was the letter:

> *Coaticook, Que.*
> *7/6/96*

> *Mr. Ken Calder*
> *Dear Sir:*
>   *This morning, while reading the paper, I saw your name and title, and my memory became fully alert. There may be*

many Ken Calders in Canada and I am writing to you in order to find out whether your family is or was connected with Moose Jaw.

The occasion for my letter to you is that about this time of year, 1945, my friend Capt. Ken Calder had just returned with the first major repatriation draft of the 1st Division. After only a few days in Canada, including less than a week with his parents in Moose Jaw, he committed suicide on the West Coast. The day before, he had written a long letter to me in which he unloaded his bitterness.

Apparently I was the only one he wrote to. His family wanted me to send the letter from Europe. It was such a bitter letter that I refused to send it to his parents. I had lost a brother in action in 1943, so I was quite conscious of parents' loss.

However, I still have the letter and would now be willing to release it to Ken's relatives. Ken had a brother who was a captain. I've no idea whether he's alive; if so where he would live.

I was a lieutenant with 2 L.A.A. Battery (Yorkton, Sask.) with Ken.

Let me know as to whether I have knocked at the right door.

John C. Gardiner

I was stunned. It was over fifty years since Ken had killed himself, and we had long ago concluded that we had learned all we would ever know about him and the circumstances of his death—and it was precious little. As we grew up, Mother had gradually abandoned her vague explanation that he had "died as a result of the war," and admitted to us that he had committed suicide. Several years before the war, she said, he had gone around with a nurse named Margaret, but they had broken off the relationship. Sometime in the autumn of 1939, they had met again at a dance or party; before long they became engaged, and shortly before Ken went overseas, they were married. A friend of Margaret had told my mother that when she asked Margaret why she had done it, she replied: "It doesn't matter. He won't be coming back anyway." When Ken did return and was reunited with her in Vancouver, he discovered that she was having an affair with a Dr. Boyd Story, and so he killed himself. Mother did not know whether Margaret had married Story or whether she was even still alive.

The name "John Gardiner" meant nothing to me, but it jogged the historian's memory in Kenneth. For decades he had carefully preserved a box of memorabilia that had come from our grandparents' home and contained the few scraps of writing connected to Uncle Ken. Sadly, none of the letters he had dutifully written to his parents every fortnight throughout the war had survived the ruthless cleaning out of the house after my grandmother's death. In more recent years Kenneth had been able to add a handful of letters that Ken had written to his American cousins during the war, but there was little else other than his service medals, some photographs and a fragment of a diary he had kept in Italy in 1944.

Among the relics, however, were two letters from wartime buddies of Ken, and these had always intrigued my brother. One, sent to our grandmother by a fellow officer, told of meeting him by chance in Vancouver the night before his death and hearing the details of his unhappy reunion with his wife. The other, addressed to Ken and clearly a response to some form of suicide letter, was from a John Gardiner. Not knowing how we might ever find Mr. Gardiner, we had resigned ourselves to his being another mystery locked away in the box of memorabilia.

Suddenly, in 1996, Gardiner's letter changed all that. A name on a piece of paper became a person, someone who not only had known Ken and served with him in Europe but possessed a suicide letter from him. It would be possible, after all the years of silence, to have Ken's words speak for themselves of his decision to end his own life. As my brother said, "It's like a voice from the past." He meant Mr. Gardiner, but the voice we wanted to hear was Ken's.

Before hanging up the telephone, we agreed that Kenneth should waste no time in writing to Mr. Gardiner; he would have to be an elderly man, and his handwriting appeared none too firm. Five days later, Gardiner telephoned Kenneth and they talked for an hour. He seemed as fascinated to have discovered us as we were to have heard from him, and he was anxious to deliver the letter in person. There was about him more than a touch of Coleridge's Ancient Mariner, a man compelled to tell his tale. In the summer of 1945 he had been chosen to receive the final thoughts of a man for whom life could no longer be endured, and for fifty-one years he had carried the burden of this trust. He had often told the story of Captain Calder to his children, who thereby became his witnesses, but catharsis would come with delivering the Ken Calder he knew to my brother and me.

Though Kenneth was about to begin a gruelling schedule of appearances before the Somalia Commission and would be leaving for a badly needed vacation in France a few days later, he invited Gardiner to spend a weekend with him in Ottawa. When I heard this, it took me all of about ten minutes to decide to fly to Ottawa to join them.

I arrived at my brother's home late in the afternoon on the last Friday in June, when Kenneth and Odile were still at work, and was greeted by my fourteen-year-old nephew, Robert. An hour later Mr. Gardiner arrived, and he was hardly the frail, white-haired, tottering figure we had envisaged from his letter. Standing nearly six feet tall, he was balding with a fringe of grey hair at the sides and back, but he stood straight-backed. Though indeed in his early eighties, he had the physique and vigour of a much younger man, and, as we were to discover over the next two days, a sharp intellect, a remarkably detailed memory and an ability to talk like no one we had ever known.

And talk Gardiner did—over drinks when Kenneth and Odile returned, over a leisurely dinner and long into the evening. He talked of growing up in a bilingual home in Montreal, the son of an English immigrant father and French Canadian mother, of his forty-eight-year marriage to his wartime sweetheart, Juliette, and his career as vice-president of the Canadian National Railways. He talked of his experiences in the Royal Canadian Artillery, of meeting Ken in England and then getting to know him in Italy in 1944, of Ken's increasing depression over his separation from his wife and of receiving Ken's suicide letter. The letter itself he did not produce, and though Kenneth and I were intensely curious, we hid our impatience and refrained from pressing him about it. When the long evening ended without its anticipated climax and I went to bed, it was with a profound understanding of the meaning of "unrequited."

It was the next morning after breakfast that we got to see the letter. Sitting over coffee in the shade of the maple tree in the small backyard, Gardiner brought out a binder and, without saying anything, handed it to me. He had meticulously arranged the papers in clear plastic sheets: the suicide letter, letters from my grandmother and my father to Gardiner, a brief history of their artillery battery, and a typed copy of a speech that Gardiner had given following Juliette's funeral in 1994 and in which he had mentioned Ken. But, of course, it was Ken's letter that I turned to first. There it was, in my uncle's own neat, steady hand:

6 July 45
Vancouver

My dear John,

Wish I weren't writing this tonight but you dared me to tell you how things are back here. You being, in my opinion, the best friend I've got, here it is: the whole shot with nothing held back. By the time this gets to you I will already be rotting in my grave but then, what does it matter after all?

After a week of "don't touch me" when all I wanted was a little love and affection, my wife Margaret whom I idolized finally summoned up courage to tell me that she had been unfaithful. I took that like a good soldier, I think, but then she put over the belly punch. She told me that she had never loved me and that she had lived with several men all the time I had been away. One in my own home town shortly after I went overseas. She won't say who he is but said I'd never reach him so something clicked into place and I asked her if he was dead. She couldn't answer that so I presume that I was right. Salute to the R.A.F.!

She has told me, John that her affair with Dr. Boyd Story has lasted for a year and only quit when I wired from Halifax. She also says that she had far more experience with the one in M. Jaw. Let me tell you about Story. Married, two sons, one in the navy. His wife is supposed to know all about it, also the navy son. The both of them told me that he couldn't get along with her so she, Mrs. Story, sleeps with some other guy and Story himself takes Margaret. That's the Canada I came home to, John. For some sadistic reason Margaret gave me the supreme insult by telling me she was not a virgin when we married. Claimed all kinds of previous experience.

John, believe me, I cried and pleaded with that girl all day to give me *another chance to start over but she turned me down. I still love her, God damn it, so I'm licked. Tomorrow afternoon when she is out I'm going to put on my serge, seal up the very small kitchen and turn the gas stove on. I want it that way, John, because I still love that girl and she killed me two days ago. Please don't feel bad, it was nice to know you because you were my buddy even if it was for only a short while. You very ably took the place of another, Fred Cooper, who died a year ago last September.*

Please don't feel that I'm doing the wrong thing. I want release, not maggots in my brain for the rest of my life. I'm sane, John, in spite of what the coroner's jury will say but I'll be out of this rotten world. I forgot to tell you that 9 out of 10 returned

*men are coming back to the same thing. This is the only victory
the German Army ever had.*

*I'm putting a condensed version in the mail for the
Commish. Of Police so they'll know why. Had to say goodbye,
John, and this is it. I'll never find happiness so I'm checking out.
Nothing can hurt me now. Good-bye old pal, good luck, may
you never know sorrow like mine. This is my farewell to you
John, you and I and perhaps Juliette if you wish. This dirty
bitch I married and still love isn't fit to clean Juliette's shoes.*

Farewell dear friends.

Ken

I had never seen a suicide letter before, but I was surprised by Ken's
cool, rational description of his disillusionment and of his preparations
to kill himself next day. This was not the voice of a deranged man
incoherently crying out; it was the composed testament of a man who
had looked around him and found his life untenable. I handed the
letter to Kenneth without much more than a softly uttered "Jesus!" I
didn't know what to say.

Why had Gardiner kept the letter for fifty-one years, long after his
children had told him he should throw it away? "Out of the thousand
men whom Ken got to know during the war, he chose me," Gardiner
said, the passion evident in his voice. "How often does a man ever
choose you to trust with his final thoughts?"

On Sunday afternoon we all went our separate ways. Not only were
we grateful to John Gardiner for having preserved and given us this voice
from the past, we had quickly developed a bond with this man in whom
the memory of Ken had been kept alive for so long. For his part, he
seemed relieved of a burden, having told his tale, not to disinterested
listeners, but to two men for whom it was deeply and intensely personal.

If a burden had been lifted from Gardiner, it had, it seemed, been
put on me. Gardiner had repaid his friend's trust by conveying his last

words to us; but now, I wondered, what was I to do with them? Gardiner's daughter, Suzanne, had told him that "it's like a Russian novel," and indeed it was the stuff of fiction. But Ken Calder was not fictional. He had existed, and his tragedy was the rarely told story of thousands of Canadian soldiers returning from war to disillusionment, to the discovery that the home they had dreamed of on the battlefields of Europe no longer existed. If Ken were to come alive again, I would have to find the truth of the life he had actually lived.

And so I began a search for that life—in military files, coroners' statements, court records, and in the memories of the remaining soldiers and civilians who had known him. What I could not then have known was that, in seeking to understand what had led to an event which had so transformed the Calders, I would discover that it had profoundly affected—in radically different ways—families beyond mine, families spread from British Columbia to Quebec. And I never expected that my search for my lost uncle would also become a search for my absent father. And, ultimately, for myself.

CHAPTER FOUR

Any search for Ken Calder would have to begin in Moose Jaw, and six weeks after our meeting with John Gardiner, Holly and I drove south through the Saskatchewan grain fields ripening on a hot August afternoon. For most of the past century Moose Jaw has suffered from its proximity to Regina, which gained immensely from being named the North-West Territories' capital in 1883, and today it struggles for a share of the province's dynamic urban growth. When Ken was born there on June 29, 1911, however, Moose Jaw was at the crest of a wave of prosperity that had begun thirty years earlier and that it has never enjoyed since. In more ways than one, Ken was the child of optimism.

Moose Jaw had been created in 1882 by the decision of the Canadian Pacific Railway to place its divisional point at the junction of the Thunder Creek and the Moose Jaw River. Almost exactly halfway between Winnipeg and Calgary, it had an excellent water supply, and within a decade it had become the most important railway centre in what would soon be the Province of Saskatchewan. It was here that the CPR joined the Soo line, which came north from Minneapolis and St. Paul, and linked western Canada with Chicago and the eastern United States. Every autumn, hunting parties from Chicago and Minneapolis rode the line north to hunt waterfowl on Lake Johnston, a few miles southwest of Moose Jaw, and folklore has it that Chicago gangsters later used the city as a temporary haven from eager federal government agents and competing gangs. Though Moose Jaw had other industries, such as flour milling and brewing, it was a railway city in 1911, with 2,500 men employed on a payroll of $250,000 a month.

The effect on the local population of the CPR's decision in 1882 had been immediate and dramatic. In July of that year there were fewer than twenty people living at the Thunder Creek–Moose Jaw River junction; by October there were over 2,500. Though Moose Jaw lost the status of capital to Regina the next year, as it would later lose the university to Saskatoon, it was nonetheless incorporated as a town in 1884 and then as a city in 1903. By 1906 its population had grown to 6,250, and five years later, at the time of Ken's birth, it boasted 20,633. So explosive was its growth that in the year between 1910 and 1911 its property assessments doubled from $13,548,402 to $27,770,453.

Like many young men and women of his generation, Ken Calder was the offspring of parents who had been drawn west by the promise of the economic boom. His father and mother had followed different but not uncommon paths to get there. His mother, Ida May Fenwick, was born in Mountbridges, Ontario, in 1882, the oldest of four children of John and Macy Fenwick. When Ida was four, her mother died giving birth to the youngest child, a girl called Macy, and two years later John Fenwick, his brother, Ida and her two younger brothers left to homestead in western Canada. Macy remained with relatives in Ontario, where she was brought up and schooled as a proper young lady, and she did not rejoin her family in Saskatchewan until she was a young adult.

Ida, meanwhile, was given a much different education. At the age of six she assumed the roles of housekeeper to the men and mother to her brothers, aged three and four, while her father and uncle built their homestead at Stoney Plain, little more than a postal address halfway between Regina and Moose Jaw. Their first home was a sod house built on the open prairie, and when the men were breaking the soil during the day, the young girl was given a rifle with which to defend the property against the Blackfoot and Cree frequently roaming the land.

When her young brothers were old enough to care for themselves, Ida was sent to school in Moose Jaw, where she took a course in tailoring and later worked in a tailor's shop. So accomplished was she in the skills expected of pioneer women that for the remainder of her life she would win numerous prizes for her baking at the Moose Jaw and Regina agricultural exhibitions and for her knitting at the Canadian National Exhibition in Toronto.

Though her training had in some ways turned Ida into a conventional young woman of her time, the rigours and responsibilities of her life on the homestead had made her unusually practical, strong-willed and self-assured. Her younger sister Macy, brought up in the urban East, was by contrast flighty and coquettish; and the two women were never close or even comfortable with each other.

When Ida inherited a modest sum of money from her father in 1933, she was given more financial independence than most women of her generation, and she guarded it carefully. In politics, too, she knew her own mind, and she was a lifelong and knowledgeable supporter of the Liberal Party. Once, when my brother and I were strolling through the grounds of the Moose Jaw Exhibition with our grandparents, she pointed to the Liberal Party booth and said: "That's *our* party." What she did not feel the need to tell us then was that Grandpa Calder—and probably her two sons—had been a supporter of the CCF since its creation in 1932. Nor did Grandpa Calder dispute her assertion that the Liberals were "our party."

My grandparents first met when Ida was about twenty. She was watching a parade on Moose Jaw's Main Street and was having trouble seeing over the heads of the men in front of her. Observing this, a handsome, dark-haired young man with a large black moustache quietly slipped beside her, pulled an envelope out of his coat pocket and placed it on the pavement in front of her. "Perhaps if you stand on this," he said, "you'll be able to see better." She was attracted to this young man with the wry sense of humour, and soon they were courting. In 1904 they were married.

Lorin Edgar Calder had been born in Brampton, Ontario, in 1880, the youngest of four children of Mary Ann and Alexander R. Calder. Alexander Calder was a stonemason specializing in marble monuments and tombstones, a gifted artist who was awarded a medal for his work by the Governor General of Canada, the Marquess of Lorne, at the Toronto Industrial Exhibition in the late 1870s. When Alexander's only son was born shortly thereafter, he commemorated his award by naming him after the Marquess, though the name was misspelled on the birth certificate.

Tragically for Alexander, the cumulative effect of marble dust on his lungs soon forced him to abandon his art and look for healthier work outdoors. In 1884 he followed a stream of migrating Canadians and moved south of the border to the Dakota Territory, where he purchased the title of a brother who had settled on a quarter-section of land. The Calder home, a one-room shanty at first and then a roomier house, soon became a social centre, and the Calders were active in building the local church and creating a literary society. In 1890, however, an influenza epidemic swept through the territory, and Alexander, never very physically strong, died at the age of forty-seven.

Lorin, ten at the time of his father's death, lived at home with his mother and three older sisters through his adolescence, and then was sent to an accounting school in Chicago. In 1902, at the age of twenty-two, he moved back north of the border to Moose Jaw, where he was able to get a job with the CPR as a hostler, servicing engines and cars. For nearly a decade after marrying Ida, Lorin worked for the railway, but as Western expansion slowed and his hours were cut, he took a job first as a yard man for a lumber company and then as a salesman in the city's booming real estate market. In the 1920s he would return to the CPR as a brakeman and then in the 1930s he would become a salesman for the Caulder (later the Co-operative) Creamery. During the Second World War, with the shortage of working men, he held both jobs, and he remained with the Creamery until his death in 1954 at the age of seventy-four.

Perhaps because he had grown up in a household of women, Lorin was a gentle, almost refined, man. Rarely drinking alcohol and never coarse, he was quiet and undemonstrative, with a sly sense of humour reminiscent of his favourite, Will Rogers. He was in many ways the perfect complement to the serious-minded and determined Ida, who, as I recall from my childhood observation, made the important decisions and set the agenda in their home.

Ida's dominance may have developed early in their marriage, the first twenty-one years of which they spent living with her father in a large and comfortable red brick house he had bought at the turn of the century just off Main Street in the heart of Moose Jaw. It was only in 1923, when they were in their forties, that the couple were able to afford to buy their own home, the house on Alder Avenue that I knew as a child. In the summer of 1907, Ida gave birth to their first child, a girl they named Edna Muriel. In the only existing photograph of her, taken at the age of five months, she looks out bright-eyed and curious, an attractive blonde-haired child with her mother's fine features. Ten months after that photograph was taken, she was dead of what was then called summer complaint, a common childhood illness of the time caused by drinking contaminated milk. Devastated, her parents buried her in Rosedale Cemetery, the first and cruelly premature occupant of what would become the family plot.

Like many young couples grieving the loss of a child, Ida and Lorin were immediately determined to have another, and fifteen months later Ida gave birth to a son, Earle Fenwick. A year and a half after that, on June 30, 1911, Kenneth Alexander was born. Whether Earle ever sensed that he was a kind of replacement for the dead Edna will never be known, but my mother always believed he bore a childhood resentment of being so soon displaced in his parents' affections by the rather quick arrival of a younger brother.

And it does seem that the boys were treated differently. When Kenneth and I, born only three years apart, were growing up, Mother had a rule from which she never deviated: she would treat her sons absolutely equally. If I got a new Roy Rogers cowboy shirt, Kenneth got one too; if Kenneth was allowed to camp along the riverbank with his young friends, I was allowed to hunt gophers with mine; and if I got a spanking for throwing crabapples at a neighbour boy, Kenneth—

though he might be only marginally guilty—got a spanking too. Mother had concluded—or had been convinced by Earle—that her husband had been damaged by the favouritism shown to his brother, and she was determined that the same would not happen to her sons.

For this or perhaps other reasons, Earle's attitude toward his mother became hostile at an early age, and their relationship was frequently contentious throughout the rest of her life. Once, when he was a young man, he exploded in anger when she, thinking she was doing something for him, mounted his shooting medals in a way he did not like. On another occasion he quarrelled with her over her refusal to bail him out of some financial quandary with money from her personal savings account.

The friction in the relationship between my grandmother and my father undoubtedly resulted from the clash of equally strong personalities. Everyone who knew him says he was strong-willed and determined always to have his own way. According to Helena Nichols, who knew the Calders well as a teenager living two doors away, Earle was overbearing: "He wanted to make sure everybody was doing what *he* thought they should. He liked to mind everybody's business but his own. If he thought that you weren't doing what he thought was the right thing, he would sure let you know about it." Once, to prove a point, she said, he staked a schoolmate hand and foot out in a vacant lot and walked away. This aggressiveness seems to have got him into a lot of fights, and, claimed a cousin, "he was good with his fists."

While Earle seems to have presented Ida with a continual struggle with someone as strong-willed and determined as herself, the easygoing and affable Ken was less challenging and easier to love. She quickly developed a close and warm relationship with him, which did not weaken when he became an adult. They were, she said years later, "always pals."

Any resentment Earle may have felt seems never to have been directed toward Ken. In fact, he was strongly protective of his younger brother, keeping an eye on him in the schoolyard and in the back alleys of Moose Jaw. The same manipulative streak that put him at odds with his mother and some of his schoolmates impelled him to intervene whenever he thought Ken was threatened by a bully or, on occasion, when his younger brother seemed to him to be about to do something ill-advised—whether it was going out with the wrong girl or looking for the wrong job.

Ken's childhood was no different from that of most children of the time. With his friend Henry Evans, whose father's floral greenhouses were located behind the Calder house, he walked three blocks around Crescent Park to attend Victoria School, the first multi-room elementary school in the North-West Territories. There, according to another classmate, Mary Lowick, he was "well dressed, quiet, nice and well liked—not the type to ever disrupt the class."

Near the end of Ken's second year of school, in June 1919, an event occurred in Moose Jaw that would profoundly affect the course of his life. When George V had declared war on Germany in the name of the British Empire in 1914, Canada was constitutionally required to join the fight. Prime Minister Robert Borden may have been irritated that London simply informed him that he was now at war, but Canadians generally approved of going to the aid of the Old Country. The population of Moose Jaw, heavily of British origin, greeted the news of war by taking to the streets in flag-draped automobiles and horse-drawn carriages in spontaneous demonstrations of patriotism. Before long, western Canadian young men were enlisting with more alacrity than in any other region of the country, and Moose Jaw became an important centre for a number of battalions: the 68th, the 128th, the 210th, the 229th, the 16th Mounted Rifles, and the 27th Light Horse.

No one could be oblivious to the military presence in Moose Jaw, as, for example, when the lieutenant-governor of Saskatchewan presented the regimental colours to the 128th Battalion on the first day of May 1916. Ken, then nearly five years old, would have been able to look out of the front windows of his home and see the entire battalion drawn up in a three-sided square and trooping the colour across the road in Crescent Park.

For sheer spectacle, however, nothing matched the return in 1919 of Moose Jaw's most illustrious fighting men, the Forty-sixth Canadian Infantry Battalion, who had gone into battle in August 1916 and had fought at Ypres, Vimy, the Somme and Passchendaele. One of its members, Sergeant Hugh Cairns, had been awarded the Victoria Cross—the day before he died—for bravery in the action at Valenciennes in the last weeks of the war. Moose Jaw's city fathers were determined that no city or town in Canada would welcome its forces home more enthusiastically.

Monday, June 9, had been declared a civic half-holiday, and at 8:30 that morning the CPR train pulled into the station, the battalion got off the coaches, and the men were allowed a half-hour to greet the families they had not seen for several years. Then a bugle sounded "fall in" and the battalion regrouped, fixed bayonets, put on its steel helmets and marched up Main Street to the Armoury, located at the Exhibition Grounds. It was, proclaimed the *Moose Jaw Daily News,* "the first time that armed troops in full battle array have marched through the streets with fixed bayonets." Moreover, it continued melodramatically, "if it were not for such men as those who returned today other troops might be marching through the streets of Moose Jaw, men dressed in the grey of the Hun uniform and to the sound of the 'Hoch.'"

The Forty-sixth Battalion, marching to the martial music of three military bands, paraded past cheering crowds on Main Street, in front of the reviewing stand on which the lieutenant-governor of Saskatchewan, Sir Richard Lake, took their last salute, up North Hill and into the Exhibition Grounds. There they were greeted by the wildly cheering schoolchildren of Moose Jaw.

Though Monday morning had been declared a holiday, the children had nonetheless been required to go to their schools, from where the teachers had marched them to the Exhibition Grounds. Those youngsters too small to walk from the far reaches of South Hill were driven there in automobiles volunteered by patriotic citizens. Seated in the grandstand

and bleachers, the children, who had begun to cheer when the bands began to be heard, went wild with excitement when the battalion entered the Grounds. It was a scene, observed the *Moose Jaw Evening Times,* "that will not soon be forgotten, when all the schoolchildren of the city, some four thousand all told, were massed . . . and presented a wonderful appearance as the Forty-sixth marched 'to attention' and swung past in beautiful rhythm. This was the signal for a tumultuous outburst on the part of the youngsters and the waving of Union Jacks."

Ken was one of those flag-waving children that day, and it is hard to imagine that the shining brass, the polished boots, the bayonets and the helmets did not have a significant impact on him. Three weeks short of his eighth birthday, he is unlikely to have read the glowing accounts carried in the local newspapers, but he may well have noticed the headlines splashed across their pages: "GREAT CROWDS CHEER BOYS HOME," "HOME-COMING HEROES GREETED BY THOUSANDS" and "MOOSE JAW TODAY GIVES THE GLAD HAND TO THE BRAVE BOYS OF THE 46TH BATTALION."

Even if Ken had read the papers, however, they would not have told him that the Forty-sixth's nickname was "the Suicide Battalion" because of its 91 percent casualty rate during the war. Nor would he have known that more than four thousand other young men from the farms and little towns of Saskatchewan were lying in graves in France and Belgium. He would not have understood that the cars lined up at the end of the parade were carrying the soldiers, some of the province's 13,209 wounded, who returned too crippled to walk. Nor could he know that within three years thirty-two of these veterans would be unable to support themselves and have to be housed at public expense in Moose Jaw's Great War Veterans Association Home.

Ken would not have seen these things. If he was like my brother and me—and so many others of our generation—in the years immediately after the next world war, he would have seen only the allure of khaki, badges and weapons, and a man's world of action, heroism and glory. Thus it is hardly surprisingly that he enlisted in the militia—the

King's Own Rifles of Canada—when he turned fourteen, and that he remained in the military in one form or another for the rest of his life.

The Non-Permanent Active Militia was Canada's meagre peace-time attempt to maintain an illusion of military preparedness. Senator Raoul Dandurand, Canada's delegate to the League of Nations, spoke for the country when he declared in 1924 that Canadians lived in "a fireproof house, far from inflammatory materials." Successive govern-ments shared his faith in geographical distance, and following the Great War the Permanent Force was allowed to shrink to four thou-sand men. Supporting this small contingent was the NPAM, which by the thirties was made up of about fifty thousand partly trained "Saturday Night soldiers."

Young men joined the militia for a number of reasons. For some, like Jack Donohue, it was simply "very much the thing to do"; for others, like Al Affleck, it was "an innocuous kind of recreation." For the officers, it carried a certain amount of prestige: a social activity with the glamour of a uniform. And for everyone during the Depression, even the modest wage was welcome. In Moose Jaw, the city fathers were aware of the economic benefits of a thriving local militia. In 1922, when the city's boom had collapsed, the *Moose Jaw Evening Times* pointed out to its readers that the pay rate for privates was then $1.25 to $1.50 a day, and that, if enough recruits could be found, the community could benefit by as much as $7,500: "This is a point that business men should not lose sight of, and they are particularly requested to interest them-selves in the matter and do all possible to prevail on men to join."

By the time Ken joined the KORC in 1925, the Calders had moved to Alder Avenue, and so it was a short walk of three blocks up the hill to the Armoury. The first such building in Saskatchewan, it was constructed in the castellated style used for Canadian armouries since 1880, a design intended to suggest a medieval castle with its crenellated roofline and buttressed walls. Here Ken would have been given uniforms left over from the Great War and undergone the kind of training described by David Bercuson: "drilling and marching and learning essentials such as first aid. Practice with actual arms consisted of an hour or two each week on the rifle range . . . with the handful of .22 rifles the regiment possessed . . . The pay was virtually nonexistent . . . the training was primitive, the weapons scarce. There were no modern weapons to speak of."

Ken and Earle joined the NPAM together, but in 1927, when Ken transferred to the Seventy-seventh Field Battery, a local artillery unit, their military careers took different paths. Earle remained in the KORC, dropped out in 1934 and then followed his brother into the Seventy-seventh Battery in 1937. By then Ken had risen in the ranks of the Seventy-seventh, becoming a sergeant in 1932 and a lieutenant in 1936. Two years later he was made a captain after he completed a qualifying course at the Royal School of Artillery in Winnipeg.

In his civilian life Ken was getting on as well as most young men in Saskatchewan could expect to in the Depression. Like many adolescents in the thirties, he dropped out of high school after grade ten, and for a while he rode the rails across western Canada looking for work that would keep him from being a burden to his family. Then, like Earle, he began working for the Caulder Creamery. But while Earle became restless after a year and left the Creamery for a series of jobs, Ken remained and was a foreman there when war broke out.

Perhaps because of their militia training, the two young men became zealous marksmen, and together they anchored a number of provincial small-bore rifle championship teams in the thirties. From time to time they liked to sharpen their aim by picking off the rats scavenging in the piles of garbage at the city dump. On one such occasion a .22-calibre slug ricocheted off a rock and hit Earle in the thigh. He sat down, a little pale, took off his trousers and proceeded to dig out the bullet with his penknife.

Earle and Ken were also ardent hunters, frequently bringing home their limit of the ducks and geese that filled the sloughs and lakes around Moose Jaw every fall. Both loved fishing and, together with their fellow marksman Fred Cooper, would fill a large tackle box with lures made from beads and feathers plundered from Fred's younger sister's sewing basket. With these they would hook large pike and walleye along the shores of Last Mountain Lake, northeast of the city.

Ken's childhood friend Henry Evans did not share Ken's love of hunting and fishing, but Cooper was an outdoorsman. Having come from England as a child, and four years older than Ken, he ran a shoe repair shop in Moose Jaw. Though closer in age to Earle, who in fact worked for him in the shop for a year or so, Cooper soon became Ken's closest friend and confidant.

By anybody's standard, both Calder boys were vigorously masculine. Though Earle might still keep a watchful eye on his younger brother, Ken no longer needed protecting. According to Ron Jones, a fellow soldier in the Seventy-seventh Battery, "Ken was a rugged individual. He was no sissy; he could handle himself."

Though Ken had become a "man's man," he was, by all accounts, handsome, charming and generous. As such, women found him very attractive. Fred Cooper's younger sister, Mona, used to hang around the shop when Ken came in and she remembers him as "sure a good-looking guy. Really good." Moreover, she says now, "he was lots of fun every time I saw him." Helena Nichols also maintained that Ken "always had a lot of fun in whatever we were doing." He would often stroll the two doors over to her house and ask her mother if he could "borrow Lena for a while" so he could take her for a soda at the ice cream parlour on Main Street.

Mrs. Nichols might have told me more. A quick and spirited octogenarian when I saw her in Moose Jaw in 1996, she reminded me that her maiden name had been Vail and that her friends and family always called her Lena. It was, in fact, as Lena Vail that our family always knew her; and when she reappeared in my life as Helena, it awakened something in the recesses of my memory. In the desk in my office at the university was an old black-handled, nickel-plated letter opener that had come down to me among the artifacts saved from my grandparents' house. From time to time over three decades of teaching, I had puzzled

over the words unevenly scratched on the blade: *All For One* on one side
and *I love Helena* on the other.

As soon as I was back in Saskatoon, I drove to the university, dug out
the opener and, staring at the inscription, began to fashion a story of
passion, perhaps of the thwarted variety. Had they been lovers, had something gone wrong, had Ken made a poor choice at some time, leaving
Lena to find and marry Bill Nichols and himself foolishly to place his bet
on Margaret? Had the girl next door always been the right one?

Holly and I took the curious relic to Moose Jaw the next time we
visited Lena. "Oh, that's nothing," she said. "Nothing happened
between us. We were just friends, nothing more." That might have
settled the matter had she not said it with the slightest trace of a sly
grin. Moreover, when she pulled out her young woman's photograph
album, she could point to a number of pictures of Ken: Ken proudly
wearing his KORC uniform, Ken and friends picnicking out at the
Pasqua Dam, and Ken, his parents, my parents and Lena at a cottage
at Etter's Beach on Last Mountain Lake. In a number of them Ken is
beaming, and Lena, with her own—is it sly?—grin, has a proprietor-
ial arm around him. Even in a more communal time, this seems more
than neighbourly closeness.

After some time Lena confided—first to my wife while they were
preparing lunch out of my hearing and then to me—that she and Ken
did "go around" as teenagers. She would have liked the relationship
to continue, but then "something happened." Pressed about this, she
explained that Earle had decided she was not the right girl for his
brother and had in his manipulative way somehow poisoned the
water. The relationship ended, though she remained friends with
Ken, and she went on to have a happy marriage to a soldier and to
raise a son. Even so, at the end of our last visit to her in 2000, when
failing health still could not dim her vitality, she suddenly and
mischievously remarked apropos of nothing: "But then there's that
letter opener, isn't there?" There was obvious pleasure in her voice and
the trace of a grin on her face.

In his twenties Ken went out with a number of women, and despite the long shadow of the Depression there was no shortage of things for young couples to do in Moose Jaw. There was the elegant Capitol Theatre, which had begun to show the fascinating new talking pictures in 1929. There was Temple Gardens, a mock-Tudor dance hall legendary in western Canada for its sprung dance floor. There was the Natatorium, built in 1932 to take advantage of the warm mineral springs beneath the city and for decades the only competition-size swimming pool in the province. In the summer there was canoeing at the Aquatic Club on the river, and in the winter there was hockey played by the Moose Jaw KORCS, a team named after the local militia regiment.

Though Ken dated a number of young women in the thirties, he developed a serious interest in only one, a classmate of Lena's—and a year behind him—in high school. Margaret Bruce had grown up on a farm fifteen miles north of Moose Jaw, the daughter of Robert Bruce, who had come to the area in 1888 after working in lumber camps in British Columbia and on a ranch south of Calgary. Her mother, Elizabeth, had been a nurse before her marriage.

If her father's name echoed that of a famous figure in Scottish history, Margaret's middle name, Lucretia—which had been her grandmother's—had classical connotations. A legendary heroine of ancient Rome, Lucretia was a nobleman's beautiful and virtuous wife who, after being raped, killed herself. Her preference for honour over life made her a traditional symbol of chastity. Of course, for many people the name took on very different connotations during the Italian Renaissance, when Lucrezia Borgia shared in the corruption and moral excesses of her infamous family.

Margaret had attended several schools in the country, but she came into Moose Jaw for high school. After graduation she went to teacher's college in the city, but decided against a career in the classroom. She then entered the School of Nursing at the Moose Jaw General Hospital, and so distinguished herself there that when she graduated in May 1935, she took the Gold Medal for General

Proficiency. A year later she became a registered nurse and before long she had become a supervisor at the Moose Jaw General.

Only one of the photographs I have seen of her suggests that Margaret was particularly attractive, but I have been told by some who knew her that she had a kind of allure not captured by the camera. Henry Evans's wife, Hilda, who in her twenties chummed around with her, claimed that "she was a very good-looking girl, but some people don't take very good pictures. Margaret was a lovely girl." Moreover, said Mrs. Evans, she was "clever. Very clever."

Whether drawn to her physical appeal or her intelligence and professional accomplishment, Ken found Margaret very attractive, and sometime in the late 1930s they began going around together. After some months, however, the relationship cooled and they went their separate ways, she to pursue her nursing career and he to continue at the Creamery.

Earle, meanwhile, had married my mother, Mildred Jane Remey, secretly in 1933, a fact that astonished Kenneth and me when Mother let it slip out one day when we were well on into adulthood. The ceremony was conducted at the home of a clergyman, in the presence of two friends, and the pair did not tell their families about it for nearly five years. When pressed about the issue, Mother explained that, the Depression being so severe in western Canada, they could not afford to live together; and, though she never said it, they likely wanted a sexual relationship, which for her had to be in marriage—and so they postponed breaking the news. A year or so later, when they decided to reveal that they were wed, a sudden death in the family rendered the moment inappropriate, and with the passage of time disclosure grew more difficult.

When my grandmother learned of the marriage, she took Mother aside and said: "If I had known that you were thinking of it, I would have told you not to marry Earle." Her concern was not with the suitability of Mother to be her daughter-in-law but with that of her son to be a husband.

CHAPTER FIVE

Like most young men in the 1930s, Ken was focused on his immediate world: his job, his friends, hunting and fishing, and the militia. Elsewhere, of course, the political face of the world was changing in ways that would have far-reaching consequences for him and his generation. In 1931, Japan invaded Manchuria, and the subsequent failure of the League of Nations to stop Japanese expansion exposed its lack of effectiveness as a political arbiter, a weakness confirmed by its virtual collapse in the face of Italy's invasion of Ethiopia in 1935. Even more ominous was the rise to power of the Nazi Party in 1932, Hitler's becoming Chancellor of Germany a few months later, and then his increasingly aggressive militarism and territorial demands. First it was his occupation in 1936 of the Rhineland in violation of the Treaty of Versailles and the Locarno Pact, then his annexation of Austria in March 1938, then his demand for the Sudetenland and the Munich crisis of the following September. As much as any Briton, Canadians wanted to believe Neville Chamberlain when, standing on the Tarmac of an English aerodrome, he waved his piece of paper and promised "peace for our time."

At the time of the Munich crisis, the Canadian public was unaware that the cabinet had already concluded that, if Britain went to war with Germany, Canada would have no choice but to follow. Prime Minister Mackenzie King, as deceived as Chamberlain by Hitler's skilfully contrived sincerity, had many reasons to hope that peace would indeed prevail, not the least of which was the delicate problem of lingering French Canadian resentment over First World War conscription. As a result, he supported the British and French policy of appeasement, and he discouraged public discussion of the stance Canada might take if war should come. With Hitler's occupation of the rest of Czechoslovakia in March 1939, however, most Canadians knew that another European war was a very real possibility.

When Great Britain declared war on Germany on September 3, Canada was no longer a colony of the British Empire. It had become an autonomous member of the British Commonwealth of Nations, and so its own declaration of war came a week later, and then only after an emergency debate and vote in Parliament. Few people had doubted that Canada would join the fight, however, and on August 25 military districts across the country were ordered to call out militia units and be prepared to guard strategically important points. By late Friday afternoon on September 1, the day before the Labour Day weekend, the Seventy-seventh Field Battery had received orders to mobilize.

For weeks Ken, Earle and Fred Cooper had been planning a weekend fishing trip to their favourite stretches of water on Last Mountain Lake, where the pike and walleye would be biting after the sluggish summer months. The outing was called off, however, when Ken was called to a mobilization parade at the Armoury on Saturday. Two days later he signed his Officer's Declaration Paper for service in the Canadian Active Service Force, the new name for Canada's Permanent Force, and three weeks after that he signed the Officer's Supplementary Declaration Paper. The second declaration committed him to serving in the CASF "if, when and so long as required" anywhere in Canada and overseas "for the duration of the present war, and for a period of demobilization thereafter should His Majesty so long require [his] services." He did not imagine—nor could anyone in 1939—that this commitment to overseas service would stretch into nearly six years. Earle, twenty-nine years old, married and not an officer like Ken, did not join the CASF.

At the beginning of the Second World War, the Canadian Army had only 4,268 regular soldiers, and so it was very dependent on militia units such as the Seventy-seventh Battery to provide a core of men with some military experience, however rudimentary, around whom the wartime army could be assembled. Since the roster of the Battery, following peacetime army regulations, was only thirty-five, a recruiting depot was set up on Main Street, and by the end of the month the Seventy-seventh was up to full strength of about 170 men.

Unlike at the beginning of the Great War, there were no flags waving in the streets of Moose Jaw and no outbreaks of public jingoism among its citizens. As Reginald Roy has said, "the nation accepted the need for war in a sombre mood." Some men enlisted because they felt a duty, but many in Saskatchewan saw the army as a place to get three square meals a day. Hoping perhaps to re-create the fervour for King and Country of an earlier age, the officer commanding the Seventy-seventh arranged for all its men to attend a special showing of Alexander Korda's new film version of A.E.W. Mason's novel *The Four Feathers* on September 12. Written in 1902, at the height of British imperial power, it is a highly romantic, Kiplingesque story of an officer given white feathers as a sign of cowardice and how he proves himself by heroic deeds in the Sudan. On its release in Great Britain in January 1939, *The Four Feathers* was splendid propaganda for a country that knew it was again heading for war. Whether it had any effect on the practical young prairie boys sitting five thousand miles away in the Capitol Theatre in Moose Jaw is another matter.

In moving from the militia to the CASF, Ken had to drop a rank to lieutenant, but he was pleased to have been made second-in-command of the Seventy-seventh while it trained in Moose Jaw. Most of the men were still only green recruits, and militia officers like Ken became especially valuable in training them, a fact that seems to have weighed heavily on him when he made his own decision to join the active force. As he wrote to his American cousin Grace, "I don't feel that I could run out on the Army now after 14 years peace-time service." Though Ken did not volunteer for overseas action with any jingoistic fervour, he was convinced that the fight against Hitler was unavoidable for Canadians—and perhaps for Americans too.

Referring to the reluctance of many people in the United States to join another war in Europe, he teased Grace about American isolationism's most famous champion: "Is Col. [Charles] Lindbergh's face red?"

The Canadian government's plans were to create two infantry divisions, one to be sent to Britain to train in the milder English climate and the other to be brought up to fighting trim in Canada. The Seventy-seventh Battery's reputation was good enough for it to be selected—along with field batteries from Winnipeg, Edmonton and Trail, B.C.—to be part of the Third Canadian Field Regiment of the First Canadian Infantry Division, renowned for its service in the Great War. Ken's pride at being part of the First Division is unmistakable in his letter to Grace: "The First Division is composed of all the famous regiments of the Canadian Army and selected units such as ourselves. We will support such units as the Princess Patricia's Canadian Light Infantry, the Cameron Highlanders, the Black Watch and the Royal Canadian Regiment." Though he was wrong about the Cameron Highlanders and the Black Watch, the First Division did contain many of the country's most illustrious regiments: the Seaforth Highlanders, the Royal 22e Regiment (the "Van Doos"), the Hastings and Prince Edward Regiment and the Forty-eighth Highlanders of Canada.

My grandmother, who had been horrified by the deaths and disfigurements of the Great War, had never wanted her sons to join the militia, and the prospect now of Ken going into active service frightened her. "Mother worries a lot about this," he confided to his cousin, "but during times like these it is best not to let the imagination run too far. The general trouble up here is the too-frequent news reports on the radio which sometimes are not so nice."

The original mobilization plan called for the Seventy-seventh to join the other artillery units to train at Camp Petawawa, in Ontario, but a shortage of proper winter quarters there meant that the Battery remained in Moose Jaw until it left for Britain. The Armoury could not accommodate the number of gunners in the Battery, so the old Moose Jaw College building, a large brick structure on the southern outskirts of the city, became the barracks. Knowing that many units across the country were housed in exhibition buildings, empty after the summer fairs, Ken enjoyed having "such luxuries as hardwood floors, tile baths, full-length mirrors, etc. Living in the lap of luxury, as it were."

The college quarters may have seemed generous to Ken, but he must have looked somewhat askance at the uniforms provided for the men he was supposed to train. Until newly designed battledress was rushed fresh from the factories to First Division units in late November, recruits were given Great War uniforms dug out of storage in the Armoury: tailored tunics, breeches, puttees and leather shoulder belts. Army boots were in short supply, so men drilled in their civilian footwear or in whatever boots could be purchased in the local stores.

If the Battery's dress was motley, its equipment was laughable. Two decades of lean military budgets meant that in the entire country there were only twenty-nine Bren guns, twenty-three anti-tank rifles, and five 3-inch mortars. The Seventy-seventh thus could train only on the hardware left over from the previous war: several 18-pounder field guns and some Ross and Lee-Enfield rifles. Even the latter were scarce enough that soldiers guarding the college were given wooden replicas of firearms with which to repel potential German saboteurs.

The inclusion of the Seventy-seventh Battery in the First Division gave an urgency to its training, under whatever conditions it might be conducted, and as the fall days got shorter and colder, Ken and his fellow officers worked to turn raw young recruits into something like capable soldiers. One of those new gunners, Stan Ingleby, remembers the officers spending "many weary hours lecturing and explaining over and over again the correct way to salute, swing the arms and pick up the step." When the training went beyond the basics, however, the officers themselves had to go to school, and Ken spent a week in Regina at a Ford Motors instruction course dealing with the new engines being built for wartime use. On his return he was asked to train thirty-nine drivers to handle every kind of vehicle from a motorcycle to a three-ton truck. In peacetime the course took a month and a half; Ken was told to do it in two weeks.

On November 21, the Seventy-seventh Battery received word from regimental headquarters that the First Division would be proceeding overseas in December and it should be prepared to move on seven days' notice. Like the others, Ken was rushed through the final round of vaccinations and inoculations for such exotic diseases as typhoid, and he had some long-ignored dental work done. There was, however, a much more important matter to attend to before he boarded the troop train to Halifax.

On the evening of September 10, the day that a CBC radio bulletin announced that Canada was at war, Ken had gone to a party. There he met Margaret Bruce, of whom he had seen little since they had broken off their relationship several years earlier. For whatever reason—perhaps the drama of the day's news, or the romance of a handsome young man in a uniform, or simply the rekindling of an attraction not fully extinguished—they began to see each other again whenever Ken could get away from the college and the training. Several months later he was able to write his cousin that he was engaged:

> Well, Grace, I have always heard that people live faster in wartime and, from what I can observe, it holds true in my case. I have even gone so far as to buy a diamond and present it to a young lady who, strange as it may seem, thinks I am all right too. I intend to buy the other ring when this war is over and I can settle down and perhaps become a responsible citizen. Mother and Dad are tickled to death and I sometimes think that they fell in love with her before I did. The lady under discussion is Margaret Bruce, R.N., who is at present Operating Room Supervisor in the General Hospital. She intends to take a six months P[ost]. G[raduate]. Course in New York starting at the end of January.

Ken's description of his engagement illustrates pride in Margaret's professional status; and it may be that the creamery foreman was in awe of the operating-room supervisor who was off to study in New York. More interesting is the suggestion that his parents were as captivated by her as he was. Indeed, my mother always claimed that at that time my grandmother saw Margaret as a "catch" for Ken, someone compared to whom she herself, a woman from the working-class area of Moose Jaw who had not gone beyond grade ten, had little lustre.

When Ken wrote his letter on November 21, he was unaware that the Seventy-seventh Battery had been told to be ready to travel, and it seems that the orders, when he learned of them, had a galvanizing effect on him—and perhaps on Margaret. On November 29, only eight days after his telling Grace that he and Margaret intended to wait until after the war to be wed, they married. The ceremony was conducted, not in either of their hometowns of Moose Jaw or Tuxford, as one might have expected, but in St. Paul's Anglican Church in Regina, with only the bride's and groom's attendants present. Earle was the best man and Lillian, Margaret's younger sister, was the maid of honour. It was only days later that their friends back in Moose Jaw, even lifelong friends such as Henry and Hilda Evans, were told of the wedding.

The marriage was thus entered into not only in haste but also in secrecy, both conditions dictated by the times. Margaret was then living in the nurses' residence of the Moose Jaw General Hospital, and since married nurses were not permitted to reside there, she would have been required to leave. Moreover, following the commonly accepted rule of the time that married women were not allowed to hold full-time jobs, she would very likely have had to resign her position. For this reason the wedding ceremony had to take place in Regina, out of the sight of hospital officials. Margaret's parents also had to postpone announcing the marriage in the Moose Jaw *Times-Herald* until August 15, 1940, nearly nine months after the event. By then the heavy enlistment in western Canada had begun to create a shortage of manpower and the sanctions against married women in the workforce had been eased. Margaret's job was secure.

It is impossible to know why Ken and Margaret married so suddenly, but they were hardly alone in doing so. There was a rush to the altar in Canada in the fall of 1939, pushing the number of marriages for the year to thirty thousand more than in 1938 and eighty thousand more than in the Depression year of 1932. According to George Blackburn, who served in the Royal Canadian Artillery in the Second World War, it was the soldier's realization that he was facing a prolonged and perhaps interminable separation that suddenly made marriage so imperative. "Facing such prospects," he said, "to postpone marriage any longer would be inhuman. To be denied some married life together, however short, before going overseas, is totally inconceivable."

When I once asked the wife of a veteran of the Loyal Edmonton Regiment why young couples, with the uncertainty of war facing them, plunged into these impulsive marriages, she snorted: "That's the stupidest question I've ever heard!" The implication, of course, was that, with a long separation before them, there was an urgency to consummate their relationship, and proper women of that period did not indulge in sex outside marriage. In the case of Margaret and Ken, however, it should be remembered that they were then both in their late twenties and hardly naive teenagers, and Margaret later claimed to have had premarital sexual experience.

There were, of course, practical reasons for marrying before Ken left for the European front. As his wife, Margaret would be entitled to the monthly dependents' allowance—providing that the Department of National Defence remained unaware that she was fully employed and therefore self-sufficient. Ken had also decided to assign a large portion of his monthly pay to Margaret for her to deposit in a savings account. He had begun to dream of moving beyond the Creamery, of owning his own hardware and sporting goods store, and the money accumulated from the dependents' allowance and his pay might eventually be sufficient to get him started. If, on the other hand, Ken were killed overseas and Margaret did not remarry, she would receive a widow's pension for the rest of her life. Ken and Margaret may have asked themselves, since they would be wed as soon as the war was over anyway, why not marry then and provide Margaret with some financial security?

The most likely reason for their impulsiveness was a quest not for financial security but for emotional security—or the illusion of it. It was common for men about to travel thousands of miles from home, family, friends and roots, men facing a separation that might last for years, to look to some sort of secure anchor at home. A married man was connected to home in a way that a single man was not: he had a wife, he had a base and he had a future. No matter that marriage was a contract that could be broken; it had the illusion of permanence.

The possibility that my grandmother played a significant part in Ken and Margaret's decision cannot be ignored. As Ken's letter had indicated, she strongly approved of Margaret, no doubt attracted by the bright, well turned out, capable, professional woman. She was, Ida probably thought, an ideal future that Ken should not let slip away, and in the present she would provide him with a solid emotional grounding wherever he might be. Ken, who had always been close to his mother and paid attention to her wishes, may well have heard these arguments from her; that at least is the opinion of one of his Fenwick cousins, George. "Your grandmother," he told me when I asked him in 1997 about the marriage, "could be a *very* persuasive woman."

And what of Margaret's reasons? When I asked her sister Lillian about them in 1997, she could not recall any. If the impulse to marry so hastily was largely Ken's, encouraged by his mother, then the Calder family legend that Margaret explained her marriage to a friend by saying "it doesn't matter, he won't be coming back anyway" has some credibility. In 1999 the respected Canadian journalist June Callwood told an interviewer that, as a young reporter in Brantford during the war, she had a number of soldiers on their way overseas tell her they were in love with her. Would she wait for them? "I gradually learned," she said, "to just say yes because . . . they'd get killed. Eleven. Eleven men that I said I'd marry were killed. Eleven." Promising to wait and actually going to the altar are, of course, very different matters, but if Margaret was uncertain and did not know how to extricate herself from a marriage she felt she was being rushed into, she may have persuaded herself that the war would eventually solve her problem.

As with so many wartime marriages, Ken and Margaret's honeymoon was brief: five days and nights in all before Ken was called back to the barracks. On the evening of December 7, the Seventy-seventh Battery marched in full kit—rifles, blankets and gas masks—from the college down to the CPR depot and straight into the rotunda underground, where family and friends had been allowed to gather to see them off. "The usual blah-blah speeches from the dignitaries," as one gunner recalled, were as much public recognition of the event as the army would allow, and from this point until they were securely in Britain their travel plans were shrouded in secrecy. All that anyone had been told was that the Battery was heading east, perhaps to a camp like Petawawa or possibly the Atlantic seaboard. As the special seventeen-coach train left the station at 2:45 a.m., Ken's friend Lieutenant Jack Eccleston got the young gunners to voice their own sentiments inspired by the hit film of that year. "We're off to see the Wizard," they sang, "the Wonderful Wizard of Oz."

When the train slipped into Regina an hour later to take on water, it was without any public warning, and each of the few passengers lingering in the waiting room was carefully questioned by railway police. For the next few days the train wound its way across Central Canada and into the Maritimes with blinds lowered, and when it arrived at the Halifax docks the men were immediately marched aboard their ship, the *Duchess of Bedford*. As they went up the gangway, some of the young gunners shouted to the dock hands: "It won't last long when we get over!"

On December 10, at noon, 7,449 men of the First Canadian Infantry Division sailed from Canada in a convoy of five troopships, two cruisers, five destroyers and one submarine. The *Duchess of Bedford* was the first ship to leave Halifax harbour, and when the gunners of the Seventy-seventh looked back for a last sight of Canada, they saw the harbour beacon flashing out the code for "good luck, good luck, good luck." Some fortunate units had been assigned to the *Empress of Britain,* the 43,348-ton luxury liner that had carried the King and Queen back to the United Kingdom from Canada six months earlier. But none of the transports had yet been stripped of its peacetime furnishings or amenities, and so the Seventy-seventh crossed the Atlantic as comfortably as any civilian passengers had six months before. Gunners found themselves in spacious cabins, with stewards to make up their beds for them, and they ate excellent meals served with silverware and crystal on linen-covered tables. The bars were open most hours of the day and there was no rationing. Coming from Depression Saskatchewan, the men might indeed have thought they had landed in Oz. Few of them, though, would know such comfort again until the war was over.

As the convoy zigzagged its way to Britain, it would need luck to avoid the U-boats prowling the North Atlantic, especially if German intelligence had learned that more than seven thousand servicemen were aboard. Few members of the Battery had seen any body of water larger than a prairie slough—or, like Ken, the expanse of Last Mountain Lake—and the ocean looked very wide and deep and dangerous. One night, recalls Stan Ingleby, the gunners on guard duty spotted an ominous black object just below the surface, cutting the water in front of the *Duchess.* "Jesus! Submarine!" they thought, and persuaded the sergeant of the guard to summon one of the ship's officers. "Oh, shit," he said, "that's a paravane." The destroyer in front was dragging these torpedo-shaped devices that glided beneath the surface of the water to slice the mooring ropes of mines.

Despite their apprehension, the gunners were amused to hear that the German radio propagandist Lord Haw-Haw had announced that German subs had sunk the *Empress of Britain,* though their amusement was tempered by the thought that their families might be hearing of these claims. They would have been even less entertained had they known that, just ten months later, the *Empress* would in fact be torpedoed off the coast of Ireland and sent to the bottom of the Atlantic. On this occasion, though, the convoy remained unscathed, and the smooth sea, reported Ken, made the voyage "a real pleasure."

Early on December 17 the convoy sailed through the morning mists of the Firth of Clyde and, greeted by the welcoming sirens of the commercial shipping on the estuary, dropped anchor at Gourock. From ship to ship Canadian soldiers began to shout "Canada!" in unison, and when word began to spread that the Canadians had arrived, the dock area filled with onlookers. Secretary of State for Dominion Affairs Anthony Eden, accompanied by Vincent Massey, the Canadian High Commissioner to Britain, greeted Major-General A.G.L. "Andy" McNaughton, the First Division's officer commanding. As the Van Doos disembarked, some began to sing "Alouette," and not to be outdone, a contingent of Western troops gave a vigorous rendition of "Hail, Hail, the Gang's All Here."

The *Duchess of Bedford,* unlike the other ships, did not remain at Gourock but moved up the Clyde to Glasgow, where the Seventy-seventh Battery disembarked. The men were immediately put on what seemed to them very antiquated and quaint little trains and taken down through Scotland to southern England. For Ken, the Britain that had existed only as the romantic stuff of books and films started to become real. Several days later he wrote to Grace of the thrill of seeing the green, lush English countryside and of glimpsing Oxford University as the train passed through the town. "I have often read of the towers and spires of Oxford," he said, "but I never expected to have an opportunity of seeing them." The journey ended in the Surrey town of Farnborough, southwest of London, where a Royal Artillery band greeted the Battery and led it on a march through driving snow to its barracks.

Back in Moose Jaw, my grandparents knew nothing of Ken's whereabouts. There had been no mention of the First Division on the radio or in the pages of the *Times-Herald* or the Regina *Leader-Post.* Indeed, if one were to judge by the newspapers of the time, the young Deanna Durbin's first screen kiss (with Robert Stack) was a more urgent public concern than the doings of Canadian soldiers. Then, on the evening of December 18, Winston Churchill, the First Lord of the Admiralty, broke the silence with an almost casual reference in a radio broadcast to the Dominions: "And yesterday, the leading division of the Canadian Army disembarked safely in one of our harbours." The next morning the British press trumpeted "THEY'RE HERE!" and at home the Regina *Leader-Post*'s headline read "CANADIANS IN BRITISH BARRACKS." Only then did Canadian papers run pictures of the troops boarding the ships nine days earlier at Halifax.

The Seventy-seventh's new home, referred to vaguely in the Canadian press only as "one of [Minister of War] Hore-Belisha's so-called 'palaces,'" was in fact Aldershot, the home of the British army since 1854. It had become the country's leading military training centre following the Crimean War, and millions of soldiers had drilled in its parade squares and trained in the surrounding countryside. Three hundred Canadian soldiers had paraded past Queen Victoria there as part of her Diamond Jubilee Review in 1897, thousands more trained there during the Great War, and 330,000 would pass through the camp before the Second World War was over. If Ken and his fellow prairie soldiers needed any reminding that they were surrounded by an illustrious history and tradition, they needed only to look at the name of their quarters: the Lille Barracks. It was part of a row of barracks called the Marlborough Lines, each named after one of the celebrated eighteenth-century victories of Winston Churchill's ancestor the Duke of Marlborough: Blenheim, Malplaquet, Oudenarde and Ramillies.

If the names on the buildings were eighteenth century, the facilities within were distinctly nineteenth century. Canadian newspapers had assured their readers that the troops were impressed by the modern quarters, with their steam heating and spacious washrooms, but in fact the soldiers were dismayed by the gloomy two-storey brick barracks that had been built during the Boer War and were rumoured to have been condemned as unfit for habitation in 1918. The rooms were damp and dirty, the kitchens had only primitive stoves, and there was no hot water for showers or baths. By chance, Britain was enduring its coldest winter since 1894—which the British officials euphemistically characterized as "inclement"—and the young men accustomed to efficient Canadian central heating were confronted by frozen water pipes and small, open-grated fireplaces fed by meagre allocations of coal. Before too many days had passed, several of the more enterprising soldiers began to break up some of the antiquated wooden furniture and even a scattering of the town's bus-stop seats for added fuel. Despite these efforts, January saw a severe outbreak of influenza among men unaccustomed to the damp climate and poor heating.

The First Division had only two days to become acclimatized and adjust to its new quarters before Sir Leslie Hore-Belisha and his War Office staff put it through a rigorous inspection. They liked what they saw. For their part, the Canadian troops were eager to get into action. Perhaps encouraged by Germany's scuttling of its pocket battleship *Graf Spee* on the day of his arrival in Scotland, Ken assured his cousin that "it is almost a foregone conclusion that the German navy is about through . . . All we have to do now to win the war is to get at the German Army and push them back."

It would be a very long time, however, before Ken or the First Division would see a German soldier. In the meantime, he wrote to his grandmother Calder in February that he was "going at it hammer and tongs": instructing drivers, despatch riders and mechanics. He was responsible for thirteen motorcycles and fifty-seven vehicles, which ranged from station wagons to three-ton gun tractors to requisitioned moving vans and greengrocer's lorries. Manoeuvres were carried out at all hours, and Ken's job was to lead a convoy on his motorcycle, dressed in trench coat, steel helmet, rubber boots and gas mask. The night exercises were especially hazardous since they were conducted without headlights on roads and trails that had become muddy in the soggy English winter weather. Ken was pleased that his company had only one gun muzzle go through a truck radiator, but the risks in such manoeuvres were brought home to him when an orderly, thrown from his motorcycle, became one of Canada's earliest World War II casualties.

The rigours of these early months of training were punctuated by moments of glamour. On January 24, King George VI, colonel-in-chief of the Royal Canadian Artillery, reviewed the First Division's four artillery regiments. "We had to drill quite lustily for the great occasion," Ken told his grandmother, "and we earned a few words of praise from his majesty and the high-priced help he had with him." The "high-priced help" were Major-General McNaughton and the Hon. Vincent Massey, and Ken said that he had "never seen so much gold braid" in his life. On February 22, the troops marched on the Aldershot parade square in a memorial service for Baron Tweedsmuir, the Canadian governor general, who had died eleven days earlier, and at the end of March, McNaughton returned to review the Third Field Regiment at the Lille Barracks.

There was also a life beyond the training field and parade square. The First Division had not taken long to set up a hockey league, though the nearest ice rink was at Earls Court, in London. In February, Ken took the train there and was delighted to report to Earle that the Saskatchewan boys of the Seventy-seventh had beaten the Royal Canadian Regiment in overtime: "We'll show those easterners how to play hockey!" The Canadians also, he added, "showed the English how to cheer a team on, how to yell for the referee's blood. None of this 'well played, old man' and polite clapping of hands for us. We made so much damn noise in that rink that the English looked at us in amazement, thinking we'd gone nuts."

On that outing, Ken stayed over in London and was able to give his brother, as one man to another, a first-hand account of Soho, London's notorious red-light district. Moose Jaw's River Street, with its hookers, gambling and drugs, had long been known as one of the roughest streets in western Canada, but Ken was unlikely to have seen much of it. Now he was shocked by the open displays of vice in Soho: "I sure as hell wouldn't go down there in a blackout! The toughest layout on God's green earth and a lady(?) in every doorway. I'll bet you could hire a murder done there for about two shillings."

Away from Aldershot, Ken was little different from any North American tourist—in peacetime or war—seeing England for the first time. One Sunday in March he and a fellow officer rode their motor-cycles to Windsor, and he pronounced the Castle, with the Royal Family then in residence, "a sight that I'll never forget." The King, in recognition of their value to Britain, was allowing only Canadian soldiers inside the Castle, and Ken was awed by the sight of royal graves dating back to the fourteenth century. Afterward, they took in the old-world charm of Eton, the famous boys' college across the Thames. To end the day, they dined at a restaurant located in what once had been the house of Nell Gwyn, the seventeenth-century actress and mistress of Charles II.

Ken's letters to his relatives, like those of all soldiers, were subject to censorship, and so they contained no specific references to military sites and only general descriptions of manoeuvres. There was, more-over, another form of censorship practised by all servicemen during the war: the self-censorship of details that might worry the folks at home. Thus, at times Ken's letters begin to sound like the BBC radio broadcasts that the author J.B. Priestley and other prominent Britons were then doing to stiffen the resolve of their own people. He assured his grandmother that he was putting on weight in England, "and that should put the lie to German propaganda claims that we're starving to death over here." Despite the precaution of a nightly blackout, there had been no air raids around Aldershot because, it seemed, "the German Air Force are too busy machine-gunning fishermen in the North Sea to come near us." "I don't want you to worry about me too much," he said, "because I always was lucky and intend to keep my head down." As for the threatened invasion of the British Isles, he wrote, "the Royal Navy has taken care of everything that sailed against it and a lot of stuff that sailed away from it, so we have no worries in that department."

If Ken was unsettled in any way during this first winter in Britain, he did not reveal it in any of his letters, even those to his brother. In December he wrote that he was pleased plans were afoot for his mother to take Margaret to visit his American relatives in North Dakota, and a month later he told Earle with apparent detachment about the arrival of the "sweetheart boat," the ship bringing the wives of some of the Battery's senior officers to live in nearby Farnborough: "This makes me chuckle when I remember that we're off to camp soon. Those dames must have more money than brains and I'm damn sure they'll freeze to death before summer."

Bringing their wives over to Britain may have seemed like a good idea to the officers who could afford their passage, but, like most of the Canadian soldiers, Ken had crossed the Atlantic to fight, and he was anxious to get into action, get it over with and go home. As he said to his grandmother at the end of May, "Next time I travel I want to take Margaret with me and I want to be wearing a sports suit instead of the battle-rompers I have been living in for the past six months."

The First Division had arrived in the middle of the phony war, or what the British called the Sitzkrieg, six months of relatively little military activity on the Continent. The spring of 1940, deceptively gentle in Britain, changed all that with dramatic developments on the Continent, beginning with the German invasion of Norway on April 9. Ken seemed about to get his wish to see action.

First there was the possibility that the Seventy-seventh would be part of an attempt to halt the German advance in Norway when 1,300 men of the Princess Patricia's Canadian Light Infantry and the Loyal Edmonton Regiment left for Scotland to prepare to mount a counter-invasion at the port city of Trondheim. Fearful of the damage the Luftwaffe might inflict, however, the British chiefs of staff cancelled this attack and the Canadians returned to Aldershot on April 26. That day Ken told his American relatives that he would not be going to Norway but, by the time the letter reached them, would likely be in France. "All that remains now," he said, "is to put in a week or so firing in a practice camp. They have transformed us from the recruit class to a 100% fighting outfit since we came here and I must admit that it is almost with a feeling of relief that we near the end of our long grind of training."

If April had brought Norway and the aborted counter-invasion, May delivered drama and confusion. In the words of the historian of the Third Field Regiment, "May was a month of alarums and excursions, despondency, excitement and frustrations." Just before noon on the tenth, when German forces began sweeping into Belgium, Holland and northern France, the regiment was flashed the codeword "Julius," the signal for it to take its assigned position in the "Julius Caesar Plan" for the defence of the British Isles against invasion. Ken's battery was confined to barracks, hard rations were drawn, machine guns were mounted and extra guards were posted at key points. Everyone spent an uneasy night. Nothing happened.

Two days later, with the reports from the Continent growing more and more alarming, the Third Field Regiment moved to Larkhill, the famous British artillery firing range situated one mile north of the ancient site of Stonehenge. Here, though converted grocery and piano-moving vans still served as transports, the Seventy-seventh Battery got to fire its guns—among them the new 25-pounder howitzers—for the first time since they had arrived in Britain. They were still on the range at Larkhill on the morning of May 24, when a despatch rider arrived with the order for the regiment to prepare immediately to move to Southampton. It was to provide artillery support for "Angel Move," a scheme to send Canadian forces to Calais or Dunkirk to restore supply lines to the beleaguered British Expeditionary Force. Gas masks were rushed from the barracks, ammunition was drawn, the vehicles were loaded, and by noon the Third Field was ready and awaiting the order to proceed. Nothing happened. The clocks ticked, the gunners sat and smoked cigarettes and waited. Finally, at 10 p.m., word came that the move had been cancelled. This frustrating exercise was repeated on the twenty-sixth, when the regiment was roused at 3:30 in the morning, sat with the trucks loaded and running by noon, and had the excursion called off in the early afternoon.

The men were told that their expeditions had been cancelled because of the dangers of mines floating off Southampton, but the real reason lay in the speed with which the German army was pushing the British and French armies to the Channel. The twenty-sixth of May was in fact the beginning of the extraordinary effort by the Royal Navy and the "little ships" (a euphemistic term for a ragtag armada of civilian sailboats, yachts and other pleasure craft) to evacuate more than a third of a million British and French soldiers from Dunkirk. Most of the troops of the British Expeditionary Force got home, but when Ken saw them back in Aldershot, they were an exhausted and battle-weary band of men needing to be identified, fed, rested and sent back to their home units. They had returned without much of their equipment and arms, making the Canadian First Division the only really armed, mobile and fully manned division in the British Isles. And no one truly believed that it would be able to stop the German invasion that was sure to come before the summer was over. For the first time since William the Conqueror crossed the Channel in 1066, Great Britain was likely to come under foreign rule.

Following the Dunkirk evacuation, the First Division was put into a defensive role. With Hitler controlling the entire Channel coastline in France, invasion could come almost anywhere, and so it was decided that McNaughton's troops, now called the Canadian Force, would be based in central England. From there, it was hoped, they would be a quick-acting and mobile reserve ready to counterattack German invasion forces at any coastal point. Thus the Seventy-seventh Battery found itself in Northampton, in the Midlands of England, where for the first time the men were billeted in English homes. Even then there remained one more chance for the unit to join the fighting in France, and it would be the closest it would come to seeing action.

On June 7, the Third Field Regiment was ordered back to Aldershot, where it was reviewed by the King and Queen, provided with new vehicles and told to prepare to move to the coast: the Canadians were to go to France as part of a new BEF. A week later the Seventy-seventh Battery was part of a convoy that wound its way through the beautiful countryside of Dorset and Somerset to an army camp outside the Devonshire port of Exeter. The units had barely settled in for the night when they were stunned to receive the order to return to Aldershot in the morning. In the process of working their despondent way back across southern England, however, their spirits were again raised when they were ordered to camp outside Southampton, where they would board ships in the morning.

As the sun rose and they looked out on the harbour, though, they saw it crowded with ships bringing back the remainder of the BEF from France. Paris had been surrendered on June 14, the British had been told that the French army was no longer able to offer effective resistance, and on the morning of the fifteenth the order had been given for all British forces to withdraw from France. The order "Return to Lille" surprised no one in the Seventy-seventh, but it was a discouraged and disheartened group of soldiers who made yet another tedious journey back to the camp. At Lille Barracks they were greeted with derisory banners that read "Welcome Home, our Heroes of Exeter," and some wag suggested that CASF really stood for "Canadians Almost Saw France."

It would be the summer of 1943 before the First Division would see battle, and longer than that for Ken. With the French surrender, the Canadian forces became more important to the survival of Britain, as McNaughton recognized in a letter: "we are now squarely set for what I have long thought was the important task, the defence of these islands." Except for the ill-fated raid on Dieppe in 1942, the Canadians would spend the next three years manning anti-aircraft posts and moving around southern England on a seemingly endless round of training exercises. They became known as McNaughton's Travelling Circus, and Ken would come to call himself "the utility man for the Canadian Corps."

CHAPTER SIX

On the seventeenth of June 1940, Ken was in the Lille Barracks, in Aldershot, when word came that France had capitulated and was seeking an honourable armistice with Germany. What France got from Hitler five days later, of course, was humiliation, its delegation forced to sign the surrender documents at Compiègne in the same railway carriage—brought out of its museum for the occasion—where the Germans had signed the armistice papers that brought the Great War to an end. Great Britain and its Empire and Commonwealth were now left to fight on alone.

Winston Churchill, shortly after becoming prime minister on May 10, the day the Germans overran Holland and Belgium, had offered Britons "blood, toil, tears and sweat"; now he was urging them toward "their finest hour." Having been a voice in the wilderness for two decades, he was now "the lion's roar" hurling defiance at Hitler. And Ken, like the British people and the men in the First Division, came to be thrilled by his rhetoric in the coming years. "Don't you just love to hear Mr. Churchill speak?" he asked his cousin Grace. "He makes everyone chuckle when he starts calling down the dictators."

In June 1940, however, there was little reason for optimism behind Churchill's infectious bulldog resolution. For ten months nothing had been able to stand up to the German army—not the Poles, the Norwegians, the Dutch, the Belgians, the French or the British. Government propagandists, the press and the public had turned the Dunkirk evacuation into a sort of triumph bordering on the miraculous—at least the men got back, they said—but Churchill knew that wars were not won with retreats. The Germans were poised to cross the Channel—and indeed Hitler had begun preparations for Operation Sea Lion, his plan for the invasion of the British Isles—and few people believed that they could be stopped. Joseph Kennedy, the U.S. ambassador to Great Britain, was advising Roosevelt that the British were finished; the American public was still predominantly isolationist, and if Britain were forced to surrender, the United States would very likely reach an accommodation with Hitler. The face of Europe would be changed for decades, if not forever, and Ken and the other Canadian troops would be returned to Canada in the most humiliating of circumstances.

In order to combat the gloom and despondency that had settled into the Third Field Regiment, the commanding officer plunged it into a rigorous series of manoeuvres and drills immediately after its disappointing return from Exeter. But the Canadians did not remain in Aldershot for long. General McNaughton had become convinced that it was no longer the best base from which his Canadian force, now clearly serving as home defence, could operate. When the invasion came, a large military camp would be one of the surest targets for German bombers. Moreover, it was difficult to disperse or conceal trucks and guns in the confining barracks areas, and it would be hard to mobilize and move quickly. Then too, spreading the Canadian units all over southern England might persuade German intelligence that the army was much larger than it actually was.

"The thing to do," McNaughton said later, "was to take advantage of what the English have—those lovely parks." Thus, in the last week of June, Canadian units were under canvas on some of the most beautiful and famous country estates in Oxfordshire, from which they were to be ready at an hour's notice to help counter an invasion from any direction. The Third Field Regiment was assigned to the grounds of Blenheim Palace, on the edge of Woodstock, about eight miles from Oxford.

Ken could hardly have found himself situated anywhere in Britain with more historic richness and relevance to the moment. Designed by

Sir John Vanbrugh and always considered the finest Baroque building in the British Isles, Blenheim had been the estate of Churchill's illustrious ancestor the first Duke of Marlborough. It was given to him by the nation in gratitude for his victory at the Battle of Blenheim, fought in Germany and in part against Bavarians, in 1704. If the Canadian soldiers camping on Blenheim's magnificent grounds needed any reminding of Britain's past military glories and how the present times desperately called for a return to that tradition, they would only have to be told that it was at Blenheim that Winston Churchill himself was born in 1874.

The Third Field Regiment had been at Blenheim only a week when it was sent south to the Surrey town of Horsley, which had been chosen as its battle position in the expected invasion. There, in forests that reminded Ken of British Columbia, the regiment spent the summer on training schemes, during which it suffered its second casualty when a gunner was thrown out of a lorry and died, as fate would have it, in front of a house named Journey's End. There, too, he told his relatives, he saw first-hand

> *the wonderful work the Royal Air Force are doing over here. I have seen battles with my own eyes that I wouldn't have believed possible. I saw three Spitfires completely rout thirty German bombers accompanied by numerous fighters. The first three spread them all over the sky where they were pounced on by other RAF aircraft which came from nowhere. And in no time at all several of the enemy were coming down in flames. Men had to bail out and were taken prisoner as soon as they landed. Shows like this give us confidence in the Air Force and the boys cheer like mad while a fight is raging.*

Perhaps in deference to their feminine sensibilities, Ken declined to tell them that one plane crashed and exploded 1,500 yards from regimental headquarters and that a gunner, eager for souvenirs, had brought back a piece of the pilot's skull.

The summer of 1940 was tense for the Third Field Regiment, but, thanks to the kind of work Ken had seen the RAF do, Hitler hesitated until it became too late to launch his invasion before the winter weather set in. At this point, with Britain unable to do anything but defend itself, what lay ahead for the Third Field Regiment was months—and perhaps years—of training schemes, manoeuvres and waiting. Ken, however, was soon given a chance to see real action, and he jumped at it.

Early in September a call went out for Canadian gunners with experience on medium, heavy or coastal artillery to serve in the Super-Heavy Railroad Group, a British artillery unit created in the Great War but inactive since then, to cover vulnerable points along the coast. Its weapons were large artillery pieces—9.2-inch guns and 12-inch howitzers—and there was even one mammoth 18-inch howitzer called the Bochebuster, which had been stored in a railway tunnel near Canterbury, in Kent. The other guns, which had not been fired since 1918, had to be retrieved from various storage sheds and railway yards, where local people had been employed over the years to keep them greased, oiled and in working condition.

Ken had joined an artillery unit when he was sixteen, and for thirteen years he had absorbed the lore of the big guns. Now he was being invited to handle the biggest guns of all in an elite British unit that he had only read about. As he said to his cousin Grace, "this is about the topmost rung of the artillery ladder. Our work is highly technical and with a gun this size we have the satisfaction of knowing that when we 'pull the string' we're going to cause Jerry a lot of concern." He volunteered immediately, and on September 6 he and seven gunners from the Third Field Regiment arrived in Banstead Wood, Surrey, where they joined recruits from the other Canadian regiments—they called themselves "the orphans of the RCA"—to form the X and the Y Super-Heavy Batteries RCA. Two days later, immediately after being inspected by General McNaughton, they proceeded to Shorncliffe, in Kent.

Ken saw a 9.2-inch gun for the first time on September 10, when the two batteries were taken to view it in storage at the railway yard in Hythe. His unit, the X Battery, comprising five officers and eighty-one men, was responsible for two guns; it took a crew of twelve to put a single gun into operation. Though the 9.2-inch shells could reach ships and landing craft fifteen miles out to sea, each gun was assigned to cover a number of beaches and the narrow paths leading from them to higher ground. Mounted on cars of the Southern Railway, the Super-Heavies were supposed to be mobile, moving quickly and efficiently along the south coast to whatever sites the Germans might choose to invade. Royal Artillery planners had not counted on English bureaucracy, however, and the X Battery soon discovered that the railway rules required that a company guard escort each train; on at least one occasion the gun crew sat for an hour on a siding waiting for a guard to arrive from Ashford. Not for nothing was there a wartime joke that the Germans would be in London in twenty-four hours providing they didn't go by train.

The X Battery did not get to fire its big guns for several months. In the meantime, it established its headquarters in some requisitioned buildings in Littlestone on Sea, near New Romney, along the southern coast. It was here, on October 10, that Ken came under enemy fire for the first time, when German planes dropped eight 500-pound high-explosive bombs and two oil bombs on the billets and gun position. Windows were blown out, and there was considerable damage to the ceilings, walls and roofs of the billets, but surprisingly, the battery suffered no casualties. Several days later, Ken was housed in a railway car when a German bomb fell two miles away, and he felt the car being shunted two and a half feet along the tracks.

Being situated along the south coast meant, of course, that Ken got a first-hand view of the aerial battles, then at their most intense, between the Luftwaffe and the RAF, and by late September he had seen more than thirty enemy planes shot down. He wanted to be more than a mere spectator in the war, but the Battle of Britain was being fought in the air and there was little that X Battery could do but drill, dig slit trenches, locate suitable gun sites, guard the guns and billets, and set up machine-gun posts for light anti-aircraft use. Ken got to man a machine gun from time to time, but, as he reported in frustration to his relatives, "nothing came low enough for me to take a welt at, worse luck. I do this little trick several times a day because I think I'll feel better about the whole thing if I'm lucky enough to make a few German feathers fly."

As the English summer turned to a wet and cold fall, any glamour attached to life in the Super-Heavies fell away. "We are living in railroad coaches on a very lonely siding at the moment," he said. "There is nothing but the odd farm for miles around, the nearest town being some six miles away. I expect that if we stay here all winter we'll be as crazy as a bunch of sheepherders by spring. The bands quit playing for us a long time ago and we're down to hard soldiering now . . . Life has become very monotonous."

The bands had not entirely quit playing for Ken, at least as far as the folks at home were concerned. Early the following February, my grandparents were thrilled to open the Regina *Leader-Post* and see a Canadian Press article about the X Battery and Ken—located, it said discreetly, "somewhere in England." By then the Battery had fired the guns to test and calibrate them, and Ken told the reporter: "You can't drive nails with these big babies like you can with the 25-pound field guns but they're terrifically powerful and accurate for the job." The mechanism was intricate, he said, but the crews had become so efficient that they were able to strip the guns for action in only five minutes from the time they received the fire order. Less exciting were the exercises simulating enemy infiltration of the gun site areas. The most recent one had called the Battery out on short notice, and for eighteen hours it patrolled muddy fields and roads looking for "enemy" vehicles and fighting off "enemy soldiers" in the chilling winter rain. "It was," Ken conceded with a grin, "a glorified wet game of cops and robbers, taken seriously."

In the end, all the training and simulated battles were for an attack that never came, and early in 1941, with the threat of invasion clearly past, the British home defence authorities decided to disband the Super-Heavies. On February 3, the Canadians received the order to turn their guns over to the Royal Artillery. "All ranks," observed the X Battery's diary, "are feeling very blue at leaving the railway guns. The officers are very disappointed at this prospect. All have worked hard to make the battery a success and the battery was becoming a well-trained and efficient unit."

Ken did not return to the Seventy-seventh Battery but spent the next month quietly in the Canadian Artillery Reinforcement Unit at Bordon, near Aldershot. While there, he got word that his grandmother had died. He had been close to her and regretted not being able to join his parents at the funeral in Fargo, but he wrote to console his relatives there. The events of the war surely distressed her, he said, and he and Earle being in uniform must have been a source of worry for her. "She is at rest now," he concluded, "where nothing can trouble her in this mad world of ours. When my own time comes I hope I will be remembered with as much respect and kindness."

While at Bordon, Ken was invited to Stowe Maries, the sixteenth-century country house of Leslie Howard, the film actor best known for his role in *Gone With the Wind*. Appreciating the presence of Canadian servicemen on their island, many distinguished Britons were welcoming them into their houses, great homes and even castles for tea or a drink. Strome Galloway, a member of the Royal Canadian Regiment, remembers meeting the writer Sir Philip Gibbs, the actress Beatrice Lillie, and the poet and Member of Parliament A.P. Herbert this way.

Howard's daughter, Doodie, has described how their home was frequently surrounded by Canadian military vehicles and every chair occupied by officers from Toronto, Montreal, Winnipeg and Ottawa. And on one occasion a lieutenant from Moose Jaw. Ken did not actually meet Leslie Howard, who was in London working on his propaganda broadcasts to North America and completing the script of the film *Pimpernel Smith*. He was amused when Mrs. Howard asked him if, coming from western Canada, he could strike a match with his thumbnail, cowboy style. Gary Cooper, she said, had tried to teach her to do it, but she always broke the match or burnt her thumb. Trying to recall the westerns he had seen on Saturday mornings at the Orpheum Theatre in Moose Jaw, Ken did his best to reproduce that manly cinematic gesture for her.

Similarly, on Christmas Day, after the officers had served the men a traditional Canadian dinner of turkey and all the trimmings, they dined themselves in the centuries-old home of Sir Auckland Geddes, who had been First Lord of the Admiralty in the Great War and the British ambassador to the United States in the 1920s. "Very charming people," Ken reported. "We swept all barriers aside and finished the evening teaching Lady Geddes a few card tricks to confound her friends with."

While Ken was enjoying the hospitality of his British hosts, Margaret was in Moose Jaw acting as hostess for visiting British and Commonwealth servicemen. She had spent the first six months of 1940 taking a graduate course in nursing in New York, where she had been treated with hostility by the American nurses of German and Italian origin. Back in Moose Jaw, she resumed her nursing career at the Moose Jaw General Hospital and was elected president of its Nurses Alumnae Association. One of her first duties as president was to award the Gold Medal for General Proficiency, the same prize she herself had won several years earlier.

As the wife of a serviceman, Margaret was also expected to take part in various activities to support the war effort and the men in uniform. She was automatically a member of the Princess Patricia's Club, an auxiliary of the Seventy-seventh Battery that raised money to send cigarettes and chocolate to the soldiers and powdered milk to the British. Throughout 1941 she attended a series of dances at what was called the Military Institute, and in October 1941 she helped organize the Victory Ball, a charity gala dance.

Among the servicemen who flocked to these dances were hundreds of young pilots from the Flying Training School of the Royal Air Force, which began operations several miles south of Moose Jaw at the beginning of January 1941. These were dashing young men from exotic places like Great Britain, New Zealand, the United States, Norway and other European nations, and they were looking for excitement. Bringing with them the newest music and dances—the Bombs a Daisy and the Lambeth Walk—from abroad, they exuded a cosmopolitanism that rendered Moose Jaw's remaining young men dull and unsophisticated in the eyes of its women. Unable to compete with such glamour, the local males grew resentful, and on two evenings in September 1944 they fought with the air trainees in front of a crowd outside the Temple Gardens dance hall, an incident splashed across the country's newspapers as the Zoot Suit Riot.

It may well be that Margaret was one of the Moose Jaw women who was captivated by the visiting airmen. In those final days in Vancouver she would tell Ken of a lengthy affair with someone in Moose Jaw during the early years of the war, a man who could subsequently not be reached. Ken's assumption that he was an RAF pilot who had later been killed may have been wrong—he could simply have been transferred to some distant part of the war—but it is not improbable that Margaret was swept off her feet by one of the dashing young airmen who came to the dances she attended.

Ken, meanwhile, was posted in March 1941 to the 109th Battery, the Trail unit that had been one of the four western Canadian batteries originally comprising the Third Field Regiment. Now it was about to become part of the new First Canadian Light Anti-Aircraft Regiment, the first such unit in the history of the RCA. The Battle of Britain had made it clear that, until the distant time when a counteroffensive could be mounted against Germany, anti-aircraft strength was more important than field artillery. No one in Canada had ever seen the need to defend the country from air assaults, so Canadian gunners had no experience of AA equipment, particularly the new

40-mm Bofors gun. Presumably because Ken had shown his adapt-
ability with the Super-Heavies and had proven a very good instructor,
he was assigned to help turn the 109th Field Battery into an AA unit.

Ken arrived at the Sobraon Barracks at Colchester, Essex, on
March 6, and four days later the 109th Light AA Battery came into
existence. A troop commander with one lieutenant under him, he was
in charge of about seventy-five men. Shooting artillery into the air was
as new for him as it was for his gunners, but he joked that "an old duck
hunter like me ought to do alright against Heinkels and such." In
April, having taken a ten-day aircraft recognition course, he became
regimental instructor on aircraft recognition along with his regular
duties. "I'll probably be a mental case in a very short while," he wrote
Earle. "We studied six aircraft per hour on the course and my head is
in a whirl. Wish the Wright Bros. had died in their infancy." Anti-
aircraft had become imperative, however, as recent outings to London
made plain to him. "Words can't describe what one of those raids is
like, and to pass through there gives you that 'all gone' feeling. God
help any Jerries that come down near some of us! Sometimes I wish
our boys would scatter them about a bit."

This letter to Earle was occasioned by Ken's receiving a cable
telling him that I had been born on April 3. He had been delighted by
the prospect of becoming an uncle and by reports that his usually blasé
brother had become "goofy" at the prospect of becoming a father.
Earle had joined the active service by that point—"I didn't think they'd
be able to keep him out for very long," said Ken—and Ken recognized
that having both sons, their only children, in the armed services was
difficult for his parents. A grandchild would give them something else
to think about for a while. What he could not know, of course, was
how much I and my brother would become the substitutes for the sons
they would lose.

In June 1940, Ken was sent to a week-long officers' training course
at Bordon, and in August he was very pleased to be promoted to
captain. He had entered the active service as an officer, and, unlike

most ordinary gunners, he was ambitious and hoped to get back his captaincy and work his way up the ranks. If a comment about his promotion made in a letter to Earle is indicative, he seems to have been particularly sensitive to people's opinions of his ability as an officer. "I'd sort of like to have this bit of news on the local city page," he said, "just to show a few sceptics that I can win promotion in the newest branch of the service without any help from the 77th."

With the promotion came a transfer to another new anti-aircraft unit, the Second Light AA Battery. Ken hated to leave the 109th because it was "a great gang," but with the Second LAA, which had originated in Yorkton, he was back in a Saskatchewan outfit. Having begun as a machine-gun battery in 1936, the Second LAA was mobilized on September 3, 1939, but did not arrive in Britain until a year later. After training on Bofors guns on the Isle of Sheppey, in the Thames Estuary, it moved to Colchester in the summer of 1941 and became part of the new Second LAA Regiment, which was attached to the First Division. Ken was battery captain, which meant he was second-in-command, his main task being administrative: providing food, clothing and equipment for the battery.

The next year was spent in various training manoeuvres at Colchester and other points, punctuated by a three-month period providing anti-aircraft protection for the Vickers factory at Dartford and for the naval base and port at New Haven. The significant events of the war were occurring elsewhere, beginning with Hitler's foolish attack on Russia in June 1941. Six weeks after that, Ken rather optimistically commented to Earle that "the way the Russians are going maybe there won't be any of the Boche left for us to tangle with. If that is the case I'll be seeing you again soon and we'll walk into the Grant Hall [Hotel beer parlour] and beller 'A hundred up and get the lead out.'" On the ninth of December, when General Zhukov's first great counteroffensive was in full swing against the German army near Moscow, he was on surer ground in writing to his American relatives that the Russians were "marvellous right now and have the Hun on the run in several areas. I still don't like the English winters. From what I hear the Hun likes the Russian one even less. Bad time of the year to be camping out."

In December, the Japanese bombing of Pearl Harbor and the American entry into the war prompted Ken to write at length to the folks in Fargo about the new configuration of the war. His family, and the relatives in the United States, had always been interested in politics, and many of his wartime letters touched on the political landscape. In January, he had reported that the American politician Wendell Willkie, visiting British leaders on behalf of Roosevelt, was well received by the general public. Several months later, he commented that they had all been much encouraged by the passage of the Lend-Lease Bill, which permitted the United States to provide war material to Britain. And he was able to tell his family that the meeting of Churchill and Roosevelt at Placentia Bay, Newfoundland, in August, a conference that produced the Atlantic Charter, "caused quite a sensation over here."

Now, he said, Roosevelt's address to Congress about the Japanese assault had been broadcast throughout Britain, and

the United States is certainly in the limelight so far as we are concerned. The Japanese attacks were almost as big a surprise to us as they were to you and everyone over here wants to see the Son of Heaven get what's coming to him. At any rate he's asked for the same dose that Hitler and Musso are in line for. While we're at it, we might as well rid the earth of all its vermin. I can't understand how anyone can be an isolationist now. Civilization hangs in the balance, but we'll win, have no doubt about that!

The entry of the United States into the war meant that Ken's American cousin Walter, who had joined the army some time before, would now likely see action, and Ken was relieved that his grandmother was not alive to have this further worry. For Americans, he added, it seemed that the war had just begun, but he could not help recalling that the Pearl Harbor attack occurred exactly two years after he had left Moose Jaw for the European theatre.

In April 1942, Ken got the chance to participate in his first large-scale battle exercise when the entire Second LAA Regiment joined the First Division on Exercise Beaver III. Playing the part of an enemy force landing near Worthing and attacking Horsham, the regiment's assignment was the protection of brigade concentration areas and paths leading inland from the beaches. An even more massive scheme was Exercise Tiger, which involved two Canadian infantry divisions and one British, a number of other units, four RCAF squadrons and one bomber group. These forces were divided into the Sussex Army and the Kent Army, and they skirmished for nine days, protecting troop concentration areas, gun sites, bridges and roads. At the end of the allotted time the First Canadian Division was the only unit to succeed in crossing into "enemy" territory.

After two and a half years of training in Britain, the First Division assumed it would be first in line when Canadian forces were put into battle, and its opportunity seemed to arrive in August 1942, when it was decided that Canadian troops would be used for a training raid on the French coast at Dieppe. To its great disappointment, however, units of the more recently arrived Second Canadian Infantry Division were chosen, and the First Division's participation was reduced to providing anti-aircraft cover at the English ports for the raiders' departure and return. The Second LAA Battery, which had been stationed at the coastal town of Eastbourne in early August, was ordered to protect Newhaven, and it was during this assignment that an incident occurred that seems to have had a damaging effect on Ken's career for the remainder of the war.

According to Chester Fannon, a gunner in the Second LAA Battery, the command to move to Newhaven came when a despatch rider arrived at battery headquarters in Eastbourne with the order "Prepare to move." Ken, says Fannon, was then acting battery commander or acting troop commander, and he dutifully prepared the unit and awaited the order to move. Nothing happened. Time passed, but no order came. Finally, the despatch rider returned and asked: "Why are you still here? You were supposed to move to the battery rendezvous."

The risks of the Dieppe raid had created a great deal of tension, and news of the delay in the relocation of the Second LAA, says Fannon, was not well received at regimental headquarters. Someone had blundered: the original command—which should have been "Prepare to move and move to rendezvous"—may have been incomplete; the despatch rider may have erred and given Ken only the first part of the order; or Ken may have misinterpreted the command. Fannon believes that a scapegoat was needed and that Ken was perfect for the role. If he had been a Royal Military College graduate, like most of the higher-ranking officers in the Canadian Army at that time, he would likely have escaped censure. The RMC club tended to protect its own, but a Westerner who had worked his way up the ladder had no such shield.

There is no record of this incident in the unit diary of either the Second LAA Battery or the Second LAA Regiment, nor is there any mention of it in Ken's personnel file. Fannon remains nonetheless convinced that the delay was blamed on Ken, that it stuck in the memories of senior officers and that it was the reason he was never promoted to major when many junior officers were advanced past him. In fact, when Fannon heard three years later that Ken had taken his own life, he was convinced that his suicide was motivated by his failure to return from Europe any higher than a captain. "I think," he says, "that he never actually got over that."

There is no way of knowing what effect, if any, the Dieppe raid incident had on Ken's military career, but there is no doubt that he believed he would be promoted before the end of the war and that some of his fellow officers in the Second LAA were surprised when he was not made a major. My grandparents were told by several of his fellow officers that he was not promoted because he was too familiar with his men, something considered inappropriate by the army. This may have been said simply to console grieving parents, but the gunners in the Second LAA I have talked to all speak very highly of him—Fannon calls him "a very, very likeable guy, a very personable man"—and it is uncommon for ordinary servicemen to remember officers with respect or affection.

In spite of—or perhaps because of—this incident, Ken remained a highly regarded training instructor, and he continued to be moved or loaned to various units. In June 1942 he had been attached to the Sixteenth LAA Battery for two weeks, and in early December he spent a similar period with the Ninth LAA Battery. In the middle of January 1943, he was transferred from the Second LAA to the Number 3 Canadian Artillery Reinforcement Unit to be a battery training instructor. From there he was loaned to the First Anti-Aircraft Brigade for a fortnight in March, and in July he was again transferred, this time to the Sixth LAA Regiment. He had indeed become the "utility man" of the Canadian Corps.

One of Ken's tasks at the Reinforcement Unit was to find volunteers for the increasing number of light anti-aircraft batteries, and one day in January he was sent to Aldershot to address a contingent of field artillery gunners and officers newly arrived from Canada. These men had been on ships for over a week, had disembarked in Scotland and endured a long ride down to Aldershot on the crowded little English trains. They were looking forward to sitting down for their first real meal in many hours when an officer announced: "I know that you men are tired and hungry and want to dig into your dinner, but we have an officer here who would like to say a few things to you, and if you give him your attention for a few minutes, we'll soon be serving the food." In this unpromising setting, Ken made his pitch.

In the audience that day were two lieutenants from Quebec: Roger Jean-Marie, a short, stocky francophone from Dixville, a town a few miles from the Vermont border, and John Gardiner, a fluently bilingual resident of St-Lambert, a suburb of Montreal located across the St. Lawrence River. Gardiner's father, Albert Austin, had come to Canada from his native England at the age of eighteen in 1906 to escape his family's destitution brought about by his own father's heavy drinking. Albert was heading for Winnipeg, but his ability to type, a modern skill very much in demand in the New World, got him a job with the Canadian National Railways the day after he arrived in Montreal. Over the years he worked his way up in the company so that by the Second World War he was the chief officer in charge of passenger service in that city.

Albert met and married Evangeline Hébert, a Québécois woman, and in 1917 they bought a spacious two-storey house on land owned by the CNR on the edge of St-Lambert. There they raised eight children, all perfectly bilingual—the rule of the house being that they had always to speak the language of whatever guest might be visiting. All the children were well educated at boarding schools, which they were allowed to choose themselves but where they were then expected to excel. John Gardiner, born in 1915, attended Collège de Montréal, and because he was bilingual and had a facility for picking up a smattering of other languages like German and Italian, he was able to get a summer job as a tour escort in the 1930s. The CNR had a joint touring venture with the Cunard shipping line and various European railways, and it needed young men to help with luggage and to interpret.

Gardiner was serving as a tour escort at the outbreak of the Second World War, not in Europe but in California, and he came home immediately to join a field artillery battery in Montreal. Since he had several years of university education, he could have entered the army as an officer, but he wanted to work his way up the ranks, in part to prove to the senior officers that he could do it on his own merit and in part to prove to himself that he could handle the job. Since his battery was not part of the First Division, most of its training was carried out for the first years of the war at the Basic Military Training Camp at Sherbrooke and then the artillery camp at Petawawa.

It was at Sherbrooke that Gardiner met and got to know Roger
Jean-Marie, though their first encounter hardly suggested they would
become lifelong friends. A sergeant by then, Gardiner was the
accounts officer, and one of his duties was to ensure that the names,
ranks and other details of the new recruits were accurately recorded.
Unable to believe that Jean-Marie was a family name, he kept changing it to "Jean-Marie Roger" on the pay list, and at each pay parade the
name was read out incorrectly. After this had occurred a number of
times, Roger burst into the paymaster's room in a fit of exasperation
and demanded to know "who's the sonofabitch who can't get names
straight?" John, never one to back away from a confrontation, bluntly
reminded him that he was addressing an NCO and that he should
watch his language. He suggested they step outside, where the shouting match continued until both men calmed down. A little while later,
recognizing, as antagonists sometimes do, that they were kindred
spirits, they decided to settle their differences over a beer or two, and
before long they had become fast friends.

Two of Gardiner's brothers, Gerry and Austin, followed him into
uniform, with Austin the first to go to Britain—with the RAF in
1942. In their family home this meant that only Austin's photograph
got pride of place on the living-room mantelpiece: for Albert Gardiner,
being in the army in Canada was merely a job, while going overseas
meant going to war. On the day John's battery sailed from Halifax in
1943, his father picked up his picture from a side table, walked over
to the mantelpiece and placed it beside Austin's.

A few days out of Halifax and a week before that January evening
in the Aldershot mess, John and Roger were aboard their ship in the
mid-Atlantic when Roger asked, "Jean, do you think there'll be a
second front soon? . . . And when?"

"Who knows?" replied Gardiner.

"Then," said Roger, "you know what we're going to be doing.
We're going to be going on schemes. For years. Like all the guys over
here have been doing for years. Training. Drills. Marching."

"I guess so," said John.

"But," continued Roger, "if we join the AA, when the Jerries come over we start working right away."

Gardiner agreed with his friend's reasoning, but neither man knew anything about getting into an anti-aircraft unit; they would just have to go to Britain and see what came up. Thus, when Ken gave his brief talk about the LAA, he was addressing eager converts, and he had barely finished speaking before the pair were on their feet and volunteering. In fact, they did it with such zeal that three of the other field artillerymen put their names forward as well, and Ken went back to the Reinforcement Unit headquarters feeling very pleased to have secured five volunteers.

John and Roger did not expect ever to see their recruiter again, and although the pair were both sent to the Second LAA Regiment, they were disappointed to learn they were being assigned to different units: John went to the Second LAA Battery, Ken's old outfit, and Roger to the Fifty-fourth LAA Battery. Both soon saw the action they had been looking for, but it was not the kind they had expected. Within six months of arriving in the British Isles, they would go into battle on European soil while Ken, who had been in the United Kingdom for three and a half years, remained impatiently behind, instructing yet more new men.

By the spring of 1943 there was considerable pressure, both within Canada and among senior army officers in Britain, to put Canadian soldiers into battle. Former prime minister R.B. Bennett acerbically pointed out that in 1942 the country's soldiers would celebrate their fourth wartime Christmas without firing a shot (he apparently did not recognize anti-aircraft fire as shots, and he seemed to forget Dieppe). Lionel Shapiro, a journalist with the Montreal *Gazette,* commented that the Canadian Army was "the first formation in the history of war in which the birth rate is higher than the death rate." The *Gazette* also ran a story under the headline "Mental Illness in Overseas Army Laid to Inactivity and Anxiety," and

Winnipeg Free Press editorials aggressively called for a full division to be sent to some theatre of war.

This insistence on Canadian participation coincided with the decision of the Allies to invade Italy. Stalin had long wanted a second front to take some German pressure off the Russian army, and Churchill, seeing Italy as less costly in soldiers' lives than northern France, pushed for an invasion first of Sicily and then of the Italian mainland. In describing the strategy to the Russian leader, he compared the Russian assault to attacking a crocodile's hard snout while Italy would be the "soft belly." Similarly, Churchill wrote to Roosevelt of attacking "the under-belly of the Axis," thus creating by his rhetoric the grossly inaccurate picture of Italy as an easy option for the Allied forces. In fact, with its many rivers, mountains and ridges, Italy was, in David Bercuson's words, "a defender's dream and an attacker's nightmare," and before it was over, 5,764 Canadian servicemen would be killed and 19,486 wounded in this soft underbelly. So difficult, in fact, was the Italian campaign that Churchill was eventually forced to change his metaphor and compare the Allies' painfully slow progress there to bugs crawling up a trouser leg.

The Canadian government wanted its troops to be part of this Mediterranean campaign, so the British agreed that their Third Division would be replaced by the First Canadian Infantry Division and the First Canadian Army Tank Brigade. On June 16, they boarded ships in Scotland, and it was not until they had been at sea for some time—Dominion Day—that they were told of their mission, though the issuance of tropical clothing had suggested they were heading for the Mediterranean. The convoy, made up of 125 vessels, had to run the gauntlet of enemy U-boats, but it was not until it reached the North African coast between Oran and Algiers that the Germans struck. During the night of July 4–5, two ships were sunk, one of which was carrying H Troop of the Fifty-fourth Battery, including Roger Jean-Marie. Roger was in charge of fifteen men, and in the terrifying confusion of water and darkness, with exploding ammunition on the burning ship sending chunks of twisted metal in every direction, he managed to have them tie four life rafts together.

At dawn, H Troop was taken aboard a destroyer, where it could be accommodated only shoulder to shoulder on the decks. Several days earlier Roger had found the sun and blue sky of the Mediterranean a splendid change from the chilly mists of the Scottish coast, but now, exposed to the sun without a hat or shirt and covered with oil, he found the heat relentless. Badly sunburnt, the men were taken to Algiers, where, in a prisoner-of-war camp from which captured Italian soldiers had been removed, they were held in seclusion for two weeks. Since they had been told of the plans for the invasion of Sicily, it was considered too risky to allow them to wander through the city.

Roger Jean-Marie thus missed the beginning days of the assault on Sicily, but John Gardiner and the Second LAA, attached to the Third Infantry Brigade, were there. D-Day—the real "D-Day" for every veteran of the Italian campaign—was set for July 10, and at two o'clock that morning the largest armada ever assembled to that time anchored ten miles off the southernmost beaches of Sicily. By first light Canadian soldiers were once again in battle on European soil.

Back in Moose Jaw on the morning of July 10, the Calders turned on their radio as they had breakfast and heard Mackenzie King tell Canadians that "armed forces of Britain, the United States and Canada are now in the forefront of an attack which has as its ultimate objective the unconditional surrender of Italy and Germany. All Canada will be justifiably proud to know that units of the Canadian Army are a part of the Allied force engaged in this attack." It may be that my grandparents shared their prime minister's pride in the Canadian role in the invasion of Sicily, but the possibility that their son was there and facing enemy fire would have made them anxious.

Though the Calders were not to know it for some weeks, Ken was continuing to train gunners in England, perhaps a victim of the old and almost universal saying among soldiers that you should "never get too good at one job or you'll never get another." Army administrators, said soldier and war correspondent Ben Malkin, "are something like Hollywood movie directors: once they put you in a certain slot, they think it's forever." Ronald MacFarlane, who had joined the Second LAA in Yorkton at the outbreak of war and worked himself up to regimental sergeant-major, learned the truth of this axiom when he revealed himself to be a capable gunnery instructor in the early years of the war. To his chagrin, when the Second LAA left for Sicily, he remained in the British Isles, and it was not until the following November, at the Sangro River in Italy, that he was able to return to the battery.

For Ken, who had been in Britain as long as any Canadian service-man, it was difficult to continue to supervise exercises when he knew that his old friends in the Seventy-seventh and Second LAA were at last seeing action. Knowing that Canadians would soon be on the battle-field, he wrote to his relatives in May that "I am still an acting Battery Commander here and in light of what is happening in other spheres I find it a dull job. I didn't come over here 42 months ago to train people to fire on the Hun properly, I came over here to fire on him myself."

In the summer of 1943, however, while Gardiner and the others were being tested by tough fighting in Sicily, Ken was still taking new men over well-trodden training grounds around Colchester and camps in southern England. On August 2, the Second LAA was protecting an infantry unit near Regalbuto in central Sicily; that day Ken was in Eastbourne presiding over a Court of Inquiry looking into a soldier who, not realizing his rifle was loaded, accidentally wounded another gunner. On September 20, the battery was on the Italian mainland, covering the Third Brigade at Potenza; Ken was in Seaford, along the south coast from Eastbourne, attending a meeting of umpires who would be judging two simulated battles in the English countryside in early October.

CHAPTER SEVEN

Even as Ken was umpiring simulated combat in the English countryside, plans were being made to send him to the real battlefields in Italy. Knowing that the Allied invasion of northern France would occur in 1944, the Canadian military chiefs wanted to have as many officers with battle experience as possible, so they sent out a call for volunteers to join the First Division in Italy. Ken put his name forward, and in late October 1943, forty-six months after he had arrived in Britain, he was sailing to the Mediterranean.

Ken spent most of November in a British North Africa Forces holding unit in Algeria, and the exoticism of that part of the world was a revelation to the young man from Saskatchewan whose only foreign travel had been to the United States and Great Britain. He wrote:

> The Arabs are a filthy-looking lot clothed in the most appalling
> collection of rags imaginable. I was in the nearby town yesterday
> and had a stroll through the Arab quarter. I have read various
> vivid descriptions of such places from time to time but never
> before have I smelt such a conglomeration of assorted smells.
> The streets are, besides being thoroughfares, apparently garbage
> dumps and worse, and one must keep a wary eye on the upstairs
> windows for obvious reasons. I have never before beheld or
> imagined such squalor and filth.

In December, Ken was in Tunisia, where he was no more impressed by the North Africans. There he saw his first soldiers' cemeteries—both

Allied and German—and noted that they were well cared for. But, he added in a letter, "for a while the Arabs thought it good business to rob the graves for the army blanket and clothing but after a few hundred had been shot in the act they gave it up as an unprofitable enterprise. Nice people, eh?"

Ken's impression of the Arabs was no different from that of most British and Canadian soldiers, but he cast a critical eye on more than just the local population. Writing to his relatives in Fargo, he commented that "there are all kinds of American soldiers over here, both black and white, and strange to say the coloured lads are the only ones who bother to pick us up when we thumb our way. For some reason or other the white boys just won't be bothered so we have decided that when we get our own transport the only Americans we'll bother to pick up will be the coloured ones." Of course, if he had tried to use an American Red Cross canteen, he would have discovered that, unlike those of the other Allied countries, they were restricted to American soldiers.

As he approached his fifth Christmas overseas, waiting in Tunisia for the order to move to the Italian front, Ken thought both of home and of Margaret. "I'd give a lot," he said, "to be back home right now with my feet under Mother's table having an ordinary meal. I wouldn't want a big spread, just whatever was on the table would do me fine. In two more days I will have been overseas exactly four years and that is a long time to have been away from good old home cooking." He was encouraged, he added, by the possibility that the war would be over in a few months, and if the men who went over first were the first to be sent home, he would be "in on the ground floor."

Margaret had written him that she had a good job in Vancouver at five dollars an hour, "so we won't have any financial difficulties after the war to bother us." The dream of owning his own sporting goods store was still alive, and so was the dream of resuming his life with her. "She'd like to have me home though," he reported, "and to heck with the job," but she insisted on working because it helped pass the time.

As eager as Ken was to go home, he was anxious to get into the fighting before it was too late. He had gone to Britain in 1939 to see action—more action, at least, than manning anti-aircraft defences in southern England—and he did not want to return to Moose Jaw having never been in battle. "I'm really glad to be out here where things are happening," he wrote. "Things look now as if this end of the war won't last much longer and I want to do a bit of fighting before the curtain is rung down."

Ken finally got his chance "to do a bit of fighting" on January 3, 1944, when he was made troop commander of B Troop of his old unit the Second LAA Battery, then located near Ortona, along the Adriatic coast of Italy. Within two days he found himself preparing his men to provide an honour guard for the visit to regimental headquarters of General Harry Crerar, who was about to become officer commanding of the First Canadian Corps when it was activated on February 1. Crerar, who himself had arrived in Italy in late 1943, was a dour, inflexible man whose belief in spit and polish, even on the battlefield, earned him the detestation of the men who had fought the German army for six months. As General Chris Vokes put it, Crerar's head-quarters "produced more useless paperwork containing more absolute bullshit than one could cover with an exploding No. 36 grenade . . . As far as I was concerned, my soldiers could go into battle in their BVDs or bare-assed if they wanted."

As an officer with no battle experience taking command of men who had seen hard combat from Sicily to Ortona, Ken could easily have been treated with the same contempt by both his gunners and his fellow officers. In fact, as he reported to relatives, he received "a very warm welcome from all the boys from the Colonel on down." The Second LAA was still heavily composed of Saskatchewan men, but the common practice of rotating officers among the units meant that the battery was now commanded entirely by men from places like Montreal, Toronto and Vancouver. With Ken's arrival, recalled John Gardiner, "they at long last had a Saskatchewan guy they could understand." And, he might have added, who understood them. According to Garnett Matchett, "as far as the battery was concerned, there was nobody like Ken Calder. The whole battery liked him." Unlike the Eastern officers—"those RMC bastards," as Second LAA gunner Harold "Eddie" Shore likes to put it—Ken was firm but fair, and played no favourites. Moreover, he would talk to the gun crews remembering that he was their officer but also that they were men enduring their own particular kinds of hell.

Ken himself must have felt like the person who has arrived late at the party, when much of the action has already happened and the relationships have been established—except, of course, that the Canadians had not been at a party since setting foot in Italy. They had met little resistance from the Italian troops on their landing in Sicily, and following the deposing of Mussolini in late July and the Allied invasion of the mainland on September 3, the Italians had surrendered unconditionally. Suddenly, Fascists were hard to find. The Germans, however, were a far different matter. They took over the country, disarmed the Italian troops, and dug in for a long and determined defence with some of their most battle-hardened divisions, led by one of the most astute military tacticians of the war, Field Marshal Albert Kesselring.

The German commander-in-chief himself could hardly have designed a better terrain for holding his ground. The Apennine mountains, difficult to traverse by anything but mule trains, run down the centre of much of Italy, and from their sides the rivers flow in old, deep gullies and ravines across the country—to the Adriatic in the east and the Mediterranean in the west. Thus the Allied armies faced a seemingly endless series of natural water defences, each of which had to be crossed by infantry terribly exposed to machine-gun and artillery fire, and each of which had to be bridged so that supplies and ammunition could reach the front. And always, it seemed, the Germans occupied the high ground, with gun turrets built into impenetrable cement bunkers along the mountainsides. Fred Majdalany, author of *The Battle of Cassino,* wrote of Italy:

A defender can fight an unlimited delaying action from one end of the country to the other. As an officer put it: "every 500 yards there is a new defensive position for a company, every five miles a new line for a division." In simple terms an advance up Italy against a strong enemy resolves itself into an interminable process of "one more river to cross, one more mountain barrier to overcome." Strategically, Italy might be a soft underbelly; tactically, it was a scaly pachydermous backbone.

Quite simply, except for the Russian front, no battleground in the European war was as formidable as that in Italy.

By the time Ken arrived at Ortona, the First Canadian Division had been blooded, and had become such a tenacious fighting force that the German troops had begun calling them "the Red Patch Devils." They had also been bloodied, and they were showing the effects. While more than two thousand Canadians had been killed or wounded in Sicily, December proved to be the cruellest month. On the fifth, the First Canadian Infantry Brigade, replacing exhausted British troops, fought its way across the Moro River, where it was counterattacked, shelled and mortared for five days. Farley Mowat, there with the Hastings and Prince Edward Regiment, remembers the Moro as "the River of Blood." Several days later, the Royal 22e Regiment (the Van Doos) was even more brutally hit while taking and holding Casa Berardi, a group of stone buildings along the side of a gully between the Moro and Ortona. Lanfranco Berardi, then a boy at the Casa, remembers having lost his shoes and being afraid of stepping outside his home because he would be walking in pools of blood. At a crossroads southwest of Ortona, the historian of the Royal Canadian Regiment recorded that "the slaughter was terrible."

Ortona itself, a town said to have been founded by the Trojans after the fall of Troy, was not an important military target, but for propaganda reasons the Eighth Army's General Montgomery ordered that it be taken. Defended by some of Germany's elite units—the crack

Ninetieth Light Panzer Grenadier Division, hardened from fighting in the North African desert, and the First German Parachute Division— it could be taken only at great cost. The Canadians—notably the Loyal Edmonton Regiment and the Seaforth Highlanders—did pay a heavy price when they captured the town over Christmas. General Vokes's comment that the struggle for Ortona made everything that had happened before seem like "a nursery tale" was confirmed by the grim casualty figures: in the month of December, from the Moro to the taking of Ortona, 695 Canadian soldiers had been killed, 1,738 wounded and 1,773 treated for sickness.

Malaria and jaundice felled many of the soldiers (even General Guy Simonds had been put out of action with jaundice), but a quarter of the men in sick bay were being treated for battle fatigue—what had been inaccurately and euphemistically termed "shell shock" in the First World War. This manifested itself, according to the psychiatrist attached to the First Division, in degrees of severity from hysteria, mutism and paralysis to the soldier who said simply, "I can't take it." Some of the lucky ones were treated sympathetically and sent to the rear, though it would take months, if not years, for them to recover from the experience. Others, like Mowat, who suffered a kind of "burnout" during the Ortona December, were reassigned—in his case to brigade headquarters as a liaison officer.

Between December and February, Canadian Army staff also identified sixty-seven men who were desperate enough to get away from the battlefield that they inflicted wounds on themselves (and it seems there were many others who escaped detection). There were, moreover, numerous cases of desertion or being absent without leave, and when a punishment camp was opened in February near Ortona, it was soon filled by two hundred prisoners.

To his credit, General Vokes recognized that the First Division had been debilitated. Writing to his British Corps commander, he commented that "the infantry units of this division will not be in fit condition to undertake further offensive operations until they have had a period of rest, free of operational commitments, during which they will carry out extensive training." The problem, however, could not be met by time away from the front; it was at the root of the Italian campaign, and it would worsen as the fighting dragged on.

There was, one officer wrote, "a sense of futility in the air," and this seems to have come from the fundamental ambiguity of the Allied goal in Italy. Aside from knocking Italy out of the war, the purpose of the campaign was to keep as many German divisions as possible occupied there and not on the Russian front or in the coming battle in Normandy. Thus, though the instinct of most soldiers was to advance, to capture territory from the enemy, a quick expulsion of the Germans would have been counterproductive. The Italian campaign had become a sideshow war, with reinforcement troops and new equipment being directed toward the battle in northern Europe rather than the struggle in Italy.

If Vokes wanted a regenerative rest for the First Division in the early months of 1944, he did not get it. For the first time in the campaign, the front became fixed, stretching from Ortona across Italy to Cassino, south of Rome, and it remained this way until late May. The sunny Italy of the travel posters turned into a land of freezing rain and inescapable mud, where the men, according to the regimental historian of the Forty-eighth Highlanders, "slept, ate, and lived in the cold slime." In fact, observed Crerar when he looked out at the landscape near Ortona, "It's just like Passchendaele," a view shared by the CBC war correspondent Peter Stursberg. "The Italian front in March 1944," he said, "looked like pictures of the Western Front. There were the same ruined farmhouses, the same shell holes full of water, the same broken, leafless trees. It was trench warfare again." What they were both describing, of course, were the entrenched, static First World War battlegrounds that first made shell shock/battle fatigue a serious problem for the British and Canadian armies.

As might be expected from a man who had just arrived, Ken showed no sign of any of this demoralization in his initial reaction to

the conditions in Italy, at least as he described it in a letter to Fargo
three weeks after his arrival at Ortona:

> *This is the warmest January I ever knew [hardly a surprising*
> *comment from a man accustomed to Saskatchewan and English*
> *winters]. We did have some rain and cold weather with a bit*
> *of snow but of late it has been warm and sunny in the daytime*
> *although it cools off considerably at night with the occasional*
> *hard frost . . . It is more or less quiet here, at least that's what*
> *I read in the papers. We shell him for awhile, then he turns the*
> *heat on us as much as he is able but so far he hasn't done any*
> *more to my outfit than come close. I'm getting pretty handy with*
> *a pick and shovel myself because below ground level is a mighty*
> *comforting place to be when the shells come down.*

Ken seems to have been practising some of the soldier's self-
censorship, so as not to alarm the folks at home, because while the
Ortona front was static, it was, in the words of historian Bill
McAndrew, "as vicious in its own way as the bitter street fighting had
been." The enemy still had to be regularly engaged, patrols made and
enemy fire endured. As in any war, the PBI—the "poor bloody
infantry"—bore the greatest hardships and faced the greatest dangers,
but the artillery were also vulnerable to shelling and air assaults.

Ken had not been in action many days before he experienced his
first "stonk," the soldier's term for a sudden, brief artillery bombardment. Harold Fretwell, a lieutenant in the Second LAA, recalls one
occasion when shells suddenly started landing near their quarters, and
Ken, another lieutenant and he dove into their slit trench. As the three
men lay crowded shoulder to shoulder there, the bombardment continued with greater than usual ferocity and for what seemed a very long
time. After a while Ken announced that he badly needed to urinate,
and the other two men had to persuade him that this was not the time
nor was the trench the place for such luxuries. It is an amusing story

told from the distance of years, but a few weeks after this episode another bombardment hit the battery, and three gunners and a bombardier—several from Ken's troop—were seriously wounded.

The enthusiasm in Ken's letters is coloured—like that of the rookie who finally gets put into the big game—by his satisfaction with seeing combat at last. "I am commanding a troop of guns," he wrote, "which is a far more exciting job than my old one of Battery Captain. We are now on the Eighth Army front so we are in pretty fast company these days. I feel great being out here after all those long years of training in England. I see quite a difference in the men too. Out here they don't have to pretend that there is an enemy up front and they all feel that they are doing something useful at last."

As battery captain, Ken had been an administrator, managing men and materials; as troop commander, he was more directly involved in the actual shooting. The battery was made up of three troops of gunners, each of which had six 40-mm Bofors guns. The firing was done by gunners directed by a sergeant; it was Ken's job to assess the terrain and the disposition of troops and equipment, and then choose the gun placements so that they actually protected the areas assigned to the battery. After that, while field artillery shoots were carefully planned and aggressive exercises following particular schedules, anti-aircraft firings were unpredictable and responsive to actions initiated by the enemy. Whereas the success of a field artillery shoot depended on how many enemy sites were hit, the effectiveness of an anti-aircraft action was measured, not in the number of planes shot down, but by how many were deterred from reaching their targets.

When Ken joined the First Canadian Light AA Regiment in England in 1941, there was a shortage of anti-aircraft units to defend the British Isles from the Luftwaffe bombers, so field artillery batteries were hastily being converted. In Italy in 1944, however, the Allies controlled the skies—having about 4,000 planes to the Germans' 450—so there was much less need for anti-aircraft protection. As a result, in January 1944 anti-aircraft batteries began to experiment with using their Bofors guns for ground shooting at bunkers and pillboxes, and from time to time for the remainder of the war they would be employed to fire directly on such ground targets.

While Ken found it exciting to be a troop commander, he hated one of his duties. Now that he was commanding men in a theatre of war, he was—like all officers—required to censor the gunners' letters, and he found it "the most distasteful job that an officer gets to do." By nature a man who kept his problems and his private life to himself, he found it repugnant to be intruding on the intimacies of other men. "But it has to be done so we get on with it so that the mail won't be delayed."

For most men, letters from home became more and more meaningful as their time overseas grew from months to years. Without access to newspapers and with only the occasional months-old magazine, they became increasingly dependent on mail to keep in touch with the life, culture, politics and sports of their city or town. In the absence of long-distance telephone calls and home leaves, letters were the only way to keep alive any sense of intimate contact with family, friends, spouses or lovers. As Jack Donoghue, a public relations officer in the Canadian Army, put it, "mail took on an importance that increased in intensity until the war ended. The morale of entire units, not just individual soldiers, would be adversely affected when mail failed to arrive when expected. After letters and parcels were distributed, those who received nothing could be easily identified by their gloom."

In a *Maclean's* article written during the Italian campaign, Peter Stursberg told the people back in Canada that the Canadian soldier's "morale depends to a large extent upon the regular flow of letters from his loved ones." Recalling his own experience in Italy in 1944, Farley Mowat explained that the soldier's world became reduced to the life of the unit, to the few hundred men with whom he was going into combat, and how important it was therefore to have some dynamic contact with home. "Most of us," he wrote later, "were also sustained by those who cared for us at home. Because they willed it so, and strained every effort of mind and spirit to make it so, my parents kept alive for me another, inner world of sanity, of trust, of love. This they made manifest through their letters—which had never before been of such vital consequence."

Ken's parents too struggled to maintain an essential connection between their son and his home and hometown through their letters and my grandmother's carefully wrapped packages of cigarettes, candies and clippings from the *Times-Herald*. But they were aging and Ken was changing, and the gulf between his world and theirs was widening. Even Moose Jaw was no longer the place he had left. In the spring of 1944 he was stunned to open his mail and read that his closest friend, Fred Cooper, had died. A shoe repairer, Fred had gone back to work too soon after having a number of abscessed teeth removed, and, unaware of any danger, he continued to grip the nails in his mouth as he had always done when he resoled shoes. His gums had become infected, the infection had raged through his system and several weeks later he was dead.

During his time with the 109th LAA Battery in England in early 1941, Ken had awakened one day to be told that the adjutant, a thirty-four-year-old man apparently in good health, had died in his sleep. "Makes one wonder about things," he had remarked then. Now his best friend's death seemed even more absurd. Too old to serve and with three children to raise, Fred had remained back in Saskatchewan—peaceful and secure Saskatchewan, about as far from the world's mad violence as one could get—yet the most harmless of actions, something he had done thousands of times before, had killed him. Dying on the battlefield, as Ken knew he might himself, made sense; this death did not. And he had always believed that, if he did survive the war, he would find himself once more with Fred in a boat on Last Mountain Lake, hauling in the big pike as they unburdened themselves to each other as only close and trusted friends can.

Newly arrived in Italy, Ken had received no mail, good or bad, for three months. Even in the years in Britain it had come only intermittently as German U-boats sank the Allied transport ships or wreaked enough havoc to render the mail irretrievably water-damaged. On the move since leaving England in October, he had been an elusive target for the armed forces postal service. But one of these days, he thought, his mail would catch up with him and he would be snowed under with letters. "I could stand that," he wrote. "I'm anxious to hear how things are at home."

Ken's Christmas parcels never did reach him, but after some weeks his mail began to come again. There were bundles from his parents and letters from Earle and the folks in Fargo, but the ones he eagerly awaited, those from Margaret, were few and spare. Over the years her letters had grown less warm, less intimate, more detached. Reading between the lines of Ken's letters home, my grandmother sensed that Margaret's correspondence had become, in her words, "cold, indifferent and far between," and she spoke to her daughter-in-law about writing more supportive and encouraging letters. As might be expected, Margaret bridled at this interference; she complained to Ken and he had to ask his mother to drop the matter.

At the same time that Margaret's letters were becoming fewer and more perfunctory, she did something else that might have signalled a lessening of her commitment to Ken. Early in 1943 she had taken another post-graduate course, this one at the Vancouver General Hospital, and in October she returned there to work. She never resided in Saskatchewan again, though for the remainder of the war her address, so far as the Department of National Defence was concerned, was 923 Alder Avenue, the Calder family home in Moose Jaw.

According to her sister, Margaret moved to Vancouver because some of her friends had done so and she preferred the weather on the coast. This may well be true, but leaving Moose Jaw was attractive for other reasons. In her husband's hometown she was the wife of a well-known local soldier serving overseas, and she was expected actively to support the war effort. There, too, she was a daughter-in-law, and if she had concluded that her marriage had been a terrible mistake, she would have come to find the inevitable—and expected—contact with Ken's parents

and extended family irksome. In Vancouver she was free of these obligations and could reinvent herself as Margaret Bruce, whose "fiancé" was
serving in Europe. Perhaps at an unconscious level, leaving Moose Jaw
slammed the door forever on the idea that she would settle down with
Ken and on his plan to open a sporting goods store.

Ken could sense that Margaret's commitment to the relationship
was waning, and he became increasingly anxious to get back and
breathe new life into it. "I want to go home quickly," he wrote his relatives from Ortona. "Hope it won't be like the last war: first over, last
home. Have been overseas more than 50 months now so you can
imagine how anxious I am to see the end of this affair." It would be
sixteen months before the "affair" was over.

Meanwhile, as the dreary winter months wore on around Ortona,
Ken inevitably became drawn into the band of brothers of the Second
LAA. In particular, he found a rapport with a lieutenant in his troop,
John Gardiner, whom he had not seen since that evening at Aldershot
when he recruited him for the anti-aircraft. Over the next sixteen
months this relationship would deepen until Gardiner became Ken's
closest friend and most trusted confidant.

Looking at the two men, it is not immediately apparent why they
felt a camaraderie. Gardiner was a bilingual Quebecker with a French
Canadian mother; Ken was an English-speaking prairie boy from
purely Scottish and Anglo-Saxon stock. Gardiner had been educated
at an excellent private school and had gone to McGill University; Ken
had dropped out of high school in Moose Jaw after completing grade
ten. Gardiner wore not only the sophistication of Montreal but also
the cosmopolitanism of one who had toured Europe a number of
times; the farthest of Ken's travels had been to a marksmanship competition in Montreal and family motor trips to North Dakota.

Moreover, while Ken was a conventional officer, understanding of
his men but respectful of military formality, Gardiner was openly
scornful of what he saw as slavish adherence to pedantic army rules.
This irreverent attitude sometimes got him in trouble, most notably

while he was training in England in the spring of 1943. On that occasion the commanding officers of several regiments had arranged a
track meet, and each of them was determined to have the bragging
rights at the end of the day. Always a capable runner, Gardiner's army
training had kept him in competitive trim, and so he was entered in a
middle-distance race. It did not take long for him to sprint to the lead,
and he maintained it until he rounded the final turn and approached
the crowd of officers and men waiting at the finish line. At this point
Gardiner spotted the regimental commanders cheering with the rest of
the soldiers, and something snapped within him. I came over here to
fight the Germans, he thought, not to play games with my fellows.
Now we're running ourselves into the ground so some major or
colonel can lord it over his cronies in the officers' mess tonight. Some
yards behind Gardiner was a captain from another regiment, labour-
ing to keep up but desperate to win. Just short of the finish line
Gardiner stopped as if to say, "You want it so badly? It's yours," and
the captain went over first. Of course, the message Gardiner had sent
to the top brass in the crowd was unmistakable, and he was called
before his commanding officer to explain his apparent insubordination. There was nothing to be said, however, and he found himself
severely reprimanded.

While Ken would never have defied his army superiors in this way,
he probably admired Gardiner's integrity. He would have been amused
by Gardiner's irreverence, but he very likely shared the man's dislike of
a thick-headed and insensitive army bureaucracy. Gardiner had come
of age in the thirties and was imbued with that period's democratic
concern for the common man, and this would have appealed to a
prairie populist like Ken, whose sense of communal responsibility had
been forged in the furnace of the Great Depression. Ideology is one
thing and action another, of course, but fourteen months in Italy gave
Ken a number of chances to see Gardiner demonstrate his humanity.

On one such occasion Gardiner found himself under fire from
German artillery and mortars in an old stone farmhouse in an area that

had been shelled for days. As he gingerly moved through the building, he found, crouched against the wall in a back room, a very old woman who was rocking back and forth on her heels and repeating over and over in Italian: "I'm afraid! I'm afraid!" "We've got to get her out of here," he told the soldiers with him, but they reminded him that it was against regulations to transport civilians more than five kilometres without a travel permit. "But you wouldn't leave your own grandmother in a hell like this, would you," he observed, and he arranged for her to be slipped out in a truck to an area away from the fighting.

On another occasion, when the Second LAA went out of the line in June 1944, a young Italian woman came to battery headquarters carrying a baby, and since Gardiner had a working knowledge of Italian, he was called to deal with her. The bambino, she said, was her sister's and she had no milk; the baby was starving. Quickly surmising that the baby was in fact hers and that the father was long gone, Gardiner explained that the army stores had no fresh milk but they did have some Carnation powdered milk. The young woman was dubious, but he assured her it was wholesome and safe but that the baby should not be given a large amount of it. He gave her a can of the powder with his carefully translated instructions, and she went on her way.

Early the next morning the camp guard woke Gardiner and said, "Your girlfriend is back and she wants to come in." It was the young woman; she was crying and the baby was very red. "The bambino is sick," she wailed. Gardiner replied, "Take me to your home and show me what you've been doing." Once inside her small house, the woman began to explain that she had followed his instructions and given the baby only a little bit of the milk. She was sure she had not given him too much.

Out of the corner of his eye Gardiner could see an old grandmother lurking in the shadows, listening to the conversation and looking guilty. On a hunch, he questioned her about the matter and she finally admitted that, yes, she had been giving the baby milk too: "She wasn't giving him enough. The bambino was always crying!"

Gardiner repeated his warning to use the milk sparingly, and he cautioned the old woman that if she gave the baby any more, he would come and confiscate it. If the child got no better, he would see his medical officer about what might be done.

Gardiner heard nothing more about the baby for a week, and then one day his batman asked him if he knew that the young woman had been coming to the camp regularly and cleaning his kit. Not only that, she had been cleaning the captain's kit, the batman's kit, the kit of everyone there—nineteen of them in all. And she had been darning their socks. Gardiner was touched and somewhat embarrassed by her gratitude, but he was also concerned for her because he knew the battery would be moving out in a few days. Conditions were harsh and, without many resources, she would have difficulty keeping her child alive; so he passed the hat among the men and collected a generous sum. The young woman, however, would not touch it. "No, no money!" she exclaimed. "But," said Gardiner, "it's not for you, it's for the bambino when food is not so easy to find." And the young woman accepted the money on those terms.

The next morning, as the convoy was moving out and down the dusty road, Gardiner's batman tapped him on the shoulder and pointed to the field beside them. Standing there was the young woman, holding the baby up so that the convoy could see it as it passed—or was it so that the baby could see the Canadian soldiers as they left? Either way, she was still standing there when the last gun crew went by and disappeared into the Italian hills.

For all their differences, both Ken and Gardiner were at heart idealistic and somewhat naive. They were honest, straightforward and loyal—and they expected others to be the same. On the battlefield, a man's life depended on those qualities, and in two savage battles in Italy in 1944, Ken Calder and John Gardiner found those elements in themselves and in the men with whom they served.

CHAPTER EIGHT

The first of the major battles that Ken fought occurred in the Liri Valley, on Italy's west side, in May 1944. The Liri gets its name from the river that runs down much of its northwest-southeast length, but the valley is in fact shaped by a number of rivers: the Sacco, the Melfa, the Gari and the Garigliano. On the northeast side lie the rugged Apennines and on the southwest are the Aurunci and Ausoni mountains. At the lower end of the valley, where it narrows and the Gari flows from the east into the Liri, the landscape is dominated by a lower ridge of Monte Cairo, and it was here that a monk, Benedict, founded the Benedictine order in the sixth century. This was Monte Cassino.

The valley is rich with military history. The Via Casilina, the inland road from Naples to Rome, was constructed twenty-five centuries ago, and there has been a town at Cassino, below the ridge, since the fourth century BC. Roman legions came south through the valley to fight the Samnites, and in the fifth century BC, General Fabius led his forces through it to face Hannibal. In the sixth century BC, Belisarius, a Byzantine commander, moved north along the road to take Rome back from the Goths, and at the beginning of the sixteenth century the Spanish general Cordoba led his army over its stones to engage the French.

For the Allied armies in the winter of 1943–44, however, the Liri had proven impassable. While the British Eighth Army had been fighting its way up the Adriatic side of Italy to a point just north of Ortona, the American Fifth Army, under General Mark Clark, had been engaged in a separate campaign up the Mediterranean coast. Landing at the Bay of Salerno on September 9, it had taken Naples at the beginning of October, but when it reached the entrance to the Liri Valley in January, it bogged down. Rome, whose liberation would be a propaganda coup and hasten the German retreat up the country, lay only fifty miles to the northwest, but it might as well have been a continent away.

What made the Liri Valley so formidable was a line of fortifications considered so impenetrable by the Germans that it was named the Führer Riegel (Führer Switchline), though Hitler ordered it changed to Senger Riegel when he thought it might fail. These defences, which the Allies called the Adolf Hitler line, ran right across Italy, but between the towns of Pontecorvo and Aquino, on either side of the Liri Valley, they seemed impregnable. Minefields and barbed wire were backed up by *panzerturm:* concrete-and-steel emplacements with 88-mm anti-tank guns mounted on them. Eight miles southeast, along the banks of the Gari River, lay another series of fortifications, the Gustav line, and overlooking everything was the monastery of Monte Cassino, from which the Germans could direct their defences.

Though some historians now question their assessment, the Allies in early 1944 believed it essential to knock the Germans off Monte Cassino, and they took four months to do it. On January 22, the American Thirty-sixth Division attempted a direct assault and was forced to retreat after suffering heavy casualties. Again on February 2, the Americans were driven back, and two weeks later, even when the 1,300-year-old Benedictine monastery was obliterated by more than 2,500 tons of high explosives and incendiaries dropped by 450 bombers, the New Zealand Corps failed to take it. On March 14, another 460 planes, many of them heavy bombers, and more than 200,000 artillery shells hit the Cassino town area, but within a week it was obvious that even this assault had failed, and the battle was called off.

To make matters worse, on January 22 a force comprising mainly American troops had landed at the port of Anzio, about fifty miles south of Rome, in an attempt to outflank the Liri defences, but a fierce

German counterattack put the Allies on the defensive and threatened to push them back into the sea. For those old enough to remember the First World War, the situation was painfully similar to the disastrous Gallipoli landing. Ironically, it was the man whose name is most often associated with that disaster who provided the most colourful description of the Anzio impasse. "We had hoped to land a wild cat that would tear the bowels out of the Boche," said Churchill. "Instead we have stranded a vast whale with its tail flopping about in the water!"

To break the deadlock at the Liri Valley, the Allied command devised Operation Diadem, a plan by which the British Eighth Army would move from the Adriatic to the Mediterranean side to join up with the U.S. Fifth Army and the French Expeditionary Force. Together they would force their way through the German defences, with the Eighth Army, composed of British, Polish and Canadian forces, spearheading the thrust. This would be done in stages, with the First Canadian Division moving forward when the Gustav line had been broken, and breaking through the Hitler line. Then the Canadian Fifth Armoured Division, newly arrived in Italy and without battle experience, would pursue the retreating German troops.

In preparation for its role in the Liri Valley campaign, the First Division pulled out of the Adriatic line at the end of April and moved first south to Campobasso and then farther west into the foothills of the Apennines, to practise river crossings and artillery firings. Units were ordered to remove all CANADA signs and their famous red patches, to drop their Canadian accents (however this might be managed) when within earshot of civilians and to maintain strict radio silence. Aside from the usual attempt to keep the enemy guessing, these measures were part of an elaborate scheme to persuade Field Marshal Kesselring that the Canadians were about to attempt an Anzio-style landing at the port of Civitavecchia, thus forcing him to draw troops from the Liri. So respected were the Red Patch Devils by this point that their presence anywhere was a signal to the Germans that an important assault was imminent.

The battle for the Liri Valley began at eleven o'clock on the evening of May 11 with a massive artillery bombardment as 1,700 guns of the Fifth and Eighth armies poured shells into the German defences. Suddenly the night sky was so bright that one soldier reported he could have read a newspaper by the light, but as the soldier quoted by historian John Ellis attests, no words can fully capture the noise of such a barrage:

> A barrage, even if it is not one's first, is a difficult thing to write about. It cannot be taken apart and described in detail, and in the mass it is so overwhelming that no broad picture of it can possibly be convincing. The noise is unbelievable . . . When some hundreds of guns are firing at once, the high shrill sound grows, until the whole sky is screaming; and when the first shells land, the earth shakes, clouds of dust and smoke arise, and the immense crash drowns the approach of shells which follow. The infantryman is a fly inside a drum; and only occasionally, when for a few seconds the guns seem to draw breath, can we hear the twanging of harps which heralds the next salvo. The uproar swells and fades and swells again, deafeningly, numbing the brain.

According to Ellis, the First World War term "shell shock," though inadequate to describe the varieties of battle exhaustion suffered by the contemporary soldier, does reflect a basic truth: "that of all the components of modern warfare, artillery and high explosives were the most terrifying, the ones that made men feel utterly dwarfed by the material holocaust around them." It was, of course, the targets of the artillery fire, the enemy infantrymen, who suffered the most from a barrage, but even a unit's own infantry or officers or gunners found the noise excruciating. A Polish officer at the Liri Valley on the evening of May 11 later wrote that in addition to the artillery pieces, "there were the mortars and anti-tank guns blazing away—the noise deafened us . . . I for one felt that if it went on for long I would go mad."

The ferocious Allied bombardment had its effect, and late in the evening of May 11 the Eighth Indian Division, the Fourth British Division and Canadians of the First Armoured Brigade crossed the Gari River. By late afternoon on May 13 the Indians had breached the Gustav line, and with the French Expeditionary Force's experienced mountain troops advancing quickly to their left along the south bank of the Liri, the Germans had to abandon the Gustav line and fall back to the Hitler line. Monte Cassino fell at last on May 18 to the Second Polish Corps, a group of men fighting so far from the home they hoped to rebuild as an independent democracy after the war; their hillside monument speaks of giving "our bodies to the soil of Italy and our hearts to Poland." The main body of Canadian troops went into action on May 17 and two days later were within sight of the fortifications of the Hitler line.

The Second LAA was assigned to protect the First Division headquarters and the bridges across the Gari River, and it moved into position on the evening of May 16. For some reason—perhaps he knew he was about to be part of a crucial battle in the Italian campaign—Ken started keeping a diary the next day. The army strictly prohibited the keeping of such diaries because, if they fell into the enemy's hands through the death or capture of the soldier, they could provide valuable information about troop deployments, equipment and perhaps strategy. A number of men—among them Farley Mowat—nonetheless kept journals, and Ken's, written in an uncharacteristically tiny hand on a small lined notepad, has survived to provide one man's perspective on the war in Italy from May until November 1944. As an artillery officer Ken was required to be more mobile than most men on the battlefield: assessing troop positions, consulting with infantry commanders and assigning gun sites. As a result, his diary is a bit of a guided tour of some of the notable elements of the battle for the Liri Valley.

Since the fighting had been going on for six days when the Canadians moved into position on May 17, Ken's first response is a reflection on the costs of the earlier struggles:

Up at 4 am and moved to occupy positions 2½ miles south of Cassino. Crossed over 2 crossroads which were under shell fire. So far lucky. B Troop guarding three bailey [portable] bridges where Maharattas [Indian troops] and Argyle and Sutherland Highlanders crossed the Gari with heavy casualties and smashed the Gustav Line. Graves everywhere and the whole place a shambles. Gave four Maharattas a decent burial. Heavy barrage on Monastery Hill and Cassino at 6 am supported by aircraft. Rumours in late afternoon Monastery Hill taken. Streams of prisoners being brought back. Some enemy shelling during the day. At this spot over 1,000 Americans perished trying to cross river and river flats last winter. 8th Army made crossing here with 1st Cdn. Tank Brigade May 12, with loss of 3 companies. Much heavy armour moving up in late afternoon. Noise terrific all day. Guns switched from Monastery Hill to 1 Cdn. Div. front in afternoon so it looks as though we have taken the place. The Yanks were giving odds of 100 to 1 we wouldn't take it. Dust and heat as usual.

If Ken passed much of the day reflecting on the loss of those who had fought there before him, he spent much of the night facing the possibility of his own death. He went to bed at 9:30 but was

rudely awakened at 11.05 pm to find whole area lit up by flares and enemy aircraft overhead. J.V.88s and Stukas dive-bombed the area, dropping H[igh] E[xplosive], incendiary and anti-personnel bombs in large quantities. B Tp fired 86 rds with 1 hit observed. Three L.A.A. regiments blasting away like hell. We scored 1 hit on fast-flying J.V.88 which almost got us. Thought I would never live to see the dawn. One J.V.88 crashed in flames 2 miles northeast. Narrow escapes on all sites but no casualties. Incendiaries almost got No.5 tractor. Nos. 1 and 4 had anti-personnel bombs in their gun pits. No.3 has 20-foot crater 50 yds from the gun.

*Gnr. Robinson missed death by inches when bomb casing landed
on his slit trench which was only 15 yds from mine. A large shell
splinter dug in the yard of earth between Lt. Chasse's hole and
mine as well. I must have been born lucky, but I have never
been more certain of death. Thought I'd had it for sure.*

What Ken had endured was a fairly large-scale counterattack by a
dozen or so enemy aircraft. Considerable damage was inflicted on
vehicles and other equipment, and though his battery suffered no
casualties, the Fifty-fourth LAA had two gunners killed and an officer
and two gunners wounded. He learned the following day that one of
the gunners had been sleeping under a petrol truck which was hit and
instantly became a ball of flames.

The next morning, as the fog at first light began to melt away and
the day became hot and breezy, Ken surveyed the battleground. The
fighting had already moved westwards, but there were hundreds of
aircraft—Allied planes, fortunately—in the sky. There was still some
shooting around Cassino, but he concluded that "it looks like the
place is in the bag. Monastery Hill and Cassino now flying Union
Jacks and Polish flags. Went as close as I could and saw that the whole
face of the mountain had been blasted away and the town practically
buried under rock. Hundreds of unburied dead and the stench terrific.
Glad to come away." Like others who saw the Liri turned into the
Valley of Death that week, Ken was struck by the profusion of red
poppies growing everywhere, as incongruous among the twisted steel
and mutilated bodies as they had been in Flanders during the previous
war. After setting up his troop office in a twenty-foot German dugout,
he "located 2 American dead near river and gave them a decent burial.
Dead for weeks. We do what we can but we have to watch out for
mines."

Burying the dead, whether your own or the enemy's, is required by
the rules of the Geneva Convention; and though it is one of the most
distasteful tasks a soldier can be asked to perform, it must be done,

too, to prevent the outbreak of disease. Though Ken had not been battle-hardened like the others through the fighting from Sicily to Ortona, he was not long in the Liri battle before he showed a kind of mettle and perhaps a certain form of leadership.

Among General Alphonse-Pierre Juin's Corps Expéditionnaire Français were the Goumiers, fierce mountain troops from Morocco rumoured to have a fondness for collecting German ears as battle trophies (as well as for raping Italian women and men of all ages). One thing they would not do—seemingly for religious reasons— was to bury the enemy dead, and when the First Canadian Division moved from Cassino into some of the area captured by the Goums, it found the hills littered with thousands of German bodies, which had been lying there for weeks in the spring sun. The throats of some had been ripped out by packs of wild dogs, and others had ballooned so that they resembled Michelin men. The grisly task of dealing with them fell to the Canadians.

According to John Gardiner, Ken decided that officers should share in the burial duties, but when he ordered a lieutenant to accompany him, the young man answered: "I couldn't do that. To see bodies like that. I'd be sick as a dog."

"Do you think any of the guys like to do this?" Ken replied. "The men have to do it. We can't ask them to do it if we won't do it ourselves."

So, with great reluctance, the lieutenant drove with him to one of the burial sites but stood at a distance, with his back to Ken as he began to enlarge a grave for a particularly tall German corpse. Exasperated, Ken said in a calm but firm voice: "Grab this pickaxe and get digging." Without turning, the lieutenant reached behind him for the axe handle. Ken handed him the severed arm of a German soldier. It was done, says Gardiner, to cure the young man of his fastidiousness, but it could well have had the opposite effect.

May 19 was a relatively quiet day for Ken as he waited at battery headquarters for orders. The First Division had reached the Hitler line and stopped, and streams of vehicles were moving along the narrow roads to provide support. The next day was different. At first light the battery moved to the concentration area—the area where troops assembled before a battle—near Pignaturo, made camp, and then proceeded to the front to support the First Brigade's Hastings and Prince Edward Regiment. The German defenders were blanketing the entire area with heavy artillery and mortar fire, and as Ken led B Troop into its gun positions, it came under fierce shelling. There were no casualties among his men, but several infantry soldiers were killed, and a sniper nearly picked off the battery major near the observation post. During this bombardment Ken laid out the guns, and in the early evening they shelled houses 3,100 yards away in Pontecorvo identified by the First Brigade officers as enemy strongholds. So successful was this assault that the brigadier commanding the First Brigade sent congratulations to the commanding officer of the Second LAA Regiment. When B Troop went out of action at 6:30 p.m., they got a round of applause from the Princess Patricia's Canadian Light Infantry, which had been watching the action from behind them. Back at headquarters, they were congratulated by the battery commander, and as Ken noted, "whole troop is in high spirits."

By May 21 the officers had been told that the First Division would attempt to smash through the Hitler line on May 23, and so Ken saw little action for the next two days. This interval, however, was anything but quiet. "Chased out of bed by shells at 9.30," he wrote on the twenty-first, "and slept all night in a ditch. Enemy aircraft overhead at 4 am and terrific A.A. barrage going up. Very jittery night." The next night, after having gone to bed at 11 p.m., he was "chased out shortly afterward into slit trenches by enemy shells. One hell of a rough night."

At first light on May 23, Ken's troop moved to the concentration area behind the infantry battalions and, with the sounds of heavy artillery and mortar shelling coming from the line just ahead, had a cold breakfast. The task of breaking through the Hitler line on the right had been given to the three regiments of the western Canadian Second Infantry Brigade, with the Princess Patricia's Canadian Light Infantry and the Seaforth Highlanders leading the assault and the

Loyal Edmonton Regiment backing them up. The Second LAA Battery was assigned to protect the Patricias.

At 5:57 a.m., eight hundred artillery guns began a massive firing, a creeping barrage designed to soften up the German defences, and three minutes later the infantry crossed the start line. Before long, as Ken's diary reveals, things began to go wrong. "Noise terrific," he wrote. "2nd Bde reporting heavy casualties by 8.30 from 4-inch mortars, nebelwerfers and small arms fire. Seaforths having a tough time. 3rd Bde on left going well. 2nd Bde stopped on first objective, calling for tanks and anti-tank guns. Streams of ambulances and hordes of prisoners passing to the rear."

For the first hour the Patricias had made steady progress, but soon the *nebelwerfers* and machine-gun fire of the Germans, who had been unaffected by the artillery barrage in their deep bunkers, slowed them down. The *nebelwerfers* were rockets fired in a sequence of six over a ten-second period, and they were especially frightening for two reasons. First, when they landed, their high concentration of explosives sent large jagged shards of rocket casing flying in every direction. Then there was their distinctive noise, which earned them the nickname Moaning Minnies because, as one soldier said, they "sounded just like a lot of women sobbing their hearts out." This noise "would start in the distance and get louder and louder, almost to a scream, and then down would come six 6-inch mortar bombs." To British rifleman Alex Bowlby, author of *Recollections of Rifleman Bowlby,*

it sounded as if the Germans were cranking up an enormous tin-lizzie. The rattle changed to a moan. The moan grew louder . . . I had time to notice the exact growth of my fear. It began in the calves, welled up through the loins and stomach, and finally struck home at the throat. As the moan changed to a deafening roar I think I screamed. A series of explosions shook the ground . . . They made any other fear I had encountered seem small beer.

Ken got his own taste of the Moaning Minnies on the morning of May 23, when he headed up to the front in a Jeep to do some reconnaissance. "Was chased down the road by nebelwerfers," he wrote. "Too much iron flying around." Later in the day he was shelled by German 88s—"had 'em bust fore and aft but we got through." Picking one's way through the artillery fire was a hazardous business, a fact borne home to Ken when, just behind the front line, he ran into a major from the Third Field Regiment still badly shaken from having had his reconnaissance vehicle destroyed by a mortar bomb.

Still, this violence was nothing as ferocious as the infantry battalions were enduring. As he approached the front, Ken saw "burned-out trucks and tanks everywhere. Corpses all over the place plus knocked out guns. Waited at cross roads and talked to Edmontons coming out. More than 50% casualties. Stray bursts of machine gun fire coming over so took cover in a slit trench. Shared whiskey with Edmontons."

The charred tank hulls Ken found were the Shermans and Churchills of the North Irish Horse, the British Armoured unit assigned to back up the Patricias and Seaforths. Because the area had not been properly reconnoitred, the tanks had been stopped by an unexpected minefield and thus became stationary targets for the potent 88-mm guns of the German fortifications. One after another the tanks had "brewed up," as someone with a macabre wit had taken to describing the ease with which the Allied tanks burst into flames and became fiery death traps. One particular enemy gun is said to have taken out thirteen Churchill tanks before it was disabled by an armour-piercing shell.

The Loyal Edmonton Regiment had been sent in to support the Patricias and to lead the final advance, but it ran into what one observer called the worst enemy fire the battalion had ever faced. It too got bogged down and, as Ken was told, suffered heavy casualties. The Patricias themselves had been butchered, leaving their commanding officer, Colonel Cam Ware, in a state of shock (one reporter commented that "his eyes were glazed" at the end of the day). When Ken talked to him at battalion headquarters the next evening, Ware told him that two-thirds of his men were casualties, that only three officers had not been killed or wounded, and that in two rifle companies only three men came back. In fact, at the end of the fighting on May 23, says David Bercuson, 59 Patricias had been killed, 118 were wounded and 17 had been taken prisoner—nearly half of the regiment's fighting strength. For the Second Brigade as a whole, the total for the day—162 killed, 306 wounded and 75 taken prisoner—was the worst single-day loss for a brigade in the Italian campaign. The western Canadian regiments had been savaged.

The day was no more successful for Ken. B Troop was supposed to move to provide anti-aircraft protection for the Patricias when they reached their final objective, the Pontecorvo–Aquino road. Since they failed to gain this position, he was unable to advance the troop, which he had left "digging in like hell" in the afternoon, and in the shelling he lost touch with it. Pinned down by enemy fire as darkness fell, he "lay in trench and shivered with cold and damp while shells burst just beyond us all night long. Enemy overhead at 4 am dropping flares and H[eavy] E[xplosives]. A.A. barrage drove them off. Very uncomfortable night and worried about B Troop because road being plastered by 88s all night."

As soon as it became light, Ken went to look for the troop and, finding it in the concentration area, led it to new positions, where it began firing at 5 a.m. The German artillery returned continuous fire, and when several 88-mm shells blew the lateral sights off one of the B Troop guns, the shrapnel killed six anti-tank gunners positioned in the surrounding bush. Ken established his troop headquarters in a burnt-out farmhouse, and in the afternoon he washed and shaved using a German helmet as a basin. He also took stock of the toll of battle: "Victoria Day. Hope the folks at home enjoy this day because by tomorrow they'll be receiving the wrong kind of telegrams. Horrible scenes near gunsites 4, 5 & 6. Dead of both sides everywhere. E Tp (5th Battery) on our left lost 14 men in the last 36 hours. Our luck still holds."

Some of Ken's old friends were not so fortunate. He heard that one of the men from the Seventy-seventh Battery had been killed by mortar bomb fragments ripping open his chest, and Glenn Rankin, a fellow officer who had gone overseas with him in 1939, had got a bullet in the leg. Killed too was the major from the Third Field who had survived his car being hit the day before. It was less than twenty-four hours since he had shared his chocolate with Ken while he tried to steady his nerves, and now he was dead. "They go quick here," Ken concluded.

Late in the day, Ken returned to the front and was incensed at the sight of Canadian stretcher-bearers being greeted by machine-gun fire as they went forward to retrieve the wounded. "Damn these dirty German bastards!" he wrote. "Were sniped at ourselves but I couldn't see anything to shoot at. Would like to get in a few licks of my own." Instead he had to content himself with going back and deploying the troop to watch a sinister-looking ravine on their right. As for himself, he said, he went to bed with both hands blistered from digging slit trenches—and his duties were not yet completed. "Officers on listening watch on radio all night," he noted. "My shift 1:30 to 4. Kept cocked automatic on table by radio just in case."

At the same time as Ken was making this entry in his illicit diary, several miles to the southwest Farley Mowat was writing to his parents that "we've just finished the best job done by Canadians in this war, and maybe in any war. In thirty-six hours First Division smashed, over-ran and passed through a defence line which the Germans assured the world was the most impregnable defence ever built . . . Our lads fought their way through the works!" Two days later he added: "With fine weather, marvellous support from artillery, tanks, the air force, and the Polish Corps in overlooking mountains, First Div has done a job that defied our predecessors in the 8th and 5th Armies for months."

Though it had been a devastating experience for the Second Brigade, the First and Third brigades had broken through the Hitler line on the left, and on May 24 the Canadian Fifth Armoured Division poured through the gap. By the next day it had crossed the Melfa River, on the twenty-sixth the town of Ceprano was in Canadian hands, and the CBC's Peter Stursberg could report that "it's becoming a mad chase in blinding dust over bumpy mud roads to keep up with the Canadian advance now." The reality was that the inexperience of the Canadian Fifth Armoured Division and the traffic jams in the narrow valley had slowed the Canadian progress. The Germans were nonetheless in retreat and, with the Americans at last breaking out of Anzio and the French forces moving quickly, the road to Rome was open.

When Ken awoke on May 25, the battlefield looked and sounded different. "It seems the Hun has left for parts unknown," he wrote. "Quiet up front." But the signs of carnage were everywhere. "Pats still getting wounded and corpses out. Minefields everywhere. Saw horrible scenes and we buried many enemy dead in our area. Results of our barrage are terrific, and there are burned-out tanks, vehicles, masses of smashed equipment, and heaps of bodies everywhere. All Cdn dead are being buried in huge new cemetery." Referring to the residual odour of cordite and the stench of rotting corpses, Ken added: "I don't like the smell of a battlefield."

Ken had come through the three days of slaughter unscathed—at least physically—but one can only guess at the effect the ordeal had on him psychologically. Even in his diary he was guarded about his own feelings and state of mind, but one comment perhaps reveals a great deal. At the end of a day of wreckage, both mechanical and human, on May 25, he wrote: "To bed at 11 pm feeling sick in mind and body." Even then he was not allowed to rest, as enemy bombers launched a raid twenty minutes later, lighting up the sky with flares and starting three large fires close to his headquarters. One blaze reached a fully loaded ammunition truck, sending exploding shells in every direction.

Ken's troop had been assigned to protect a section of the road between Aquino and Pontecorvo, which had been part of the Hitler line, but since the Allies dominated the Italian airspace, the next few days were mainly spent regrouping and taking care of the dead. May 26 was a hot, dusty day and the "whole battle area [was] becoming most offensive to the nose. The stench and flies are horrible." It was essential to bury the dead as soon as possible, but mines made this a hazardous job, and Ken had to leave one German body to the sun and the flies because it lay in a minefield. If he needed any reminding of the residual dangers lurking in the earth, he got it a day later when four gunners in the Fifty-fourth Battery were badly injured when one of them struck a mine with a pick while digging a gun pit.

With all the death and decay and the millions of flies and mosquitoes, it was inevitable that the soldiers would be hit with dysentery. By May 29, Ken reported that all of B Troop had been levelled by it, and he himself was "too weak to get out of bed all day." The next day he was still "beat out with a combination of dysentery, flies, dust and heat. Wish I had a case of cold beer." On June 1, though still weak, he had to move his guns to provide protection for the First Division headquarters area near Ceccano, during which he observed that the "whole troop was glad to leave the scene of so much death."

Ceccano, however, was yet another scene of shattered vehicles, tank hulls, crashed planes and graves, and Ken was taken aback when he came across the wreckage of a Seventy-seventh Battery gun and tractor: "Direct hit by shell. Seven graves including that of Sgt. Percy Latham. They never had a chance . . . Wish the industrial strikers could spend a day with us," he added, a bitter reference to the labour strife going on in Canada at the time.

The Canadian servicemen abroad had little access to news from home except through letters, the occasional old magazine and brief items in the *Maple Leaf,* the army newspaper that had begun in Italy in February 1944. Like Ken, however, they were all aware that, while they were enduring the privations and perils of the Italian battlefields, able-bodied men back in Canada were building homes, establishing careers and drawing good paycheques. Four weeks before Ken's remark, Farley Mowat had written his parents about hearing "how much we all owe to the industrial workers who, with unselfish dedication, have declined to enlist and instead are saving the world by producing so much of the wherewithal for war. When they aren't on strike for higher wages, like the Quebec aluminum workers. We feel for them. Some of us would like to feel for them with the business end of a bayonet."

As the Italian campaign wore on, Ken became increasingly and particularly bitter about the servicemen who would not volunteer for overseas duty—called zombies, the living dead, by the fighting men. Mowat too grew more and more contemptuous of the zombies as the year went on, but in his Liri Valley letter he chose to echo the St. Crispin's Day speech of Shakespeare's Henry V before the Battle of Agincourt in pitying them for having been home abed when heroes were being created in the field:

> This day I am proud to be a Canadian, and I am prouder still to belong to the "band of brothers" who volunteered for overseas service. Today I don't despise the Zombies who refuse overseas duty—I pity them, for they will never know what it is to be a man among men. Men! Not supermen, just men, who have learned to act together from no selfish motives, but as comrades willing to risk death for one another. After the busting of the Hitler Line, the squirmings of the politicians and the war profiteers and the other gutless wonders at home won't bother us as much. By God, we *know* who *we* are, and what *we* amount to.

But, one might ask, would anyone—*could* anyone—who had not been beside them on the Liri Valley killing grounds that May ever fully know these men again?

Even in the short term, as it turned out, public attention soon turned away from the Canadians in Italy. On May 27, as the day neared when Rome would be liberated, the Second Brigade invited the Second LAA Regiment to march with it in the victory parade in the Eternal City. The invitation, however, had not counted on the American Fifth Army's egocentric and anglophobic General Mark Clark, who was determined that it would be only his American soldiers whom the newsreels would show "liberating" Rome. When General Alexander argued that the Eighth Army deserved to be represented, Clark is reported to have told him that if the British attempted to enter the city, he would have his troops fire on them. Thus, when Clark entered Rome on June 4, two days after the Germans had declared it an open (undefended) city, the only Canadians in the triumphal march were a few who were part of the combined American-Canadian First Special Service Force.

Even the reflected glory of the fall of Rome, the first Axis capital to be taken by the Allies, lasted only two days. On June 6, the Allies launched Operation Overlord, the massive assault on the beaches of Normandy, and instantly the Italian campaign was pushed to the back pages of the world's newspapers. Though the tenth of July in Sicily and the third of September in Italy had been bloody and significant D-Days, the immensity of the Allied assault in northern France meant that, in the public imagination forever after, "D-Day" would mean only the sixth of June.

In the eyes of the Allied soldiers fighting in Italy, their role soon seemed further diminished by the unfortunate comments of two prominent British politicians. First, an article in the *Eighth Army News,* a paper distributed widely to British and Commonwealth troops in Italy, reported that Roosevelt had suggested to Churchill that the United States should provide all the land forces for the Pacific war. To the soldier huddled in a slit trench or crossing a river under a hail of machine-gun bullets, the prime minister's response was flippant and insensitive: "We can't let your chaps have all the fun."

More infuriating was the comment attributed to the American-born Nancy Astor, Britain's first female Member of Parliament, who was reported to have referred to the Italian veterans—of all nationalities—as "D-Day Dodgers." Whether intended or not, it seemed to be a denigration, a suggestion that the Italian campaign had been a holiday and that the men had avoided the real fighting, which was in Normandy. Angry at first, the soldiers soon responded with irony, taking the title with pride—a pride that is still apparent today at Italian campaign veterans' reunions—and composing a song that was sung to the tune of the German favourite of the time, "Lili Marlene":

> *We are the D-Day Dodgers, out in Italy,*
> *Always on the vino, always on the spree.*
> *Eighth Army skivers and their tanks,*
> *We go to war in ties and slacks,*
> *We are the D-Day Dodgers, in sunny Italy.*
> *We are the D-Day Dodgers, way out in Italy.*
> *We're always tight, we cannot fight.*
> *What bloody use are we?*

Though sung with defensive sarcasm, the question was one that began to haunt the Canadians in Italy more and more through the summer and winter of 1944. They had suffered more than three thousand casualties in the Liri Valley, and they had fought well—well enough for the Eighth Army commander, General Sir Oliver Leese, to call the First Canadian Division the best infantry division in Italy. In the days following the battle, however, the Allies failed to build on the success. Had General Clark led his Fifth Army inland instead of into Rome, the German Tenth Army would have been destroyed in a pincer between the Americans on one side and the British and French on the other. Had Leese moved his Eighth Army more expeditiously along the Liri Valley, fewer German troops would have escaped to fight another day. As it was, Field Marshal Kesselring was able to withdraw his army north to another formidable series of defensive fortifications, the Gothic line, and the Canadians who had thought that the Liri Valley battle would speed the end of the Italian campaign soon found themselves being asked to mount yet another murderous assault.

CHAPTER NINE

Having broken through the Hitler line and forced the Germans to retreat north, the First Canadian Corps came out of the line on June 7 and, bitterly disappointed at being denied a chance to see Rome, moved south to Piedimonte d'Alife, in an isolated region north of Naples. There, for the next seven weeks, it remained in reserve but hardly inactive. Ken's diary summed up the period laconically: "All ranks working like hell." For its part, the Second LAA Regiment was put through extensive drilling in infantry tactics, ground shooting and anti-aircraft practice; and it took part in two brigade-level training schemes. During this period, as well, each of the three batteries in the regiment was reduced by one troop and some of the gunners were transferred to the infantry, which was beginning to suffer from lack of properly trained replacements.

On June 11, in the middle of writing a letter to the folks in Fargo, Ken learned that he too was being transferred, though not to the infantry. Officers were being redeployed throughout the regiment, and as one of the senior captains he was made second-in-command in the Fifty-fourth LAA Battery. This meant working with Gardiner's friend Roger Jean-Marie, whom Ken had seen only occasionally since recruiting him into the anti-aircraft at Aldershot. It also meant working under Major John R. Pepall, the battery commander and a bit of a legend among those who served in artillery regiments in Italy.

Pepall, a Toronto man and an RMC graduate, took command of the Second LAA Battery in England and led it from the Sicily landing to the capturing of Ortona, when he was transferred to the Fifty-fourth

126

Battery. In both units he became famous for his idiosyncrasies, in particular his obsessive-compulsive habit, perhaps induced by stress, of endlessly looking at his watch. Like many officers, he had a pocket watch that he hooked by a strap to his battledress and kept in a chest pocket. He would take it out of the pocket, study it for a moment, then put it back. A minute or two later he would repeat the procedure; and this would go on throughout briefings, conversations and meals. To the amusement of his men, claims one veteran, he would put his watch back in the pocket, pause for several moments and then turn to another officer and ask the time. Some mischievous souls took to entertaining themselves by waiting until the watch was put away and then asking innocently: "What's the time, sir?"

"Damned if I know," the major would reply, and out would come the timepiece again.

In Ron MacFarlane's words, Pepall "was academically bright, with a good mind for mathematics—essential in an artillery officer—but he didn't have an ounce of common sense." Unlike the watch habit, this deficiency had serious consequences on the battlefield, and it may be the reason that he became intensely disliked by most of the men who served with him. John Gardiner became one of those men on the day he arrived to join the Second LAA Battery in England and was ordered to a meeting of officers at four o'clock. Since he was travelling by rail, he was a prisoner of the train schedule and of the driver sent to meet him, but with some haste and good luck Gardiner got to the meeting room just as the clock struck four. This was not good enough for Pepall, however, who chastised him in front of the other officers. "A good officer," he said, "is always five minutes early."

Matters were far more serious once the battery got into action in Sicily. In one week, says Gardiner, Pepall sent him forward three times to do reconnaissance on possible gun sites. On each occasion, Gardiner discovered that his commanding officer had misread the maps and sent him behind the German lines, and he had to scramble to avoid being captured or killed.

Gardiner also remembers an incident in December, just after the battle for Ortona, when a fellow officer, Jim Wood, came to his tent one evening to say that "the old man wants to see us right away."

"But," said Gardiner, "Battery HQ is four or five miles away and it's pitch dark. Surely we can wait till the morning."

"Better go now, John," replied Wood. "The despatch rider says it's important."

The trip to headquarters, in the dark and through the December rain and mud, was hazardous, especially since German artillery and planes were still active. When they eventually got to Pepall's tent, the adjutant informed them that "the old man" was playing cribbage and could not be disturbed; they would have to wait. So the two men took shelter in a storage tent while the card game went on, and Gardiner, not content to remain idle, began poking around and discovered several cases of beer. Having been limited to the standard ration of one bottle a month, the pair found the opportunity too good to pass up, and they happily consumed several bottles before they were finally summoned by the major.

When Gardiner and Wood got to Pepall's tent, he asked, "Did the adjutant tell you why I called you here?"

When they replied, "No, sir," he was perplexed. He thought awhile and then said: "Oh, yes. I remember now. It's this. I learned a long time ago that an officer who is too friendly with his men is not a good officer. I just thought I should tell you that."

At this point, recalls Gardiner, Wood, who was well over six feet tall, drew up to his full height and answered: "Well, sir, according to your rules, you must be the best damned officer in all of Italy!" He then grabbed Gardiner by the arm and said, "Let's go!" and they got away before the major could respond. Gardiner remembers his companion being so furious at being summoned for such a triviality that he could still hear him swearing as they went to bed that night.

Ron MacFarlane got a taste of Pepall's bureaucratic inflexibility just after the Hitler line breakthrough, when the battery had mounted its guns on a hillside west of Monte Cassino and was living in caves. It had been decided that, with overwhelming Allied air superiority, anti-aircraft units would fire at night only if the enemy aircraft were visible and had committed hostile acts; otherwise, night fighters would drive them off. Pepall passed the order on to his battery, telling it not to fire until he had determined that it was necessary.

Several nights later, German planes began a heavy raid on infantry and field artillery sites in the valley below the battery, but no Allied aircraft came to drive them off. MacFarlane watched as enemy bombs exploded among the troops, and he waited for the battery commander to give the order to fire. Unable, finally, to sit idle any longer, MacFarlane yelled to his gun crew, ran to their site and began firing. Before long the other crews joined them and, though they might have brought down only one plane, drove off the bombers.

The reactions to MacFarlane's behaviour were not long in coming. Early the next morning he was summoned to the Seventy-seventh Battery headquarters, where its major asked him who started the shooting. "I think it was me," replied MacFarlane.

"Well," said the major, "I'm recommending you for a decoration because you saved a lot of lives out there last night."

Arriving back at his own battery, MacFarlane spotted a despatch rider waiting for him and, before the man could get a word out, said, "I've been expecting you." Yes, the messenger confirmed, the old man did want to see him.

"I understand that you were the first to fire last night," Pepall began. "Even though I had given orders that there was to be no night firing."

"But," replied MacFarlane, "there weren't any night fighters and the Third Field were getting the hell bombed out of them. I thought somebody should do something about it."

"Well, I'll have to court-martial you for disobeying an order in the face of the enemy," said Pepall. "You know that."

"I knew that when I fired," MacFarlane replied. After a pause he added: "But, sir, I think it only fair to tell you that the officer commanding the Seventy-seventh wants to decorate me. You might want to talk to him." And in the end, recalls MacFarlane wryly, he did not get decorated, but neither was he court-martialled.

Serving as second-in-command to John Pepall must have been difficult for Ken. He believed in army discipline and order, but he was not inflexible nor was he insensitive to the needs and concerns of the men. He would have been the link between Pepall and the men, the officer to whom they turned when something irked them, the buffer between their indignation and their commanding officer's foibles. And in the seven weeks in reserve in the summer of 1944, when the soldiers were recovering from the ordeal of the Liri Valley, there were lots of reasons for them to be indignant. In addition to seemingly pointless ceremonies and parades, there were silly new rules such as the one limiting the number of cigarettes each man was permitted.

The First Canadian Division had suffered 1,231 casualties in breaking through the Hitler line, and one-quarter of these were iden-tified as neuropsychiatric—that is, battle exhaustion—cases. Though many senior officers had little sympathy for such men, it was at least recognized that the division as a whole needed rest and recreation, and so a number of the soldiers were granted leave to go to seaside rest camps at Bari and Salerno. By July they were allowed to join American servicemen in seeing Rome.

Ken too took the opportunity to relax. As soon as the Canadians had been settled at Piedimonte, he caught up on his correspondence, explaining to his relatives with delicious understatement that "I have been far too busy of late to do any more writing than was absolutely necessary." He was similarly muted in writing about the fighting in the Liri. "The defences of Cassino, the Gustav Line and the late Adolf Hitler Line," he said, "are now a memory only, but at the same time they provided me with a few thoughts of my own that I will never forget." What Ken could not tell his relatives—what no soldiers wanted their families to know while the action was still going on—was what Farley Mowat was later able to say about the intensity of the fighting in the Liri Valley after the war: "There was a bestiality here that was beyond comprehension."

Like many of his men, Ken took a week's leave—in his case to the seaside town of Amalfi, where the army had taken over an old hotel and converted it into an officers' rest centre. Set in the stunning coastline south of Naples, Amalfi had long been a fashionable vacation site for the European rich and titled, and more recently it had served as a leave centre for German officers. For seven days Ken was able to enjoy the stunning view of the Gulf of Salerno, the mountainside covered with geraniums, oleanders and flowering shrubs, and the man-made wonders such as the ninth-century Cathedral of Sant' Andrea. Almost as enjoyable were a real bed and clean sheets, good meals, a reasonably well stocked bar and some tranquillity. It was the last tranquillity he would experience for many months, and the last leave he would take until the end of the war.

Around the time that Ken was relaxing in Amalfi, the German Tenth Army's chief of staff, Generalmajor Fritz Wentzell, was lamenting, "If only I knew where the Canadians are!" Find the Canadians, he was convinced, and you would know the point of the next Allied attack. Thus, when the First Canadian Corps did return to action, its movements were designed to confuse German intelligence, beginning with its move back north on July 26 with all markings, signs, flashes and regimental insignia removed. Passing through the Liri Valley again, Ken noted that, even two months after the fighting, "Cassino is still stinking to high heaven." More pleasant was the evening in Rome he was able to snatch when the battery stopped for the night at a staging area outside the city. By the first of August they had reached a concentration area at the ancient city of Siena, about fifteen miles south of Florence, and four days later, three battalions of Canadians moved into the part of Florence south of the Arno. The Germans still occupied the larger section of the city north of the river, which had been declared open and therefore not to be shelled, but they continued to bombard the Canadians on the south bank. Ken got close enough to the action to see that there was "heavy shelling during the night. Street fighting in the town. Snipers prevalent." Driving into the southern outskirts, he drew fire from a German 88-mm gun but managed to stay ahead of the shells.

The Canadian action in the front line in Florence lasted only three days, and when Ken turned in on the evening of August 9, he wrote: "Early start tomorrow. Where to?" The next day's start, once again undertaken with complete secrecy, was at 4 a.m. and the destination turned out to be a concentration area near Perugia, thirty miles south of Florence in the middle of Italy. "Rumour has it," he observed, "that we have foxed the Hun and will hit him in a soft spot where he least expects to see Canadians. He still thinks we are around Florence."

The rumour had a grain of truth in it, but the situation was a great deal more complex than Ken or any of the soldiers in the Canadian Corps knew. Largely because of American pressure, the Allies had decided to launch an amphibious assault on southern France on August 15, and to do so three American divisions and the entire Corps Expéditionnaire Français were withdrawn from Italy. Losing the American divisions hurt, but the loss of the experienced French mountain troops was especially damaging to the Italian campaign.

Following the Allied breakthrough of the Hitler line at the end of May, the Germans had made an orderly retreat to the Gothic line, another series of fortifications stretching across northern Italy from Pesaro on the Adriatic coast to La Spezia on the west side. General Alexander had intended to focus the attack on this line in the mountains north of Florence, but since this would be difficult without the French, he decided that the Eighth Army would strike at the ten-mile gap between the Apennines and the Adriatic coast. Churchill had long nursed the dream of British forces driving through northern Italy to Vienna, but the reality was that the Italian campaign was being continued to keep Kesselring's twenty-five divisions occupied there rather than in France. This was to be accomplished with diminishing resources, since any new men and equipment were being channelled to the armies in northern France. Thus, in Farley Mowat's words, the Canadian troops were "the unwitting pawns in a gigantic bluff. They did not know that for the next six months they would be committed to a desperate and largely hopeless battle."

The Canadian Corps had been moved secretly to Siena as part of the original proposal to break through the Gothic line north of Florence, but when that plan was jettisoned, all secrecy was abandoned and it was sent openly into Florence, as Ken had heard, to "fox" German intelligence. When it was withdrawn and sent to Perugia—and then to the Adriatic coast—it was again with all markings and insignia down in the hope of convincing the enemy that the Canadians were still around Florence.

If Ken and his fellow soldiers thought the Gothic line would be "a soft spot"—and why would they not when the commander-in-chief of the Eighth Army, General Sir Oliver Leese, parroting Churchill, proclaimed, "Gentlemen, we march on Vienna!"—they soon learned otherwise. The Adriatic section of the Gothic line was thirty miles deep, and the Canadians had six rivers to cross to reach their goal of Rimini. In key locations the Germans had cleared the landscape of every bush, tree and building; and they had built Panther gun turrets into steel-and-cement foundations, set up machine-gun posts, put down extensive layered minefields, gouged anti-tank ditches into the earth and spread barbed wire entanglements across the countryside. Manning all these defences were the most proficient German troops in Italy. When the American journalist Martha Gellhorn saw the battle-field, she commented that "there is no soft place where there are mines and no soft places where there are long 88-mm guns, and if you have seen one tank burn with its crew shut inside it, you will never believe that anything is soft again."

Looking over the German fortifications, the Saskatoon Light Infantry's Howard Mitchell concluded grimly: "The Hitler Line was terrible. This could only be a stupid slaughter." General Vokes, on the other hand, confidently predicted that his First Canadian Division would cut through twelve miles of the Gothic line in the first twenty-four hours. Noting this in his diary, Ken commented: "Hope he's right."

On the afternoon of August 25, Ken wrote to his cousin about the intensity of the fighting. "Jerry flung a few at us last night," he said, "so instead of writing to you as I intended to I was down in my fox-hole smoking a cigarette and murmuring 'pass friend' every time I heard that WHEEEOOO—CRACK!" It looked as if the Eighth Army was about to shift into top gear, he added. "Remember the date of this letter and you will probably know what I'm referring to by the time this reaches you."

A few hours after Ken finished his letter, in the darkness of the Italian evening, the assault on the Gothic line began when four Canadian battalions slipped across the Metauro River, and at one minute to midnight 350 guns began a bombardment of enemy positions. The Fifty-fourth Battery was assigned to protect the First Division headquarters, and as Ken looked out during the afternoon of the twenty-sixth he was surprised to catch sight of General Alexander's staff car bearing Winston Churchill to an observation post at the front. The prime minister liked what he saw there, and four days later the Allied forces had reached the main Gothic line defence along the Foglia River.

On August 30, when the Canadians launched a ferocious three-day assault on the Gothic line, Ken was acting commanding officer of the Fifty-fourth Battery, Major Pepall having left the previous day for a field artillery conversion course. Ken's first act was to leave battery headquarters to see for himself what was happening at the forward positions, and he noted that "the battle is gaining momentum by the hour." The next day he was able to report that "our infantry is well into the Gothic Line now and going strong. Swarms of bombers over, and the din is terrific with strong enemy return fire. All our armour moving forward. Enemy dead still unburied round and about. Not so good when the wind blows from certain directions."

The "armour" was the Fifth Canadian Armoured Division, General Hoffmeister's "Mighty Maroon Machine," which had struggled in the Liri Valley but now was tearing through the surprised German defences. On September 3, Ken observed the anniversary of the beginning of the war by writing: "Five years of war and this day finds us chasing hell out of the Hun after making a 20-mile breach in the Gothic Line." The Canadians had moved so efficiently, in fact, that they were well ahead of the British V Corps, made up of one armoured and five infantry divisions, who were on their left.

Many historians believe that if armoured reinforcements had supported the Canadian Corps at this point, the Eighth Army could have driven far up into the Po Valley and outflanked the Gothic line. The British senior officers hesitated, however, allowing the Germans to fall back to another defensive line near Rimini, and the opportunity was missed. Progress was slowed, and it was not until September 21 that Rimini was taken—and then the Canadians had to stand by while the honour of entering the town was given to a Greek brigade. The next day, the Canadian First Division came out of the line and moved back south to Riccione.

From the crossing of the Metauro River to the fall of Rimini, the Canadian Corps suffered more casualties than during any other comparable period in the Italian campaign, and the brutality of the fighting is etched in Ken's diary. He had resumed being second-in-command of the Fifty-fourth Battery on September 2, when Major C.S. McKay returned from hospital leave after commanding the Second LAA Battery, but he was still doing reconnaissance along the front line. There he saw "the usual wreckage and corpses all over the place . . . Our shells have flattened everything and enemy dead are sometimes found in heaps by the roadside. When dead enemy are found they are incinerated with flame-throwers or buried by bulldozers." In the seaside town of Pesaro, he said, there was "horrible destruction where the Hun blew whole streets of houses down and felled all trees to get field of fire. Dead horses, mules and men here and there." Before setting up battery headquarters in a vineyard near Rimini, a detail of his men had to bury a number of oxen that had been blown to bits by a direct hit on their stable. "All the boys," he added, "are eating grapes now."

If by now the "wreckage and corpses" were "usual," so too was the almost constant enemy artillery and aerial bombardment. Sleep could be only sporadic when the skies became lit by enemy flares and the ground shuddered from high explosives, anti-personnel bombs and incendiaries. The enemy's arsenal was lethal, but so were the battery's own ammunition trucks, exploding as they were hit and sending metal flying all around them. With their engines shut off, the German planes were gliding so close, said Ken, that "I could have hit him with a shovel! . . . I can remember better nights."

Casualties were high among the gunners. Four of Ken's men were hit by enemy shelling when they were trapped on a road across the Foglia River, and two men were killed at their gun site near battery headquarters. Sixty-three members of the Third Field Regiment, which the Fifty-fourth was covering, were killed or injured when their position was radioed to the Germans by a spy hiding on a hillside (he was shot on the spot). The battery nearly lost its new commanding officer when McKay's Jeep was blown to pieces and his slit trench raked by 88-mm fire for several hours. "Cooled the Major off by other methods than freezing, to quote Damon Runyon," observed Ken.

Perhaps the most telling entry in Ken's diary for this period is the one for September 9: "It seems I missed a day somewhere. Oh well!"

In the midst of all the bloodshed, brutality and chaos of the assault on the Gothic line, a strange form of democracy came to the battlefield, and Ken found himself in the thick of it. Back on May 10, when the Canadian Corps was preparing for the Liri Valley, the Liberal government in Saskatchewan had called a provincial election for June 15. Recognizing the large number of Saskatchewan men and women in the armed services outside the province, it provided for three Armed Services Voters' Representatives to be elected in the fall. One would be chosen from Canada and Newfoundland (excluding Saskatchewan), one from the United Kingdom and northern Europe, and one from the Mediterranean theatre. Those elected would serve as regular Members of the Legislature but without party affiliation.

Though he had been an active member of the trade union at the Co-operative Creamery, Ken had never been formally involved in politics. When some men from the Second LAA Battery, which he had left three months earlier, came over to suggest that he represent them in the election and that they could easily find the twenty-five signatures needed to endorse his candidacy, he began to find the idea appealing. The provincial election had been a convulsion in Canadian politics: the CCF under Tommy Douglas won forty-seven seats to the Liberals' five, and it formed the first socialist government on the North American continent. Like his father, Ken had always been attracted to the new populist movement, and this sympathy grew during his years at the Creamery. Though he understood that the Service Representatives would not be connected to any party, it would be exciting to be present at this political experiment in Saskatchewan. Of course, it would also be a way—seemingly the only way outside being severely wounded—to get home and try to salvage his relationship with Margaret.

On September 15, in the midst of the First Canadian Corps's preparations for the assault on Rimini, Ken attended a nomination rally at the Second LAA Battery, still made up largely of Saskatchewan men, and he returned to Fifty-fourth headquarters feeling that "the boys thought my platform reasonable. We'll see." The men did indeed think his platform reasonable, and they voted unanimously to make him their candidate.

In this battlefield election, of course, there could be little of the usual electioneering. Reporting for the Regina *Leader-Post,* Maurice Western compared it to the student elections in western Canadian universities—except that there was an intense earnestness to the soldiers' concerns about life in Canada and the problems of readjustment they would have on their return. "Everywhere in Italy," he wrote, "one is impressed by the gulf between interest in rehabilitation and factual knowledge of measures actually proposed or on the statute books." Many of the men, he added, had time to think and worry, and they needed to know what awaited them. "The idea that they can be satisfied with back issues of *Maclean's* or *London Opinion* is quite fallacious."

None of the fourteen candidates in the Mediterranean region could fail to recognize that repatriation and readjustment were on every serviceman's mind, but not all candidates presented clearly articulated platforms. Ken did, and five days after being nominated he accepted the offer of the army newspaper, the *Maple Leaf,* to print any candidate's program. "The military member from the Mediterranean," he began, "must consider the appointment to be a full-time responsibility, be prepared to advise the provincial government on all service problems, and take a vigorous interest in all postwar plans for active service personnel."

Ken's platform stressed nine points: pensions, rehabilitation, employment, farming, education and training, small business loans, care of the ill and disabled, defence, and immigration. The federal government, he said, should immediately announce a demobilization policy of "first in, first out," with preference being given to married men with children. Disability rates should be increased, and dependent mothers of men killed in action should have pensions equal to that of widows. There should be a national employment survey to determine the availability of jobs, their types and requirements, so that knowledge and skills acquired in the services could be related to what was needed in civilian employment. There should be free education, including post-graduate study, for veterans; low-interest loans for establishing small businesses; maintenance of a permanent active militia, with preference given to veterans; an immigration quota until the veterans were fully repatriated; and "generous pensions and opportunities for a life of usefulness and self-respect for disabled veterans."

One of the most interesting and thoughtful of Ken's proposals—one that ought to have sat well with Tommy Douglas's government—

was his call for the government to purchase arable land and lease it to veterans qualified to work it:

> A soldier's settlement scheme must not be allowed to become a dumping ground for all types of discharged soldiers without regard to their qualifications or to the suitability of the farms provided. The government should purchase, at prewar prices, the large tracts of unoccupied arable land now held by mortgage and land companies. Each individual unit should be soil tested to ensure that it can produce a good living for the soldier and his family.

It is not hard to see why this platform appealed to the men in the Second LAA Battery, one of whom was Chester Fannon. Fannon would later become the unofficial historian of the Second LAA and keep a rich variety of memorabilia about his war experiences, including a yellowed cutting from the September 20 edition of the *Maple Leaf*. It was Ken's platform, which had so impressed him that he wanted his parents to see it, and across the top was his note, scrawled years earlier on an Italian battleground: "We'll have a vote soon and I hope he gets in."

In the end Ken did not get in, but he came a respectable sixth to Lieutenant-Colonel Alan W. Embury, the commanding officer of the Saskatoon Light Infantry and a man with all the right credentials. He was the son of Brigadier-General J.F.L. Embury, a decorated First World War officer who later became a prominent judge in Saskatchewan. An RMC graduate, a lawyer in civilian life and a supporter of the Conservative Party, he might have seemed certain to win the nomination of the SLI. On the first ballot, however, Embury trailed a private who was arguing for monetary reform.

The ensuing argument and strong feeling, according to one officer, "almost disrupted the outfit," and the SLI's Major Howard Mitchell was convinced it was a mistake to try to introduce democratic principles into a rigidly hierarchic military setting. The vote, he said, was "a very disgusting spectacle. We were an army unit on active service where the life of everyone was dependent on the discipline of everyone respecting the chain of command. It was utterly fantastic to think that ordinary humans could step out of that role for an hour and listen to the Commanding Officer of the Battalion compete against those under his command for a popular job." On the final ballot, Lieutenant-Colonel Embury narrowly edged out the private.

The vote for the Mediterranean Service Representative took place in late October and early November, and no Canadian election has ever been conducted under more challenging conditions. The battle-ground had moved up the Adriatic coast, the Germans were still offering fierce resistance, and the weather had turned wet and cold; so, officers had to move from outpost to outpost, often under German shelling, to collect ballots. Almost three thousand votes were gathered this way, and on November 10, having the advantage of representing the largest unit of Saskatchewan men in Italy, Embury was declared the winner.

Ken must have been disappointed to have lost the chance to get back home, but a week later he attended a public meeting where Embury talked of leaving soon to take his seat in Regina. Along with one other candidate, Ken thanked his own supporters and congratulated the member-elect, expressing confidence that he would vigorously pursue the problems facing servicemen. That faith may have been somewhat undercut by Embury's cautious remark that "the present allotment of home leave is not adequate, but I think it is as large as they can make it under the circumstances. Winning the war still comes first." For Ken and the very large majority of Canadian servicemen in Italy, that victory still seemed frustratingly out of reach.

Earle and eighteen-year-old Ken at Etter's Beach with Ken's friend Lena Vail.

Pre-war Ken relaxes on the steps of the Calder home with Mickey, who remembered him on his return from Europe.

Ken and Margaret's wedding photo, taken a few days before he went to war.

6 July 45.
Vancouver.

My dear John,—

Wish I wasn't writing this tonight
but you dared me to tell you how
things are back here. You being, in my
~~opinion the~~ best friend I've got. here it
is: the whole shot with nothing held
back. By the time this gets to you I
will already be rotting in my grave but
then, what does it matter after all? After
a week of "don't touch me" when all I
wanted was a little love and affection,
my wife Margaret whom I idolized finally
summoned up courage to tell me she
had been unfaithful. I took that like
~~a good soldier~~ I think, but then she
put over the belly punch. She told me
that she had never loved me and
that she has lived with several men
all the time I was away. One in

When Ken left Margaret for overseas duty, he thought they were as inseparable as they appeared in the shadow on the wall of the Calder house.

John Gardiner as Ken knew him in Italy, 1944.

Ken taking a break from artillery training exercises in Britain, 1941.

Margaret, Earle and the
author's mother in
the early years of the war.

Earle enjoying his greatest success
as an army training officer.

Brigadier Sherwood Lett, CBE, DSO, MC, in 1945, when Ken's suicide presented him with a family dilemma.

Juliette, who waited for John Gardiner and married him three days after his return from Europe.

Robert (in hat) and Kenneth with their grandparents several years after the war.

Robert (far left) and Kenneth Calder (far right) at dinner in 1997 with two of their uncle's closest wartime friends (from left to right) John Gardiner and Roger Jean-Marie.

CHAPTER TEN

"24 September, 1944.

And the rains came! Also Ralston."

This entry, the briefest in Ken's wartime diary, is rich in both humour and meaning for Canadian veterans of the Italian campaign. By the time he wrote it, they had already endured a terrible winter on the Adriatic coast, and now they were about to face the worst autumn in Italy in twenty years. On September 20 the weather broke and it began to rain. It rained for twenty consecutive days, and then at frequent intervals for the rest of the winter. In the mountains the rain turned to sleet and men died of exposure. On the plains it turned the land to a quagmire and made progress nearly impossible. For every serviceman it made life unbearable.

For understandable reasons, most accounts of war focus on the drama of the fighting and the killing, and we tend to forget that soldiers endured less spectacular but sometimes equally debilitating hardships such as vile weather. One American officer in Italy later wrote that "the worst part of the war was not the shooting or the shelling—though that had been bad enough—but the weather, snow, sleet and rain, and the prolonged physical misery that accompanied them." A British officer remembered the rain filling the slit trenches, often the only refuge from the shellfire. The average man "was permanently soaked to the skin, and permanently in danger. He spent his days in the bleak surroundings of stunted decapitated trees, hundreds of waterlogged shell holes, unburied corpses of . . . soldiers, sopping blankets and discarded ration tins . . . The greatest enemy by far was the mud." John Guest, author of *Broken Images: A Journal* and an artillery captain like Ken, described sitting in his tent with the feet of his bed standing permanently in water:

> It is ten o'clock in the morning and I have—rare thing—deliberately postponed my visit to the guns until this afternoon . . . The ground for fifty yards outside is MUD—six inches deep, glistening, sticky, holding pools of water. Great excavations in the mud, leaving miniature alps of mud, show where other tents have been pitched in the mud, and moved on account of the mud to other spaces in the mud. The cumulative psychological effect of mud is an experience which cannot be described.

In the words of the American Bill Mauldin, "Mud . . . is a curse that seems to save itself for war."

Throughout the autumn of 1944, Ken's diary reflects the misery being inflicted by the weather: "My tent leaks" (September 20), "Cold and blowing all night" (September 30), "Rain started again at dawn" (October 1), "Cold, wet miserable day. Everyone thoroughly soaked. Rained heavily all night" (October 2), "Still raining" (October 5), "Starting to rain in the afternoon. By evening the whole place a quagmire" (October 17), "Rain started at 4 pm and continued steadily all night" (October 21), "Raining all day" (October 22), "Rained all night" (October 25), "Dull day with heavy rain and high winds. Bridges going out everywhere" (October 26).

Though he had escaped the various bombardments unscathed—as if he had a lucky star—Ken had been ill several times earlier in the year. After the Liri Valley he had twice been levelled with severe dysentery and had contracted malaria. Now, in the wet and cold of the Italian autumn, he was being hit with the inevitable colds and flu. On October 3, after two weeks of continuous rain, he wrote: "Have a bad throat and burning nostrils, so don't have to be a swami to guess what's coming. To bed at 3 am feeling tough." "As I thought," he noted the next day, "have a pip of a cold," and on October 5: "Spent whole day in bed." And lest anyone imagine that a day in bed on the battlefields of Italy meant warmth and comfort, during a sustained downpour two weeks later Ken commented that he "refused to get up and lay in wet ditch."

This last comment suggests more than just obstinacy in the face of inclement weather; it is the statement of someone who is beginning to find no reason to get up, someone becoming exhausted spiritually as well as physically. Alex Bowlby, a British soldier enduring the same conditions not far from Ken, described the desolation brought on by the weather and the seemingly endless war:

A storm sprang up in the night. It was still blowing next morning. It was still raining too. After breakfast Jeffreys and I stood watching it stream down the windows. The year's fall set off a wild train of sadness. I thought of the dead, unburied in the rain, or ourselves, waiting our turn, and of all the hopeless futility of war.

"It makes you think, doesn't it?" said Jeffreys.

I looked round at him. Jeffreys stared straight ahead. His face was so sad I had to look away.

"You know," he said slowly, "I've had four years in a duty platoon. That's a long time. They've never given me a rest . . . The trouble is that once you prove yourself reliable they shit on you. They use you. They use you till you—"

He broke off with a shrug.

"Oh, well," he said, smiling. "Who knows? Perhaps I'll get one just the same."

His words coming on top of my sadness brought me to the point of tears. There was nothing I could say. Perhaps I had drawn off some of his sadness. It felt like it. When he walked away I sat down on my blankets and wrote a sonnet called "The Dead." It came straight out, and the sadness passed into the words.

October 2 may have been such a day of desolation for Ken, a man like Jeffreys who had served five years without seeing his family or his wife. From dawn until dusk it was bone-chilling and wet, with a rain that drenched every tent and every soldier. In the afternoon the Germans began shelling the area, and they kept up the bombardment until nightfall, when periodic raids by enemy aircraft kept the men huddled for shelter in the waterlogged slit trenches. "It was," wrote Ken, "the kind of day you think about home."

Sadness made Bowlby write a poem. It must have been a kindred sadness or some sense of hopelessness that made Ken produce a drawing that was found among his wartime relics after his death. Sketched in pen and ink, it depicts a human skull, lower jaw missing, resting on a book. It is, of course, hardly original in theme or form, but its morbidity speaks volumes about Ken's state of mind as the Italian campaign dragged on.

But Ken was hardly alone. For everybody in the Allied armies in Italy in the autumn of 1944—fighting men and occasional visitors alike—the melancholy was palpable, hanging over the troops like the grey Italian morning mists clinging to the hillsides. After Rimini, in late September, the Canadian advance slowed, and as winter set in there was no longer any exhilarating talk of destroying the German army on the Romagna plain, of forging through to Vienna or of driving across the Adriatic to meet the Russians in the Balkans. There would be no dramatic breakthroughs to shorten the war—as Ken observed on October 4, "the dopes who think the war will be over soon should be here to see for themselves."

The Allied soldiers in Italy knew that any spectacular break-throughs would come in northern Europe, that the world was focused on the battle in Holland and the invasion in southern France, and that the Italian campaign had become merely a sideshow. Their task was not to defeat the German divisions opposite them but merely to keep them engaged and away from the fighting taking place on the second front. The result, as Strome

Galloway, an officer in the Royal Canadian Regiment, said, was that the goal was never clear to the soldiers: "Eighth Army was to keep bashing on, the weather, the flooded rivers notwithstanding. Impossible goals were chosen—the line of the Santerno River was to be reached. As to *why*, nobody at the fighting level was ever told." And as the First World War had proved and the British artilleryman John Guest discovered in Italy, no kind of combat is as demoralizing as that without any real advance or obvious purpose:

> Though we didn't always go forward in the African campaign, it was nearly always exciting, and one kept oneself fully wound up. But now . . . we've done nothing but sit and wait and wait. When one has to be in the army one can compensate one's loss, if one is advancing or fighting, by all sorts of day-dreams of the end being in sight. But nothing is more depressing than the awful waste of sitting still in the army. I don't mean the waste of the huge military machine—one doesn't think about that— but personal waste.

Though it became bogged down, the Italian campaign remained as deadly as ever, and at battery headquarters at the Rubicon River in the middle of October, Ken wrote: "R[oyal] C[anadian] R[egiment] cemetery beside us. Bigger every time I look at it." And, judging by the next day's entry, he was grimly prophetic: "RCR cemetery growing." Strome Galloway later explained that "our rifle companies were always under strength, the reinforcements poorly trained. The eyes of the world were now on the great destructive battles of the Second Front. By October 1944 we were floundering in a backwater of the war . . . Life was sour indeed."

So sour was life for the Canadians in Italy that Eldon Davis and other padres in the Third Field Artillery Regiment created the Padre's Hour, a time when the men could meet to give voice to their discontent. After "long years of fear and loneliness and despair," said Davis, the soldiers were feeling forgotten as the world's attention was directed elsewhere: "Mostly, though, there was quiet despair . . . the kind embodied in the expression 'how long, O Lord, how long?'" The war had become, in the American Ernie Pyle's words, "a flat black depression without headlights, a revulsion of the mind and an exhaustion of the spirit."

The Canadians, however, had another growing source of exasperation unknown to Pyle's GIs, Guest's British gunners or indeed any of the other Commonwealth troops fighting in Italy. They had the zombies, the nearly 100,000 servicemen back in Canada who had been conscripted but declined to serve overseas. This situation, unique among the major participating nations in the Italian campaign, had come about because in 1939 Prime Minister Mackenzie King, to placate Quebec, had promised no conscription for overseas service. All Canadians fighting outside the country would be men, like Ken, who had volunteered to do so.

In June 1940, Parliament had passed the National Resources Mobilization Act, which authorized conscription but only for defence of the home country. Two years later the minister of national defence, Colonel J.L. Ralston, tendered his resignation because he was convinced of the necessity of conscription for overseas service, but he was persuaded by King to stay on. By the middle of September 1944, however, when shortages of men, in both Italy and northern Europe, were not being adequately filled, Ralston decided to visit the fronts and assess the situation for himself.

Ralston was seen by the Canadian soldiers in Europe as part of a government they detested, hence the whiff of contempt in Ken's comment "Also Ralston." But that does the man an injustice. During his nine days in Italy he met with as many Canadian troops as he could, inviting them to explain their difficulties, particularly with regard to reinforcements, and he learned that if the First Canadian Corps continued in action, its pool of reinforcements would be exhausted in three months. Moreover, the reinforcement situation was so grim that wounded men were often rushed back to the front too soon, and artillery gunners were being converted into inadequately trained infantrymen.

Ralston became convinced that there was a manpower crisis in the Canadian forces in Europe, and he promised the men that something would be done, that he would not let them down. He was as good as his word. When he returned to Ottawa, he advised the prime minister that it would be necessary to send conscripted troops overseas. At this point the wily King took Ralston's 1942 letter of resignation out of his desk drawer and announced that he was now accepting it; General Andrew McNaughton would be the new minister of national defence, and he would persuade enough zombies to volunteer for overseas duty.

McNaughton's recruitment speeches to the zombies fell on deaf— indeed, frequently hostile—ears, however, and in November 1944 he recommended that 16,000 NRMA men be sent overseas. King reluctantly agreed, and eventually 13,000 were sent—amid public protests in various parts of the country—to Europe. In the end, 9,700 of these men got to the Continent and fewer than 2,500 saw action on the battlefield. Not one zombie ever reached Italy.

The zombies had many reasons for refusing to fight: some were pacifists, some were men who felt they had been ignored during the hardships of the Depression and believed they owed the country nothing, and some had personal reasons for wishing to remain in Canada. But to the long-serving men in Europe, for whom the only way home was to be wounded three times, they were detestable—the "living dead," as the term "zombie" suggested. The poet Douglas LePan, an artillery gunner in Italy, wrote of the reinforcement crisis that "it is impossible to exaggerate the bitterness" of the men doing the fighting.

It is possible, however, to get a sense of the soldiers' loathing in Farley Mowat's accounts—both those written during the heat of battle and those recollected in tranquillity after the war. Having read a *Liberty* magazine article about the complaints of zombies with respect to their pay, their leaves and the pressures to sign up for overseas service, he wrote to his parents in June 1944 about the "whining bastards . . . Makes me want to puke up everything I've eaten for a week." In December he reported that German radio propagandists were having a field day with the stories of Canadian conscripts burning the Union Jack and attacking those few who did volunteer to fight: "I have to tell you that we are becoming so ashamed of our so-called country that some of us don't give much of a damn if we ever see it again." And one of the NCOs in the Hastings and Prince Edward Regiment, he said, wrote in his diary: "Shame and hellfire for Mackenzie King and his whole rotten, louse-bound crew. May they rot in hell with the Zombies that they love!"

Strome Galloway too saw the resentment boiling in the First Canadian Corps, but, he said, "some gentler souls were less blasphe-mous than most against the 'Zombies' and put their thoughts into poetry." Though he would likely have laughed at the idea of being one of the "gentler souls"—especially after the effects of ten months of brutal fighting—Ken was one of those who expressed his outrage in verse.

Anyone who doubts that poetry is the central literary experience, the form to which people turn when they wish to express their most deeply felt experiences and emotions, need only look at the response of men to war. Historians have estimated that in the initial months of the First World War there were more poems produced—and published—than at any time previously. Many of these verses were written, not by the Siegfried Sassoons or Wilfred Owens, but by ordi-nary soldiers, men who had never put pen to paper before and who very likely had grumbled when their schoolteachers asked them to read and memorize a bit of poetry. Now the enormity of what they were facing and enduring seemed to call for the apt metaphor, the stark image or the evocative word; and in the mud of the trenches or the chill of an outpost they scribbled their lines on cigarette packages or maps or the backs of envelopes.

The Second World War was no different, and neither were the Canadian servicemen. Shortly after the *Maple Leaf* was created in Italy in January 1944, it began to receive poems by Canadian soldiers, and by May the flow of verses was steady enough that the editors introduced a new section called Rhyme and Reason. Here the soldiers could publish their efforts, in most cases simple rhyming couplets or doggerel in imitation of Robert W. Service, but always honest work and frequently deeply felt and moving.

Back in Moose Jaw, Ken had never shown any inclination to write poetry. It was Earle who read poetry and in later life could still quote lines, while Ken was more the conventional young man interested in hunting, fishing and sports. Now, on the battlefields of Italy, as he explained it to the relatives in Fargo, he was experiencing something that would lead him to try his hand at verse:

> *What worries the boys who have been at it for five years now is when can we expect to go home if only for a leave? The call-ups at home who won't go active are called zombies (walking dead) and there is a big controversy as to whether they should be made to take over or not. As you can readily see, they would not be the sort of soldiers we want and would in all probability lose all the ground we've gained but there it is. Personally I think any infantryman who has been at it for five years is past due for a glimpse of home. All we need is something other than a weak-kneed Gov't which will take the issue in hand and do something.*

Ken had seen more than enough at Ortona, the Liri Valley and the Gothic line to recognize the old truth that in any war it is the Poor Bloody Infantry who endure the greatest hardships, and he knew that any reinforcements who might arrive in Italy would be infantrymen, not artillery officers. Only very indirectly—through ending the transfer of artillery officers and men to infantry units—would reinforcements perhaps enhance his own chances of being granted a home leave. His disgust with the zombies, therefore, would seem to be an expression of disinterested concern for the situation of the ordinary foot soldier. That said, it is hard not to believe that at the heart of his anger lay a feeling of despair and helplessness about the seemingly endless war and his own entrapment in it.

In any case, as he went on to explain, "in a moment of weakness I penned the accompanying effort of blank verse and am taking steps to see that it gets into the home papers as undoubtedly it will. We were told recently by a lad who made a trip to Canada that the zombies were worried about how the soldiers overseas felt about them. I think I have answered their question":

Answer to a Question

Dedicated to the Non-Active Service Personnel in Canada

You, who have never heard the sound of shells,
Have never trembled from a mortar bursting close,
Have never seen your friends lie mangled, dead,
Nor fought beside them when they went to meet their God.
You know not what it means to live in winter
Crouched in a burrow scraped from oozing mud,
Nor yet, to stand and say farewell
To a friend who faced death with a smile.

The flares at night, the diving planes,
The awful tearing sound that chills the spine,
You know them not, nor have you seen
Men rise to heights which you will never gain.
You, who have never sailed in a fighting ship
And manned her guns in heat or freezing cold,
Or flown through hell, while friends on either side
Plummet to earth, a blazing ball of fire.

You ask us what we think of men like you?
Who stand apart, content to serve at home,
Cov'ring your shrinking souls with heroes' garb,
While girls in England die beside their guns?
Have you forgotten Singapore where British girls
Chose to stay and tend the wounded men?
Where are they now, and where, we ask,
Are your brothers, cousins, friends, who heard the call?

What do we think? The answer's plain.
We who have known these things which you do not,
Pity you, each one of you afraid
To take your rightful place with fighting men.
You'll never know the pride men feel
Who come through hell and live to tell the tale,
That brotherhood, sharing every joy and pain,
Founded on common danger and pride for work well done.

We see the crosses standing stark and think
Of friends who lie beneath the winter sky.
We ask, how can our home breed such as you
And call you men, while heroes gladly die?
The men who fight don't want your kind.
We'll finish this with what we have.
Five years of war, and yet you waver still!
Be not afraid, stay home, we'll carry on—alone!

Sending his poem to Fargo, Ken explained that "war is not always as bad as I make it sound, but sometimes it is and I have had every experience I have written of with the possible exception of the Navy and the Air Force. I don't think I could have insulted the zombies any more but they did want to know what we think." In the end, however, no zombies heard what Ken thought of them. For whatever reason, the newspapers to which his mother forwarded his poem, the Moose Jaw *Times-Herald* and the Regina *Leader-Post,* declined to publish it; perhaps their editors were afraid of exacerbating a volatile situation in the country.

Ken's poem was published—in the November 4 issue of the *Maple Leaf,* where ironically no zombie would ever see it; the only readers were active overseas servicemen like himself. Like all contributors to the paper, Ken had to secure the permission of his commanding officer, and in order not to compromise his position as battery captain he signed his verses simply "K. (R.C.A.)." To his amusement, this anonymity allowed him to overhear the critiques of the unsuspecting men under him, all of whom felt that the poem spoke for them.

Addressing even the converted of the First Canadian Corps may have given Ken some form of catharsis, but it did not entirely wash away his anger. Writing to his relatives in early December, he dismissed his poem as "that piece of nonsense," but its subject was still very much on his mind. "Back home the zombies seem to be slugging it out with each other to keep from coming out here; if I had that poem to write again, I think I'd add a couple of verses or so."

CHAPTER ELEVEN

Through most of the autumn of 1944, Ken remained the battery captain of the Fifty-fourth LAA Battery, and it was while he was there that he heard that his former commanding officer, Major John Pepall, had been severely wounded. It seems that in preparation for an attack on German positions near Cesena, on the Savio River, Pepall, then commanding the Seventy-seventh Battery of the Third Field Regiment, had joined the colonels from three infantry battalions and gone forward to do some reconnaissance at the front line. Along the way they came to an open field within the sight and range of enemy guns, so the colonels crouched down and moved slowly and painfully through a ditch skirting its perimeter. Pepall, apparently lost in his own thoughts, continued plodding across the open expanse, with the others shouting: "Get down, Major! Get down! You'll get yourself killed!"

"Nothing to worry about!" Pepall replied. "I'll be all right!" And he was. Miraculously, it seemed, nothing happened.

All four officers got to the rendezvous point safely, decided on the gun placements and began the return journey. At the field the colonels again took to the ditch and the awkward crouching walk around the edge. Pepall, though, perhaps feeling quixotically invulnerable or simply oblivious of the danger, began to retrace his steps across the exposed terrain, but this time his luck did not hold. German gunners must have been surprised to see a lone enemy officer casually strolling along in such an exposed site, and they opened fire. Artillery shells began exploding near Pepall and moments later a fragment of jagged metal ripped into his chest. The medics were able to get him back to headquarters, but a day later, at the age of thirty-seven, he was dead.

It was an absurd way to die, and one member of the Second LAA Regiment, recalling the man's eccentricities, commented that "it was a fitting end for John Pepall." What Ken thought of the matter is not known, but, since the Fifty-fourth LAA was covering the Third Field Regiment at that time, he heard of the major's wounding within hours and noted it in his diary. The next day, October 22, he added simply: "Major Pepall died early this morning."

A little more than three weeks later, on November 15, Ken was transferred back to the Second LAA to serve as battery captain, where he remained for the rest of the war. In addition to being back with the Saskatchewan men, he was again working and living closely with John Gardiner, whom he had seen only occasionally since June. Within days, however, the friends found themselves seriously at odds.

Talking with various officers on one of his reconnaissance sorties, Ken had learned that Pepall was lying in an unmarked grave, either because of error or because someone had removed the marker. When the Commonwealth War Graves Commission staff came to relocate the body, now sixty miles behind the front line, to one of the Canadian Army cemeteries, they would have great difficulty finding it. Ken came to Gardiner one day and said, "John, we've got to do something about Pepall."

"Why?" replied Gardiner.

"Because he's lying there in some farmer's field and soon nobody'll know where the hell he is. No one from the Third Field seems to be doing anything about it. And I can't get anybody to go back with me to put a marker on it. You know how the men feel about him."

"And I feel the same way," said Gardiner. "The man nearly got me killed three times in Sicily. I've never disobeyed one of your orders, Ken, but this time I'm going to. I'll be damned if I'll go."

"But," Ken insisted, "the man has a wife and family back in Canada. For their sakes, we can't leave him like this. You wouldn't treat a dog this way. Besides, I need you to explain to the Eyetie farmer what I'm looking for."

"Hell, Ken," Gardiner replied, "these Italians can sell us vino and women without knowing a word of English. Go down there, show them the cross and say, 'Canadese tomba.' They'll know what you want." And that ended the matter so far as Gardiner was concerned.

Who can tell what lay behind Ken's insistence that the grave be marked? It may have been simple common decency, a conviction that no one who falls in action should go unrecognized, or merely a good and conventional officer's sense of propriety. In any case, he proceeded to make a cross on which he carefully stencilled the essential details about Pepall, ordered a driver to take him back behind the line, found the grave and planted the marker. Some months later Pepall's body was exhumed and given a proper burial in the Canadian military cemetery in Cesena.

When Ken returned to the Second LAA in the middle of November, the battery was out of the fighting at the divisional concentration area near Riccione, and it remained there until the end of the month. During this time the men rested, were entertained, and trained in small-arms fire, equipment maintenance and anti-aircraft firing. Many of them were given seven-day leaves, which they gladly used to visit Rome and Florence, by then in Allied hands.

Ken, however, went nowhere. In fact, for a number of months he had declined to take any leave, perhaps because, as the Seaforth Highlanders' Robert McDougall observed, "when the pressure's off the spirit sags. Some [soldiers] remember their loneliness, and a great many unhappily remember more of the self than they do when the going is tough." So, while other officers eagerly took two or three days away from the line, grateful to find somewhere away from the shelling, the killing and the cold, Ken remained at the front. When they urged him to join them, he replied that he no longer got any pleasure in his leaves, that he would just as soon stay in his tent. This surprised his friends in the Fifty-fourth Battery and began to trouble them enough that they went to Gardiner about it. "It just doesn't make any sense," they said. "He just wants to sit there instead of going down the line and relaxing."

Gardiner too was concerned, but for a different reason. He knew Ken well enough to realize that he had an almost ritualistic respect for anniversaries: he could tell you the day war was declared, the day he left Moose Jaw for Britain and the exact number of Christmases—it would be six this year—he had spent away from home. In a few days it would be November 29, the anniversary of Ken's wedding, an anniversary that in five years he had never once been able to celebrate with his wife. It would be a very difficult day for him.

Gardiner knew he had to do something, so he explained the situation to the battery's commanding officer, who agreed that he should take his friend down the line for a couple of days of relaxation and talk around the twenty-ninth. As he had done with the others, however, Ken refused to go. Nothing could sway him, so Gardiner fell back on an alternate plan. The battery headquarters was then situated in a five-room school, and the major agreed that Ken and Gardiner would have the last room at the end of the hall for the evening. No one was to come in or interfere. "It's Ken's evening," explained Gardiner. "He can decide what he wants to do." In fact, confessed Gardiner many years later, "I wanted to get him so goddamned drunk that he'd fall down. I'd strip him and put him to bed, and for one night at least he'd sleep."

Getting Ken falling-down drunk was not as easy as Gardiner thought. "We started," he recalls. "We drank rye, we drank Guinness, we drank anything we could find. And he wasn't falling." They were running out of booze when Gardiner remembered that, from Ortona to Cassino to Riccione, Ken had been lugging around a bottle of champagne he had bought for the day he would be reunited with Margaret. So he said: "You're from Saskatchewan. You people out there are like the Yanks, you don't know anything about wine or champagne. This is lousy champagne. We'd better drink it. I'll buy you a bottle of real champagne before you leave, and you're not leaving tonight, right?"

Ken did not disagree, but, he said, "we can't drink champagne out of these goddamned army tin cups."

"It has to be glass, does it?" replied Gardiner. "Of course, you know that the Canadian army doesn't supply wineglasses." Ken shrugged, so Gardiner wandered down to the far end of the building where the cook was sleeping. It was now 2 a.m., but he took his chances and woke him, saying: "You remember when that women's group—the IODE or something—sent us some pickles a while back. You still got some?"

"Sure," said the cook. "But what for?"

"The captain," replied Gardiner.

"The captain wants to eat pickles at two o'clock in the morning?"

"No, to drink champagne. Out of the pickle jars. He doesn't want to drink it out of a tin mug."

So the cook emptied and rinsed two jars. Gardiner went back down the hall with them and told Ken, "Here's your glasses."

Ken looked at the labels still on the sides and said, "But they're pickle jars!"

"What the hell's the problem?" his friend replied. "Is there any rule against drinking champagne out of pickle jars? Go on, drink up."

And so they continued into the early hours of the morning. Gardiner does not recall that they ever discussed Ken's relationship with Margaret, but their conversation, the voluble and wide-ranging talk of two men drinking themselves into a stupor, was repeatedly punctuated by one comment from Ken. "Five years married," he would mutter over and over again. "Five nights with my wife!"

It may be surprising that so little of the talk that night was about the source of Ken's distress: his relationship with Margaret. Gardiner's intent, though, had been to help his friend forget his difficulty, not to push him to remember and address a problem that could not be solved on a battlefield in Italy. The pain Ken was enduring is perhaps best described in George Blackburn's comment that "none of the books you'd read about the miseries endured by soldiers in the last Great War prepared you for the cruel torture a soldier endures from too vivid a recall of his young wife."

It is possible, too, that the two men's behaviour that evening was dictated by a certain form of the military ethos. Both Ken and Gardiner were officers, expected to be disciplined and emotionally self-controlled, and baring the difficulties of one's personal life—even to one's fellow officer and friend—might have seemed a sign of weakness. Five years in uniform and months of rugged combat would have led Ken to erect the shield against visible signs of emotion depicted by American infantry lieutenant Paul Fussell: "I compressed my lips very tightly and kept them that way for some time. This ritual tightening-up constituted my sole defence against all my natural impulses to weep, scream, or run away."

In his letters to his American relatives, too, Ken seems to have hidden his feelings behind a mask of jocularity and optimism, a posture that is quite at odds with, say, the anxiety and cynicism Farley Mowat freely expressed in writing to his parents. Of course, we do not know how open Ken was in his letters to his own immediate family or with Margaret, but it is worth noting that nowhere in the diary which he kept through most of 1944 is there any comment on his feelings about his marriage. Was he gripped by a form of denial which prevented him, even in the intimacy of his own thoughts, from recognizing that his marriage would not likely survive a separation of more than five years? And thus led him to continue to idealize Margaret and to count on her to provide the normalcy of a married life when the war was over?

Ken could not hide his depression in the Christmas greeting he sent to Fargo a week after the anniversary evening. Even in the worst of times he had always managed to make his letters cheerful and optimistic, but he clearly struggled to make this one positive. "I haven't been writing very much lately," he began, "due to one thing and another, mainly the war." For a month, however, the war—the worst of it at least—had been miles away, as the Second LAA had been taken out of the line. In June, when the First Division had gone into a rest period after the Liri Valley, Ken had plunged into his correspondence. Now, it seems, something—apathy, exhaustion or depression—made it difficult to put his thoughts on paper. Despite his best efforts, those thoughts he did manage to put down betrayed a debilitating resignation.

He was delighted, Ken wrote, to receive their two parcels, but he would not open them until Christmas Day; he was determined not to have another Christmas like the previous one in Tunisia, when he spent a miserable day without a scrap of mail. "Things here," he went on, "are about like the papers say only they don't go into detail about the mud and cold like I could," adding with some pride that he had managed to construct a stove out of an ammunition box and a piece of drainpipe.

Out here we are still slugging it out with the Herrenvolk and according to the map we're not losing. That is as it should be, I guess. In ten more days I will have been overseas five years and right now I would willingly hand over to some newcomer if I could. About all I have to show for the past five years is that I'm a little broader in the beam and a trifle grey at the temples.

As the winter of 1944–45 dragged on, Ken seems to have become increasingly conscious of having aged considerably in the five years since he left Moose Jaw. He was still only thirty-three, but he felt like an old man. In a letter to Fargo written on October 3 he had commented that he was "as grey as a badger, in top shape but getting old fast," and in early January he said he hoped that "you don't all get a shock when you see me next. I hardly think I've gotten any younger in appearance." In February he wrote to his cousin Grace that "your comments about people looking like the wrath of God sure apply to me! Every time I look at my mug in a shaving mirror, I flinch!"

More and more, as Ken looked into his mirror, he could not fail to see that he had changed during his years in England and Italy, that he was not the same man who had gone to war in 1939. And not, therefore, the same man who had married Margaret. But how could he know what kind of changes had occurred in her in his absence? She had sent him few photographs of her while he was in England and none since he had been in Italy, and when she did send one in December 1944, it was startling. "I notice that she has aged a good five years since I've been away," he said, as if speaking of a distant cousin rather than his wife. "I guess I have, too."

Inescapably, despite Margaret's letters—or because of the scarcity of them—the only woman Ken knew was the one he had left in the railway station in Moose Jaw five years earlier. With his world shrunk to the life of the battery, his fellow soldiers, the enemy across the line, the next shoot and the killing, how was he to comprehend her life in a Canada that was both getting on with business as it always had and changing in so many ways? Or indeed understand someone who was getting on with her life in a world so different from his?

However apprehensive he felt about his relationship with Margaret, Ken continued to nurse his dream of taking up his married life with her and opening a sporting goods store. Sometime in the cold and mud and gloom of the Italian December he sat down and on the back of an army-issue Christmas card calculated how much money they had saved since he had been overseas. Throughout the war he had been sending $118 of his $150 monthly pay to Margaret to put into a savings account, and this would now amount to about $7,000. Then, too, there was the monthly dependents' allowance, which, having worked continuously, she would not have needed to use. As well, he would be given a service gratuity, a payment of fifty cents for each day served during the war, which by the end of hostilities would be at least $1,600. Add in the $100 clothing allowance and one month's pay on demobilization, Ken figured, and by December 1945 he and Margaret would have around $11,000 in savings. In 1946 this would be enough both to buy a house and to start a respectable business. And with his experience as battery captain in directing the day-to-day operations of a large number of men, he was confident he could successfully manage his own store.

Writing down these figures may have been Ken's way of making the future seem more tangible, but even his calculations, stretching as they did to the end of 1945, betray his realization that it might still be years before he would get home. The Allies' winter campaign had bogged down, and there was no longer any talk of pushing the Germans back to Vienna. "The Herrenvolk in front of us," reported Ken, "seem to be far from discouraged even yet. Things here remain pretty much the same and our theme song might well be 'There's One More River to Cross.' When we fought in the mountains they used to say 'chase him off that ridge ahead and we're in the clear.' Now they say 'chase him over that next river.'" As he looked ahead to 1945, he hoped that "this year will see the end of hostilities, but one never knows because, after all, this is a crazy world and a crazy war."

Even if the Russians and the Allies in northern Europe forced an end to the war in Europe in 1945, there was no guarantee that Ken would be sent home. Who could know how large an army of occupation would be required and how long it would be needed? Then there was the war in the Pacific, where the Japanese were determined to fight to the last man to defend their home islands. Canada's contribution to that campaign would come, not from the zombies, but from the battle-hardened veterans of the war in Europe, and it was rumoured that the First Division had already been selected to go. Ken's war might grind on for several more years.

And grind on it did in the early months of 1945. At the end of December, Sir Harold Alexander, the new Supreme Allied Commander in the Mediterranean, called a halt to further offensive operations in northern Italy, recognizing that, in the words of one of his regimental commanders, his forces had "only enough strength left to lean against the Hun." This did not mean that the fighting stopped, however; there were still the patrols, the shelling, the reconnaissance missions and the snipers, and by mid-February Ken could report that two of his closest friends had been killed already in the new year. Then, too, there was the freezing rain, the snow, the mud and the desolate landscape. And there was the realization that the battles that would win the war were being fought elsewhere. "There was nothing to be done," wrote Farley Mowat years later, "except endure."

But many of the men found the life unendurable. More and more soldiers—British, American and Canadian—went absent without leave, while numerous others took the more serious step of deserting, a crime no longer punishable by death as it was in the Great War, but one that nevertheless brought the risk of a lengthy jail sentence in harsh conditions. As Bill McAndrew demonstrates in *Battle Exhaustion,* the neuropsychiatric cases in the Canadian Army in Italy increased as the weather worsened and morale declined. Many such casualties were soldiers who had long before begun to wonder why they were being asked to suffer and die in a sideshow campaign, but a growing number of the burnout cases were men who had many months of commendable service and who remained dedicated to the cause. Among them were good officers no longer able to face being responsible for their men as well as for themselves.

Though he confessed to being "fed up with this war," Ken did endure, clinging, as so many others did, to friendship and to simple, familiar rituals such as Christmas. "Our Christmas was fairly good," he reported.

> *We had too much to eat and drink and everyone had a mountain of Christmas mail and parcels. I was very lucky indeed as I had saved everything for weeks and had lots of things to open. We loaded ourselves with candy etc. and visited every home in the village so that the kids could be happy too. The parents were very pleased at such antics on our part. Anyway the soldiers and the kids both had a wonderful day. There were only limited attempts made during the day to keep the war going, by both sides, so it was not too unpleasant.*

At the end of the day, Ken joined the other officers in the army tradition of serving the men their Christmas dinner and then taking guard duty at two in the morning. While he was doing this, the commanding officer of the First Division, Major-General Harry Foster, was sitting at his table summing up the day. "Tomorrow," he wrote, "we return to the cold reality of the war and all its ugliness but we won't forget Christmas 1944, because for 24 hrs men became human again and war seemed very far away."

The cold reality of the war did indeed return and it kept its hard grip on the troops for the rest of the winter, but the men found other opportunities to become human again. Like most of the Canadian soldiers in Italy, Ken's first impression of the Italians had not been positive, and he wrote from Ortona in early 1944 that "I can't say that I admire them very much." First, he shared the widely held sentiment that the Italians were merely political opportunists; he was convinced that "the Italians are all violently anti-fascist now but I believe they would change back again just as quickly if the Germans started to win." Then, too, there were some aspects of the centuries-old patriarchy that offended his prairie Canadian idea of the roles of men and women. "Some of the sights I have seen have been revolting, to say the least," he wrote. "The women apparently do all the work and we see them daily, plodding along the roads with great loads of stuff perched on their heads (they carry everything that way) with the men following along behind with their hands in their pockets." As often as not, the men were riding mules, and after seeing this several times, Ken and Gardiner took to ordering the men off at gunpoint and putting the women in their place. They knew, of course, that as soon as they got over the hill the men would reclaim their position. Besides, quipped Gardiner once, the men were not strong enough to carry the loads.

By the middle of their second winter in Italy, however, Ken and Gardiner saw the Italians differently. In part this was driven by their need to experience again, as they did on Christmas Day, some semblance of family life, even if it was among strangers with whom

Ken, at least, could barely communicate. It was also the inevitable result of their being billeted in Italian homes, a practice made necessary by the severe winter weather in the more northern part of the country.

On one such occasion in the middle of January, when the Second LAA Battery was assigned to cover the Corps Artillery gun area near Ravenna, Ken and Gardiner were billeted in a home in the small village of Godo. In the family were a six- or seven-year-old girl named Rina and an older boy named Rino, and since Gardiner could speak some Italian, he and Ken became exotic *Canadesi* uncles and began to entertain them. With the help of an old dictionary they played word games, thus giving the children a bit of an education denied them by the wartime turmoil and the men a chance to improve their fluency in Italian. Before long, Ken and Gardiner were teaching the young pair the basics of arithmetic.

There were thousands of such children who were temporarily adopted by the troops, and even today you can find Italian men and women in their late sixties who speak with tears in their eyes of the Canadian soldiers who befriended them during the war. At the time, however, the army discouraged such close association with the children because Fascists still loyal to the Germans would often pump the youngsters for information about the Allied units. Moreover, when the troops were ordered to move to a new location—even to the front— the children would want to go with them. In this they were often encouraged by their parents, who saw it as one way to ensure that the children would be fed. Thus, when the Second LAA was sent back south to a camp near Ancona in early February, Rino desperately wanted to go along as kitchen help, and Ken and Gardner had difficulty explaining that this was impossible. The two men themselves had a melancholic time saying goodbye to the children.

Even as Ken and Gardiner were leaving Godo, plans were being made to send them very much farther away than Ancona. Senior Canadian Army officers had long disliked the First Canadian Army being split between Italy and northern Europe, and in late January 1945 the Allied command agreed to Operation Goldflake, the transfer of the troops in Italy to Belgium and Holland. In preparation for this move Ken's battery was sent farther south to Montefiore on February 21, where it rested and did maintenance work on its guns and vehicles. On March 6, with all divisional patches, regimental titles, campaign ribbons, service chevrons and badges removed from their uniforms, and all signs of their Canadian identity blacked out on their vehicles, they left the Adriatic coast for the last time. Working their way through the Apennines once more, the convoy made its way to Foligno, then Pontessieve and finally to Livorno (Leghorn) on the west coast of Italy.

On March 13, the Second LAA Battery sailed from Livorno in a brigade convoy, and forty-eight hours later it docked at Marseilles. The next morning it began a six-day trip up the Rhone Valley in France, stopping nightly at staging areas in St-Rambert, Mâcon, Les Laumes, Sens and Cambrai, and finally arriving at a concentration area in Rumst, a Belgian town between Brussels and Antwerp, on March 21. As they travelled, the soldiers were forbidden to speak to civilians and to discuss—even with other military personnel—the identity of the units or their destination. As a result, on the day the First Canadian Corps began arriving in Belgium, the German high command was convinced it was still in reserve around Ancona.

The secrecy surrounding Operation Goldflake meant, of course, that from mid-February until April 23, when the move was officially confirmed, there was nothing in Canadian newspapers or on radio about the location or operations of the First Canadian Corps. None of the outgoing mail from Italy was delivered for two months, and in the vacuum created by the lack of news, rumours spread in Canada that the Corps had been sent to the Far East. It was, recalls Farley Mowat, a difficult and apprehensive time for the families back home.

This interruption in the flow of Ken's letters to Fargo has left us without any record of his thoughts about leaving Italy after fourteen months of battle, but he likely shared the eagerness of most of the

Canadian soldiers to join the rest of the Canadian Army in the decisive battles in northwestern Europe that were bringing the war to an
end. Certainly his first letter from Holland, written on April 25, is
charged with an energy and optimism that had been missing in his
correspondence of the previous eight months:

> *Well, folks, you probably have heard ere this that we have changed
> our location somewhat and are now looking at windmills instead
> of jackasses! Here we are in Holland and extremely busy. Saw a
> bit of Germany recently and it was as it should be—hammered
> flat! The people of Holland have given us a royal welcome and
> we in turn have given the Wehrmacht a first-class going over.*

The Second LAA Battery had indeed been busy, though its first
two weeks in northwestern Europe, around Rumst, was a pleasant
interlude of rest and reorganization after the long trip from Italy. For
the first time since they had left the Adriatic, the troops were billeted
in public buildings and private homes, where they were welcomed as
liberators. As well, the men began to be given nine-day leaves to the
United Kingdom, which most of them had not seen since they sailed
for Sicily nearly two years earlier. Ken, however, preferred to stay with
his unit and get the job done.

Ken saw his "bit of Germany" on April 3, when the First Division
moved to a concentration area near Kleve, in the Reichswald Forest,
which Canadian and British forces had taken in the middle of
February. Here the vehicles were fine-tuned and calibrated, and,
finally, the men were ordered to sew back on their badges, ribbons,
chevrons and especially the division's famous red patch. Since the
Germans had not pulled their 120,000 troops out of western Holland,
the Canadians were ordered to move north into the Netherlands to
trap them there.

On April 7, the First Division moved across the Rhine to take up
gun positions at Emmerich, and on the eleventh it went into action,

crossing the Ijssel River and attacking westwards toward Apeldoorn, which fell a week later. The Second LAA Battery's assignment was to provide cover from air attack, but it was also issued Bren guns and PIATs (hand-held anti-tank weapons) with which to fight German land forces. These soldiers, Ken told his relatives, "don't measure up to the standard of the German Army in Italy though they do everything they can think of in the way of devilishness."

The teenaged boys and old men thrown into the final months of battle by a desperate German army could never have fought with the skill and tenacity of Kesselring's crack Tenth Army veterans, but among the German soldiers still in western Holland were many SS troops and Dutch SS men for whom surrender meant humiliation and likely vicious reprisal from Dutch partisans. And so they fought, said Farley Mowat, "with the particular savagery that only civilized men who have abandoned civilization can achieve."

If the SS troops had abandoned civilization, months of brutal fighting had worn some of the civilized veneer away from all of the soldiers, German or Allied. The jocular remarks about beating the German army in Ken's early correspondence had, with each battle in Italy, been replaced by an increasingly absolute and unforgiving hostility toward the enemy. Thus, if the towns in the Reichswald area were "hammered flat," it "was as it should be" (the identical phrase Farley Mowat used to convey the same sentiment in a letter written five days before Ken's—though Mowat had added, "I only hope we don't go soft on the job"). And when the Dutch underground tipped the Canadians off about pockets of German resistance, Ken took pleasure in directing his troop's Bofors guns in ground shoots. "Had the time of my life one day recently," he wrote to his cousin, "when I cleaned out a railway station. In the past I had a hobby that came in especially useful on that day."

Though Ken does not describe the "hobby" that he employed, it must refer to a sport he shared with Earle to keep their shooting eyes sharp. On bright moonlit nights back in Saskatchewan, the two young

men would take their .22-calibre rifles to the garbage dump outside
Moose Jaw and wait patiently. Before long they would spot the dark
forms of rats foraging through the rubbish, and if their reflexes were
quick and their hands steady, they would rid the dump of some of its
vermin. Now, less than ten years later, the man who had shot nothing
larger than a goose in his life was relishing cleaning human "rats" out
of railway stations.

If Ken's attitude seems harsh, it is nonetheless understandable.
Like all the Allied troops, he had been shocked by the destruction in
Holland and by the severe starvation he saw everywhere. Moreover, on
April 13 the concentration camps at Belsen and Buchenwald had been
opened up and the world began to learn of the depths to which
humanity could sink. On April 23, two days before he wrote his letter
to Fargo, Ken read of these horrors in an article in the *Maple Leaf,* so
it is not surprising that his description of cleaning out the railway
station is prefaced by a statement about the immense suffering
imposed by the Nazis:

> *The people here are actually starving and I see kids with rickets*
> *everywhere. On top of that the Hun is flooding the country by*
> *blowing the dykes, and the people tell me that it will take at*
> *least 15 years before the land will be productive again. We also*
> *know all about what has been found in the concentration camps*
> *in Germany, so all these things are not going unnoticed by us.*

With Apeldoorn taken, the Second LAA Battery took up a position to cover a stretch of the road from Apeldoorn to Amersfoort to
the west, but it also took on infantry assignments. Working with a
company of the Dutch National Battalion, composed largely of resistance fighters now equipped by the Allies, the battery made sorties
north to the coast of the Zuider Zee, flushing out pockets of German
diehards. Unlike their counterparts in Italy, however, many Germans
knew that the war was lost and were prepared unhappily to surrender,

and the patrols brought back a large number of prisoners. One sweep up the coast to Elburg on April 2 netted eighty-seven prisoners of war.

Henk Hulshof, a platoon commander in the DNB and interpreter for the Second LAA, remembers accompanying Ken and his driver, Harold Shore, as they went on patrols through the Veluwe, the wooded area of central Holland. After the months of being under-equipped and undermanned in Italy, Ken was surprised by the new equipment, new vehicles and large stores of ammunition supplied to the troops in northern Europe. He was, in Hulshof's word, "enraptured" when his battery was given a set of new Swiss-made, four-barrel Oerlikon anti-aircraft guns. The Dutch commander's most vivid recollection was an occasion when he and Ken had to deal with a large mine depot near Apeldoorn that the Germans had wired to explode. A delicate task at any time, they had to take great care to cut the connecting wires without triggering the explosives.

The war was winding down, however, and by the time Ken wrote his letter to Fargo the Canadian Army had ceased most of its operations in western Holland. The Dutch were starving to death—the daily food ration had fallen to 250 calories, a tenth of an average man's requirements—and it was more important to get food to them than to round up more Germans and Dutch SS. By April 29, the Germans and their puppet Dutch government had agreed to a truce, and supply planes and convoys began to move into the area. For the Second LAA Battery and for Ken, the fighting was essentially over.

From the time of their arrival in Belgium, the civilians had treated the men of the First Canadian Corps with a warmth beyond anything they had experienced in Italy. Beer flowed more freely, and there were parties and dances in Rumst, Apeldoorn and other towns. Seen as heroic liberators, and tanned and fit in contrast to the starving Dutch men, they were attractive to young women too long deprived of romance; and so, according to one Dutch journalist, the Dutch men who had been beaten on the battlefield in 1940 were beaten in bed in 1945. Several thousands of these women became Canadian war brides.

From all accounts Ken was driven by one idea throughout that liberating spring: to get back to Margaret. Hulshof recalls that "he never went to dancing parties in Apeldoorn or other towns. He said: 'My wife is knitting balaclavas for the Canadian Army overseas; she is doing her share of winning the war.'" There is undoubtedly a large element of irony in this comment, since Ken knew that Margaret had never knitted balaclavas or socks for the servicemen, but he did believe that she shared his commitment to the war effort.

After five and a half years of separation from his wife, it would not have been surprising—nor unusual in a Canadian soldier overseas—for Ken to have had some sort of fling, but there has only ever been one suggestion that he was unfaithful to Margaret during the war. Her family are convinced that he developed some sort of liaison with a woman while he was stationed in the United Kingdom, and my mother herself once said that she had heard he had formed some kind of relationship over there. If he did in fact have an affair, it did not last, and according to John Gardiner and other officers who knew him well, he was never involved with any women in Italy or Holland. "We were a bunch of renegades," says Harold Shore. "No two ways about it. But not Ken."

Ken simply wanted to get back to Margaret, and with the war clearly winding down, this was now more than just a dream. And so, shortly after the First Canadian Corps had arrived in Belgium, he put in a request for home leave. A man no longer needed to be wounded three times to get back to Canada, and, being married with five and a half years of continuous service, he stood an excellent chance. Even so, he dared not count on it. "I have nothing to report so far on my proposed home leave," he wrote on April 25. "I'm not counting on anything, being wise in the ways of the Army. I'll believe it only when I'm coming *down* the gangplank in Canada."

CHAPTER TWELVE

At a quarter to ten on the evening of Friday, May 4, 1945, the Second LAA Battery, then encamped at the regimental concentration area near Kootwijk, in the central Netherlands, received an order from divisional artillery headquarters: "Cease fire w[ith] e[ffect] f[rom]. 0800 hrs. 5 May, 1945." Two days earlier the German forces in Italy had surrendered, and now for the Canadian soldiers in northwestern Europe, and for Ken Calder, the war was over.

Hostilities did not officially cease until Colonel-General Alfred Jodl signed the surrender papers at General Eisenhower's headquarters in Rheims in the early hours of May 7. When this news was flashed to Canada, it triggered jubilant headlines and wild celebrations from Halifax to Victoria. In Moose Jaw the front page of the *Times-Herald* proclaimed: "ALLIED VICTORY IN EUROPE." On Alder Avenue my grandparents, for the first time in five and a half years, did not have to live with the fear that this might be the day their son lost his life to a German bomb or bullet. The next morning they expressed their gratitude at a national thanksgiving service at St. Andrew's Church.

In Vancouver on May 7, Margaret would have been awakened by three blasts of the city's air-raid sirens at 7:04 a.m. As the day wore on, she would have seen the crowds spilling onto Granville Street as they sang, danced, drank and hugged their way through a day of celebration. Her own mood must have been much different. The German surrender meant that Ken would be coming home soon, and her long-postponed crisis, the one she had hoped not to have to face, would have to be confronted.

The revelry of May 7—and that of the next day's official VE day celebrations—was a luxury to be enjoyed by civilians far from the battlefields. For the soldiers who had experienced the horrors of the fighting, there was only a feeling of relief and exhaustion. At General Eisenhower's headquarters, said his companion Kay Summersby, "no one laughed. No one smiled. It was all over. We had won, but victory was not anything like what I had thought it would be. There was a dull bitterness about it. So many deaths. So much destruction. And everybody was very, very tired." American infantryman Paul Fussell, recovering from a shrapnel wound in a military hospital in Épinal, observed the day by drinking a can of beer he had been saving, but, he said, "there was no pleasure in it." For the soldier in the field, artillery officer George Blackburn later wrote, there was no celebrating even on hearing the King's VE day radio broadcast: "Everyone is tired, emotionally drained, and with unlimited opportunity for sleep many find it difficult to drop off in the disconcerting stillness. While others, who haven't been conscious of having dreamt in months, start having dreams and nightmares."

One of the waking dreams of many men was, of course, of being reunited with their wives or lovers, and so, said Blackburn, "every time you get a chance to be alone, you study snapshots and try in vain to recall the sound of her voice." Ken had not heard Margaret's voice for five and a half years.

For Farley Mowat, soldiers about to be repatriated and reunited with loved ones faced "a chill wind." Writing to his parents from Amsterdam, he described the overriding emotion of VE day as befuddlement, confusion about what would happen now that the long-cherished dreams of the future were about to become the present:

The only home we've known these years past has been that amorphous entity we call "the unit." Herein lay our trust when we learned to distrust that other home across the western ocean. I don't know who I'm the most sorry for—the fellows who will go rushing back to smash their own patiently nurtured dreams, or Canada, which will have to receive them and ingest them. Someone is due for the hell of a big bellyache.

Ken had—not always patiently—nurtured his dream of returning to Margaret and the marriage begun only a week before he had departed for Europe. So, even as the ceasefire was silencing the guns on May 5, he left Kootwyk for a repatriation depot in Britain. As one of the '39ers, a married man with sixty-five months of overseas service, he qualified to be among the first officers to be repatriated.

Ken took his leave of his men in the battery and said goodbye to John Gardiner, promising him that he would let him know "how things were" back home. They would, they vowed, have a beer or two together back on Civvy Street in Canada. He invited Henk Hulshof to visit him in Saskatchewan, and, having bought a new trench coat for the journey home, Ken gave him his old one, frayed and mud-stained from the Italian campaign. Shortened by Hulshof's wife, it was proudly worn by their eldest son for years after.

Ken made his way to the coast and several days later was in the Second Canadian Repatriation Depot, near Aldershot. As he made his way through that army town, then vivid with Union Jacks and flags of the Allies, colourful bunting and victory slogans, he must have thought of his arrival there in that cold and gloomy winter of 1939–40. A sixth of his life had passed since that first British Christmas. Did he realize, I wonder, how much the years between had transformed the young lieutenant who had come so earnestly to fight the war? Did he, like so many thousands of servicemen, now feel like an old man?

On the eighth of June, Ken left the British Isles aboard the *Samaria*, a 30,000-ton troopship used earlier to transport German prisoners of war to Canada. It was a far cry from the luxurious *Duchess of Bedford*, but the soldiers had been told that, if they wanted to get home quickly, they would have to take what they could get. More than two thousand eager servicemen opted for the *Samaria,* among whom were twelve veterans of the disastrous Dieppe raid. On board too were 576 excited and apprehensive British war brides and their children.

On the morning of June 12, with the *Samaria* almost halfway across the Atlantic, its passengers awakened to the news that the Canadian public had re-elected Mackenzie King and his Liberal government to a comfortable majority the night before. Eight days later, when the military vote was counted, the servicemen of Canada would take away King's Prince Albert seat; as a local sign proclaimed, "This town liberated by the Canadian Army." Apparently forgetting that he had been publicly jeered by Canadian troops in Britain in the summer of 1941, the old politician whined: "Cruel it should be my fate, at the end of the war, in which I have never failed the men overseas once, that I should be beaten by their vote." Ken was not one of the soldiers who pretended to be from Prince Albert so he could vote against King, but as a man who had not been given home leave in five and a half years of overseas service, he had as good a reason as any of them to believe that his prime minister had failed him.

At 5 a.m. on June 15, as the sun was rising over maritime Canada, the *Samaria,* together with her sister ship the *Scythia,* entered the harbour at Halifax. Within five hours their passengers were transferred to eight troop trains of fifteen cars each, and at the rate of two an hour the trains left for Montreal, Toronto and western Canada. The crush of returning servicemen had caused the railways to cancel all sleeping-car accommodation for civilians and to curtail dining-car service for them. Travel priority was given first to the wounded and then to military personnel returning from overseas to a posting within Canada. At many stops women's auxiliary groups gave the troops cigarettes, chocolate and soft drinks. For men so long accustomed to field rations or the dehydrated food of a beleaguered Britain, the real butter and milk of the dining cars seemed luxurious.

When Ken's train reached Montreal, it had to stop for an hour at the Pointe St-Charles railway service yards to take on fuel and ice for its cooling systems. Gardiner had alerted his father that Ken would be passing through, and as the chief officer of CNR passenger service in Montreal, Albert Gardiner had lists of all servicemen travelling by rail. Spotting Ken's name one day, he picked up John's fiancée, Juliette, and together they went down to the yards and began looking for his car. Aboard the train were nearly nine hundred virile, battle-weary but supercharged young men crowded at the windows and doors, and the sight of the slim, dark, attractive woman strolling down the platform was as electrifying as if Betty Grable had suddenly materialized before them. At Juliette's funeral in 1991, Gardiner reminded her family and friends how for years after she would get an amused sparkle in her eye when she recalled the shouts and whistles of admiration which greeted her that day.

Gardiner also told the mourners of Ken's own captivation by her, as if the words of praise of a friend dead for forty-six years somehow authenticated his own love. A week after leaving Montreal, Ken wrote to him of their meeting and said that

> *one look at her and I know right away why you spend so much time not helling around with other dames. Boy, is that little girl ever in love with you. After recalling your homely mug I can only come to the conclusion that you must have used drugs! Certainly a fine little girl, John, and if I ever hear of you not treating her right I'll personally come down there, tear your arm off and beat your brains out with it!*

Ken's train had a one-hour stopover before continuing its westward journey, and, reported Juliette, he was thrilled that she and John's father had come to meet him. For his part, Albert Gardiner was so taken by Ken that he did everything he could to persuade him to spend a few days at their home in St-Lambert. John had often written of his good friend from the Prairies, and it had not been so long before that Ken had said goodbye to him in Holland. Letters might be informative and intimate, but a serviceman did not always tell his family about his true condition or state of mind, and talking to a man who had so recently seen him was reassuring to his father and his fiancée.

Since he had been designated the officer commanding the train and was also anxious to get home, Ken turned down Mr. Gardiner's offer. He had wired Margaret from Halifax to ask her to meet him in Moose Jaw, and the prospect of being with her once again made the rest of his journey seem interminable. In Winnipeg he watched the joyous bedlam as hundreds of Manitoba veterans sought out their loved ones in the packed railway terminal. In Regina the next day, Union Station was similarly jammed to overflowing, so that the military police had difficulty in clearing a path through the crowd. As the men made their way into the station rotunda, the building was rocked with cheers.

Ken looked for Margaret's face in the crowd of wives, lovers, friends and relatives, but he was bitterly disappointed. Awaiting him in Moose Jaw was a letter from her telling him that she would not be meeting him there. If he wanted to see her, he would have to go to Vancouver. Judging by her letter, Ken wrote to Gardiner, "Margaret is all of a dither. Wish I was out there."

For his parents, of course, it was a time of relief and joy. To Ken's eyes they had aged considerably, but they were rejuvenated by his presence. "We are living," his father wrote to a sister, "in a state of much rejoicing this week. Kenneth's safe arrival home has renewed our youth to a very, very great extent." Even their aged Boston terrier, Mickey, he said, remembered Ken and made a big fuss over him.

Ken's family had him with them for a week before he left for Vancouver, but, to his mother's lasting regret, they had to share those few days with so many others. Though he had been granted a one-month disembarkation leave, he had to report almost immediately to the army depot in Regina to discuss his future. He was offered the chance to join the war in the Pacific or to serve in the army of occupation in Europe, but he declined both invitations. Among the officers returning from overseas duty he was identified as one who had been an instructor and "had considerable administrative ability," so it was agreed he would be employed in an administrative capacity somewhere in Canada.

While he was in Regina, Ken also dropped into the head office of the Co-operative Creamery, where he was warmly greeted. Whenever he wanted his old job, said the general manager, it was there for him. As well, there was his dream of owning his own sporting goods and hardware store in Moose Jaw, which was now possible. But Margaret might want to remain in Vancouver, and an army posting there would mean that he could join her. He decided, therefore, to report to the military authorities at Pacific Command at the end of his Vancouver trip to see what might be available.

Ken's week was also taken up by what he found to be a surprising number of social events. He still had a number of pals in Moose Jaw—though, sadly, his closest friend Fred Cooper was not there to greet him—and they were eager to see him. Two days after his return he joined a number of other recently returned soldiers as guests of honour at a special meeting of the Canadian Legion. Several days later he spoke to the local Lions Club about his experiences in Italy and Holland. Then, too, he noted in his letter to Gardiner, the "uncle business" was "pretty much a full-time job." There were his two nephews, Earle's sons, and two nieces, daughters of Margaret's sister, Lillian. Just as one of his nephews had been named after him, one of the little girls, Peggy, had been named after Margaret.

Recounting his week of wining and dining to Gardiner, Ken remarked that there was "lots of good food in this burg," but this jocular remark is deceptive. Three days after his son's return, his father wrote to a sister that "we can see that the experiences of the past 5 1/2 years have aged him some and his face looks thin. He has a very small appetite, having been on light rations, and he does not eat much at a time. Food seems to fill him up quickly, but in time he will get over this. It's so wonderful to see him home without injury."

In June 1945, my grandfather could be forgiven for assuming that his son had come home "without injury." So too could the millions of other Canadian parents, wives, brothers and sisters who looked at their returning men and women, saw that they possessed four limbs in working order, had their eyesight and were not disfigured by burns or scars, and concluded that they were sound and whole—and ready to slip back into their pre-war jobs, their families, their marriages and their communities as if they had never been away.

Nearly six decades later we know differently; we recognize that soldiers returning from the battlefield have to be treated differently. In July 2002, eight hundred men of the Princess Patricia's Canadian Light Infantry and the Lord Strathcona's Horse were scheduled to return to Canada after a six-month tour of duty in Afghanistan as part of the coalition forces fighting to oust the Taliban and destroy the Al Qaeda terrorist network. Though they were subject to some rocket attacks and conducted three extended missions in search of terrorists, these soldiers were not engaged in any major battles, and except for those men mistakenly killed and wounded by American bomber pilots, they suffered no casualties. Though they endured cold winter weather and desert heat and dust, together with the dangers of poisonous snakes, spiders and scorpions, they had amenities that would have been the envy of the Second World War serviceman. They had the opportunity to telephone home, mail was carried regularly and quickly to and from Canada, and before too many weeks had passed, gym equipment was flown over to relieve the boredom.

Even before the end of this operation, however, the battalion's senior officers discerned unmistakable signs of stress in the troops. This came, they determined, from such unfamiliar practices as carrying their personal weapons everywhere they went and having always to be prepared to kill if necessary. There was, moreover, the claustrophobia of living in a constricted area for months on end. As a result, said the chaplain, "our coping mechanisms to deal with little things are kind of stretched right to the limit . . . We're tired living in this climate and living under the cumulative stress that's here." Even the positive experience of forming close bonds with fellow soldiers, she added, would make re-entry into Canadian life difficult: "This has become normal. We're going back to a world that's going to look abnormal to us."

To help the soldiers deal with their stress and bridge the two worlds, the Department of National Defence put together a $2-million reintegration program. The men were briefed at their base in Kandahar and then flown for a week of rest and relaxation at resort hotels on the island of Guam, in the western Pacific. There, psychologists, psychiatrists and combat stress specialists flown in from Canada counselled them on such topics as family reintegration, work reintegration, the home front and suicide prevention. In addition, hiking and sightseeing tours were arranged, and time was allotted for relaxing on the tropical beaches in the thirty-degree temperatures. Since Guam is heavily Americanized, with Hard Rock Cafés and Kmarts, each soldier was given a per diem of $95 to enable him to readjust to North American consumer society. This time on Guam, said the chaplain, was "giving us all some corporate time to do the closure, and some personal time to rest and reflect and start to put this six months of living into perspective—because we're going back changed people."

For their families, the possibility of being reunited with husbands, fathers, sons and brothers who were not the men they had known six months earlier was unnerving. When one woman's husband telephoned to say that "I'm going to be different when I get back," she was frightened. "You've known him for thirteen years," she said, "and then, all of a sudden, he's going to be different. It's scary. There's no other word to describe it."

To deal with this fear, wives and families went to a Military Resource Centre for counselling sessions designed to familiarize them with the problems the soldiers might face as they again became peacetime husbands, fathers and sons. The men would be given fifty-five-day leaves on their return, and counsellors would check with them periodically to see how they were adjusting.

The wisdom of this enlightened and sensitive reintegration program seems borne out by the rash of murder-suicides that broke out among returned American veterans of the Afghanistan campaign. And if a soldier at the end of a six-month tour of duty providing security for a military base requires such assistance and understanding to fit back into civilian life, what of the Second World War veterans who had been away from home for more than five years? Who had fought their way into Ortona, through the Liri Valley, and up the sodden and muddy Adriatic coast of Italy? Who had struggled through the machine-gun and mortar fire on the beaches of Normandy, overcome desperate, determined and battle-hardened German troops, and witnessed the starvation and suffering of the Low Countries? Men who had not heard the voices or seen the faces of their wives and families for nearly six years, many of whose parents, grandparents and siblings had died in that time and could be mourned only in some slit trench or barracks thousands of miles away? These men stepped off the troop trains, were taken home and were assumed to be unscathed by their experiences.

To Ken's childhood friend Lena Vail, back living at the family home two doors away while her husband was overseas, he seemed different, distant and preoccupied. Standing in her front yard one morning, she noticed him come out of his parents' house and head up the street to the Armoury. In what now seemed another world, she used to watch a boy stride purposefully up the hill in his militia uniform; now a battle-weary man with who knew what intent made his way past her front door. Eager to talk to him for the first time in nearly six years, she shouted a greeting, but to her disappointment he gave only a brief reply and a little wave of the hand, and continued on his way. She never saw him again.

It is not surprising that Ken might prefer the atmosphere of the Armoury to a conversation with a neighbourhood friend. The military world he had inhabited so fully for the past five years was not one that could be left easily, even for the familiar and comfortable world of home. Ronald MacFarlane recalls that, for months after he returned from Europe that same summer, he spent much of his time drinking with other veterans. They were the only people whom he could really talk to, who really understood what he was talking about. For him and for Ken a gulf of vastly different experiences lay between them and the people of home, and this could be bridged only slowly and in small steps. As the British soldier-poet Siegfried Sassoon observed of returning Great War veterans, "the man who really endured the war at its worst was everlastingly differentiated from everyone but his fellow soldiers."

Describing the disorientation of the soldier returning to his home, the English writer H.M. Tomlinson wrote: "You really have come back from another world; and you have the curious idea that you may be invisible in this old one. In a sense you are unseen. These people will never know what you know . . . They will never understand. What is the use of standing in veritable daylight, and telling the living, who have never been dead, of the other place."

The returning veteran, said Tomlinson, is like Rip Van Winkle awakening from his sleep, except that Rip had lost only some years of his life; save for the length of his beard, he had not changed. "But the man who comes back from the line," Tomlinson claimed, "has lost more than years. He has lost his original self." And how can a profoundly changed man slip easily and comfortably back into the old world? "It is curious to feel that you are really there, delighting in the vividness of this recollection of the past, yet balked by the knowledge that you are, nevertheless, outside this world of home, though it looks and smells so close; and that you may never enter it again."

Looking back fifty-eight years later, I think it very likely that Ken, so long away from home, shared Tomlinson's sense of alienation. Of his expectations of what awaited him with Margaret in Vancouver, I am much less certain. Here the evidence is conflicting, suggesting a deeply troubled man who fought, in the face of distressing evidence, to resist accepting a conclusion he found unbearable.

At the very least Ken must have known that it would be very difficult to re-establish a relationship interrupted by a five-and-a-half-year
separation. He could hardly ignore Margaret's reluctance to write him,
and the lack of intimacy and warmth in the few letters she did pen.
Moreover, her move to Vancouver, away from their hometown, from
their families and friends, and from their plans for the future, was the
action of someone wanting to distance herself from her past—and,
more importantly, the past that linked her to him. According to
Garnet Matchett, a fellow officer in the Second Light Anti-Aircraft,
Ken had told him of this growing estrangement in Italy, and Matchett
had advised him to cut his losses and forget her.

And then there is the question of how much, if anything, Ken
learned of Margaret's affair with Dr. Boyd Story during his week in
Moose Jaw. Several days before he left for Vancouver, he dined with
her parents and pronounced Mrs. Bruce's cooking as good as ever.
Nothing in their conversation or manner suggested that he was
heading to a crisis with their daughter. Several people have told me,
however, that Margaret's affairs—particularly the one in Moose Jaw
cited in Ken's last letter to Gardiner—were known to a number of
people. One of those may have been my father, if an anguished letter
he wrote to John Gardiner three months after Ken's death can be
believed. He had been aware of Margaret's behaviour for two years, he
said, and castigated himself for not warning his brother about it: "I
had mentioned to Mother that trouble was brewing, but she exacted
my solemn promise not to speak to Ken about it and I was therefore
restrained from doing so."

If Earle did not talk to Ken about Margaret's infidelity, someone
seems to have forewarned him. Dining with his boyhood friend Henry
Evans and his wife, Hilda, on the evening before his departure, he told
them: "I'm going out to the coast, and they tell me I'm not going to
like what I find out there."

With this evidence of Margaret's growing estrangement from him,
how could Ken have eagerly left Holland at the first opportunity, have

written Gardiner from Moose Jaw that he wished he were with her already, and have left for Vancouver with an expectation that she would return with him? The answer, I suspect, is that he had kept a dream alive for five and a half years, a dream that had become increasingly idealized the longer he was away from the reality, and he was unable to let the dream die. He may, moreover, as people so frequently do when confronted by a lover's rejection, have successfully blocked out what he did not want to accept. Or he may have believed that, whatever distance had developed between Margaret and him over the years, he would be able to overcome it when he was again alone with her. After all, when they were last together, it had been in the glow and passion of their brief honeymoon, and could that passion not be rekindled?

And so, I think, Ken boarded the train to Vancouver knowing that it would not be easy to win Margaret back but that he could do it. For five and a half years he had been an officer—a good one, too—solving problems and commanding men. This was just another problem to be solved, a conflict to be resolved, a battle to be won. The terrain—the human heart and its vagaries—was different from the battlefields he had known, but a man with a strategy would win.

But what if he couldn't win? As he packed his good clothes, his still unfamiliar civilian dress, he carefully wrapped and placed among his shirts his army-issue automatic pistol.

CHAPTER THIRTEEN

On the evening of July 6, eleven days after Ken had left for Vancouver, the Calders were finishing supper at 923 Alder Avenue. It was Friday, so my grandfather was back home from his road trip through southern Saskatchewan. He had been delayed by having to repair a cooler for the owner of the Owl Café in Ponteix, but it had been a good week. The July heat had hit the Prairies and the Creamery would be pleased with the sheaf of ice cream orders he had brought back with him. The next day, as he had done each Saturday morning for a decade, he would file the orders in the Creamery office on Caribou Street. His Dodge sedan—blue like every car he ever owned—had taken a beating on the dusty gravel roads, but a washing and simonizing on Sunday would have it looking like new.

My grandmother too was feeling pleased. On the previous day she had again won first prize for her much-acclaimed angel food cake at the Moose Jaw Exhibition, and her oatmeal cookies had taken second place. On Saturday my grandfather would take her up the hill to the Exhibition Grounds to collect her ribbons, they would look at the displays and the young people on the daring new rides, and have tea and a piece of pie at the church booth. In a few weeks she would bake another cake and they would take it to the much bigger Regina Exhibition.

My grandmother had just finished clearing up the supper dishes when the telephone rang in the front hall. It was a long-distance call from Vancouver. They had heard nothing from Ken since he had left for the coast, but the voice at the other end of the line was not his. It was Margaret's, which surprised my grandfather because she had rarely called them since she moved to Vancouver. Now her voice was hardly recognizable. She was in some distress, and struggled to get her words out. "I . . . I hardly know . . . how to tell you this," she began. There had been a terrible accident, she stammered. The gas in the kitchen stove had been left on and Ken had been asphyxiated. He was dead.

⁓

Ken's body was brought back to Moose Jaw by a captain of the Pacific Command of the Canadian Army, and on July 14 a military funeral was held in St. Andrew's Church. Thirty-three years earlier his parents had watched him being christened at its font; now they sat devastated before the flag-draped casket on which lay his officer's cap and his Sam Browne belt. As the procession left the church on its slow journey to the cemetery, with muffled drums and the Regina Military Band playing the dead march from Handel's *Saul,* they could look out the car window and see the house to which they had brought Ken as a baby. When the pallbearers—members of the Seventy-seventh Battery recently returned from Europe—lowered the coffin, soldiers of the District No. 12 Depot of Regina fired a final salute into the afternoon sky and the bugler's mournful sounding of the last post drifted across the prairie air.

Two days after the funeral, a Court of Inquiry was convened in Regina to determine the cause of Ken's death. Margaret, who told the court she was then staying with the Calders at 923 Alder Avenue, recounted the event:

On Friday, July 6th, 1945, at approximately 3.45 hrs in the afternoon, I returned from a shopping trip to the apartment which my husband, Capt. Kenneth Calder and I occupied. Before I got to the door, I could smell gas. I unlocked the door and went in. The kitchenette door was closed, I opened it and saw my husband sitting in a chair. The three gas jets in the gas stove were open, I closed them and dragged my husband into the living room and opened the windows. I also opened the bathroom door because there is a ventilator in the room. As far as I can remember, I tried artificial respiration for a couple of minutes and then phoned a doctor. I was unable to reach one, then tried artificial respiration for a few minutes more, then phoned for an ambulance. I phoned the doctor again unsuccessfully, but left a message, then carried out artificial respiration until the ambulance arrived. When it arrived the crew were going to take Capt. Calder to Shaughnessy Hospital, but I suggested that they continue artificial respiration. They did so and phoned for the inhalator squad. The inhalator squad arrived and applied a Pulmonator for approximately 45 min. Then two members of the Police Department came in, at this time I became ill from the gas fumes in the suite and possibly from shock and I asked permission to leave the apartment. This was granted by a member of the Police Department and I left the building escorted by Dr. Boyd Story, who had by this time arrived. Some time later, I went back to the apartment and the sum of $ [here the transcript is unclear] was turned over to me, and I signed a receipt for the same and gave the receipt to a member of the Police Department. Capt. Calder's body was then placed in the ambulance and then taken to the City Morgue.

What Margaret did not tell the Court of Inquiry was that the doctor whom she called when she discovered Ken unconscious in the kitchenette, Boyd Story, was her lover. Nor did she tell the court that, far from going shopping that afternoon, she and Story had been consulting a lawyer to see if there was some way for her to secure a divorce. Given the strict divorce laws of the time, she was almost certainly returning to the apartment after being told the dismaying news that it would be very difficult, if not impossible, to get a divorce if Ken was not willing. Her adultery provided grounds for him to divorce her, if he wished, but not for her to divorce him.

∽

For more than fifty years after Ken's death, the Calders knew "Boyd Story" only as a name woven into a family tragedy. In Vancouver in February 1997, the name began to take on a human shape for me when I met his sister, Evelyn Lett—then a hundred years old—and his older son, David. With their co-operation, and some digging into various archives, it began to be possible to envisage the man, the "other man" in Ken's and Margaret's marriage.

Fourteen years older than Margaret, Boyd Story was born in Wawanesa, Manitoba, in 1898. One of the founders of the town, Story's father owned a general store and was reeve of the municipality. He moved his family to Vancouver in 1910, drawn by the booming economy there, but returned himself to Wawanesa several years later to try to save the business, which was then failing in the hands of relatives. Boyd remained with his mother and the other children in Vancouver, where he went to school and then spent a year at the local branch of McGill University (which would eventually become the University of British Columbia). During the First World War, he attempted to join the air corps but was disqualified by a heart murmur resulting from diphtheria suffered in his childhood. Since his father needed him in the store at Wawanesa, he returned to Manitoba. He entered the University of Manitoba Medical School in 1919 and graduated with honours in 1924.

Boyd Story opened his first practice in Admiral, Saskatchewan, and later went into partnership with another physician in Shaunavon. Western Canada was then gripped by the Depression, however, and like other doctors he soon found he had few patients who could afford to pay their bills. In 1937, supported financially by his brother, Roland, and his sister Evelyn's husband, Story moved back to British

Columbia and interned at the Vancouver General Hospital. Six months later he resigned from the College of Physicians and Surgeons of Saskatchewan, explaining that, with a mother, a brother and two sisters living there, Vancouver felt like home.

Story opened a general practice in an office on Alma Street, and with his wife, Marian, and two sons, David and Robert, moved into a spacious house on a corner lot in the fashionable Point Grey area near the University of British Columbia. All was not well, however. He had already begun to drink heavily, and by 1943 he had become a severe alcoholic—so severe that he was being treated with electroshock therapy. The nurse brought in to see him through these difficult treatments was Margaret Calder, recently arrived in Vancouver, and Evelyn Lett and David Story both maintained that she very likely saved his life. Before long, Margaret was working as Story's office nurse and became his lover.

By all accounts Boyd Story was a handsome and congenial man. Though only five foot six, he was always very athletic. As a young man in Wawanesa, he was such a good baseball player that businessmen always found a job for him so that they could be sure of having him on the local team. At university he was a skilled tennis and basketball player. A man with a good sense of humour, he was known to joke with his patients as they went into the operating room.

Even with his alcoholism, Story was a catch, and according to David, Margaret set her sights on him; she "wanted my dad." Before long it became obvious to his family that his marriage was in trouble, and Evelyn and his other siblings assumed he was planning to marry the nurse from Saskatchewan. To Evelyn, Margaret was always known as Bruce, and everybody but Boyd was led to believe that she was merely engaged to an artillery officer serving in Europe. Even as late as 1997, Mrs. Lett needed to be convinced that Ken had been more than just Margaret's fiancé.

꩜

It is not surprising that Margaret, on finding Ken unconscious in the kitchenette, would first call Story to ask him what to do before phoning for an ambulance. If she did get through to him, however, he almost certainly told her that he could not possibly come to her aid. If he had treated Ken medically, and Ken died anyway, Story's being her lover—and thus someone who stood to benefit by Ken's death— would make his position untenable in the eyes of the Medical Association. It would even look very suspicious in the eyes of the law. She was on her own, Story would have told her, but he would come when he could.

In Margaret's testimony Boyd Story's name appears almost casually, and the Court of Inquiry did not ask her about him or their affair. Nor did it ask her whether this was the reason for Ken's suicide. In cross-examination she answered only factual questions about his military history, and then suggested that he had been physically and emotionally unbalanced. He had recently suffered two attacks of malaria, she said, and had been unwell for several days. To the question of whether he had been wounded or had suffered any shell shock, she replied no, "but at times his letters appeared queer." In the days leading up to his death he had "seemed restless and moody at times."

This Court of Inquiry was not a trial. Its purpose was to gather information, and the court had already been given a much more thorough picture of the circumstances leading up to Ken's suicide. On the day after his death, the Vancouver coroner, Dr. J.D. Whitbread, filed his report, stating that the doctor who went to the apartment and certified the death, E.A. Campbell, "knew the situation well." In other words, Story and his relationship with Margaret were familiar to the close-knit medical community of central Vancouver, and Campbell was likely an associate and friend of Story. Captain Calder, Campbell was thus able to say,

> found on his return back to Canada that his wife wished a divorce, stating that she didn't care for him any more, but that

she had been living with Dr. Boyd Story. Apparently Dr. Story had been ill and Mrs. Calder, who was a trained nurse, had nursed him—then had been Dr. Story's nurse at his office. She also had been doing special work at St. Paul's Hospital. Capt. Calder apparently was very upset over this condition and started to drink heavily for the past week. Calder had pleaded with his wife to return home but she would not do so.

Attached to the coroner's report were three notes in Ken's handwriting found in the apartment by the police at the time of his death. One was addressed to the Commissioner of Police, a military officer's orderly attempt to leave a clear and unambiguous record:

Sir:

Sorry to give your boys such a distasteful job but I cannot face life any longer and I'm taking the easy and sure way out. I intend to gas myself early this afternoon while my wife is out talking things over with her lawyer. I am Captain Kenneth Alexander Calder, late of the 2nd Cdn. Lt. A.A. Regt. I have recently returned from Holland after 67 months overseas to find my wife Margaret as cold as chilled steel. Finally she told me she has committed adultery with Dr. Boyd Story of 3897 W. 15th Ave., for about a year. She has also told me that she had an even longer affair with someone in Moose Jaw, our former home, but refuses to name this man. I spent 24 hours pleading with her to start over again or, in effect, give me another chance but she has refused. I don't want to stretch a rope for murder so I'm getting out the easy way because I prefer the coward's way out instead of a future existence with maggots in my brain. In spite of all she has done, I still love her and living without her is impossible.

Kenneth A. Calder Capt.
Royal Canadian Artillery.

A briefer but more impassioned note was addressed to Margaret and suggested that, in his pleas for her to return to him, Ken had threatened to take his own life:

Sorry I finally broke a promise to you but I'm too big a coward to do anything else. I still love and adore you in spite of everything that has happened. I'm remembering now the words of Canon Lee "Until death do us part." My love for you has lasted that long. I'm awfully tired now, can't fight any more.
Goodbye darling

One other terse note was found in the apartment, obviously something Ken had scribbled in his final hours. Written on a page of the *Reader's Digest*, in the margin of an article about the heroism and sacrifice of soldiers on the battlefield entitled "No Greater Love," were the lines: "These are the only people who count. The enemy has never hurt me but my own wife has killed me."

After hearing Margaret's testimony and the brief statement of the officer who escorted Ken's body to Moose Jaw, the Court of Inquiry concurred with the coroner's report: "The court finds that Cap. Kenneth Alexander Calder died from asphyxia and carbon monoxide poisoning due to artificial coal gas fumes, and that this was a suicide."

While the Vancouver City Police and the Department of National Defence were satisfied that they had determined the circumstances and cause of Ken's death, my grandparents knew almost nothing. As civilians, they were not permitted to attend the Court of Inquiry, and the court saw no reason to forward a report of its findings. Margaret returned from her court appearance in Regina, told them what she wished to of her testimony and left for Vancouver a few days later. They never saw her again.

It is hard to imagine the pain my grandparents must have endured in the weeks following Ken's death. There was, of course, the grief, the numbing sense of sudden loss, that engulfs anyone at the unexpected death of a loved one. For five and a half years they had worried about their son, and when, in the summer of 1943, photographs of dead or missing Saskatchewan servicemen became a daily feature of the local newspaper, they steeled themselves against the arrival of the dreaded telegram. But when Ken had returned unharmed, at least so far as they could see, they relaxed and let their guard down. Losing him now seemed incomprehensible. My grandmother wrote to John Gardiner on July 27 that

> *it does not seem possible. After all those long years of waiting and praying for his safe return, and having him with us just one short week, a week that literally flew past, we saw him leave for the west, thinking he & Marg. would be back before his leave was up. Then the shocking news . . . I'm so sick at heart, I just feel as if the very bottom has fallen out of everything. Ken and I were very close, always pals, he was so considerate, and always thoughtful of Mother. He was a wonderful letter-writer all through the long years of war, so many people remarked that he deserved a medal for correspondence, and we did enjoy his letters so much. Some of my letters never reached him and are being returned to me. It almost breaks my heart to think he never got them . . . I am so upset, really, sometimes I wonder how I can go on. It's so terrible.*

Three months later, my father told Gardiner that "Mother and Dad have aged 20 years."

Ken's death, however, was not simply a devastating loss. There was the nagging unanswered question of how and why he died. For my grandparents, the thought that Ken took his own life was unbearable. They lived in an age when suicide was considered shameful, a sign of weakness in the person who committed the act and failure in those close to him. Then there was the welter of bewildering and complicated thoughts—most notably a sense of impotence and guilt—surrounding the suicide of a loved one. For some time my grandparents, encouraged by Margaret and others, were able to tell themselves that Ken's death was accidental. Even then, my grandmother predictably began asking herself what she might have done to prevent it. "There was so much we planned to talk over with him when he returned," she wrote to Gardiner, "we had little chance to talk while he was here owing to lack of time and so many friends making demands on his time, etc. I regret so much that I did not have a chance to talk over their future. I might have done some good, I don't know."

My grandparents were tormented by not knowing whether Ken's death could have been prevented. And they might never have known had it not been for a chance encounter Ken had on a street in Vancouver on the afternoon before he died. This they learned of, almost in passing, from a card of condolence sent by Captain Jack Eccleston, a fellow officer of Ken's from the original pre-war Seventy-seventh Battery. A lieutenant at the beginning of the war, he had witnessed Ken's signing of his Supplementary Declaration Form, his volunteering to go overseas. They had gone to separate units during the war, but, said Eccleston, he had been in Vancouver and had talked to Ken the evening before he died. My grandmother immediately replied to the card, pleading with him to tell her anything he could about Ken's condition that evening.

Captain Eccleston wrote back on July 29 to explain that on the afternoon of Thursday, July 5, his wife, Mary, was shopping on Granville Street when she recognized a man standing on a corner. It was Ken, and as she approached him, she could see immediately that he was preoccupied and troubled. Her face was the first familiar one, other than his wife's, that he had seen for nine days, and he seemed eager to talk to her. Mary invited him back to the house, where she and Jack were dining with Jack's parents. After dinner, said Eccleston, Ken told him about his reunion with Margaret:

> *Margaret avoided telling Ken about her affairs with Dr. Story and others for about three days, she did everything possible to*

avoid it, kept other people around, sleeping powders and so on. Ken couldn't understand her attitude at all, he had absolutely no idea of anything being wrong, he blamed Margaret's attitude on nerves and overwork. On the Monday he decided to try to brighten her up, and he had a grin from ear to ear when he told me this part, he went out to the shops and bought some groceries and flowers while Margaret was at work and returned to the apartment and started to prepare supper. Oh yes, he said while he was out he had a haircut, shave and shampoo. He arranged the flowers on the table and peeled potatoes and started to fry the meat. He said he was really happy and was enjoying his first job in a kitchen of his own, he even had an apron tied on. When he figured it was nearly time for Margaret to come home, he put the water for tea on, and then Margaret came in. Ken said he was standing there in the middle of the kitchen and had a big grin on because of the apron and everything.

Margaret didn't say very much but told him to turn off the stove and sit down and have a drink. She then told him of her affair. Ken was hit badly, he didn't know what to do. Margaret went ahead and ate the supper Ken had cooked while Ken just sat there. He didn't have anything to eat from that time on until he had supper with us.

Ken said he was amazed at the change in Margaret, she was hard and callous. She wasn't emotional at all and didn't show any emotion at all until later when Ken threatened to drag Dr. Story through the courts and take every cent off him. It was only then that she showed emotion and she told him he wouldn't dare.

Ken had Margaret get Dr. Story over next day and he went over it all with the two of them and tried to find some reason or some method of restoring his married life. He was still willing to take Margaret back even after all she had told him. He talked to them all day but they wouldn't give him any satisfaction. Ken

didn't know where to turn to for advice, he was feeling pretty
bad about the whole thing and the main thought he had on his
mind was how his mother would take it. He mentioned that
several times, that worried him an awful lot.

Talking about his troubles to friends, continued Eccleston, seemed
to lessen some of Ken's desperation, and before he left, he formed a
plan. He would persuade Margaret to take the train back to Moose Jaw
with him—either to start their marriage over again or to have her
explain the situation to his mother. When he left the Ecclestons he was
in much better spirits than when he had arrived, and so Captain
Eccleston was stunned when he turned his radio on in the early hours
of Saturday morning and heard that Ken was dead.

Whatever optimism Ken had mustered in talking to the Ecclestons
evaporated between the time he left them and when he wrote his
despairing final letter to Gardiner. One can assume that Margaret
refused to accompany him to Moose Jaw and that her decision to
consult a lawyer on Friday afternoon told him absolutely that she was
finished with him. If he returned to Moose Jaw, it would be alone, and
it would be up to him to explain to the people there his failure to keep
his wife.

At the end, of course, Ken chose not to reveal his agony or justify
his suicide to the people in Moose Jaw, his parents or his brother.
Instead, he wrote to a man whom he had known for little more than
a year. This distressed my father, who had always seen himself as his
younger brother's protector, but it is unsurprising to veterans of the
battlefield. Writing of the Hastings and Prince Edward Regiment's
second year away from Canada, even before it had been in battle,
Farley Mowat commented that "within it every man now knew his
comrades as he had perhaps never known his own brothers. The
Regiment had become the home of the spirit and of the flesh." And
when such a group of men shared the dangers and hardships of the
battlefield, this sense of comradeship became intensified beyond

anything known in civilian life. "When a man is wounded, in trouble, or needs help," writes Richard Malone, "his instinctive reaction is how to get back to his own unit, his friends—in effect, his home." William Manchester, wounded in the American assault on Okinawa, even discharged himself from the safety of the hospital so he could return to his unit. "It was an act of love," he explained. "Those men on the line were my family, my home. They were closer to me than I can say, closer than any friends had been or ever would be. They had never let me down, and I couldn't do it to them. I had to be with them."

Manchester's loyalty would have been understandable to the Canadian soldier Jack Currie, for whom

the friendships you make in battle are different from any other kind of friendships. The guy you served with in battle is different than the guy you went to school with, the guy you live with, or the guy you work with. There's something between you and the men who fought alongside you that's different than anything else. Perhaps it's just that you both faced death together and during that time a special bond was welded.

And so it was to John Gardiner, the man with whom he had formed a special bond on the battlefields of Italy, that Ken wrote his final, explanatory letter. Eleven days later, Gardiner was sitting on a log in a grove in Holland, devastated by his friend's words. He sat there for a very long time. Finally he thought he was composed for the return journey to the Fifth LAA camp, but when he went back to retrieve his cap in the mailroom, his face betrayed him.

"Bad news, Lieutenant Gardiner?" inquired the sergeant.

"Yes."

"Your wife?"

"No."

"Your family?"

"No."

"Well," said the sergeant, "would you like to talk about it?"

Gardiner thanked the man, but he had things he needed to do back at his own base. For all Gardiner knew, Ken might not have gone through with his suicide plan, and might yet be dissuaded from carrying it out. With the help of the regimental padre, who had more influence than the ordinary serviceman and could arrange for a cable to be sent without the usual censorship delay, he immediately wired some words of encouragement to Ken, sending it to the Regina military depot to be forwarded to him.

The next day, Gardiner wrote a letter that began "it is still impossible for me to grasp what I would like to tell you." Then he mustered every argument he knew to give his friend reasons for living:

> *You alluded to your having taken the news as a good soldier and also that you tried to make up and start a new page; for this I must admit you are a better man than I am. Very few can find the moral courage needed to offer such a generous forgiveness.*
>
> *Your life still means a lot to your folks, Ken; therefore you must try and sear that terrific hurt and do your best to comfort your parents in their old age to come. You [may] say that this would mean sealing yourself forever with people of another generation and that in those long years overseas you have dreamt of other things for your future. [But] I know that you always loved kiddies, remember Rino and Rina, those two kids at Godo. I offer as a solution that some day after you have settled down in Civvy St. you look around and should you find some little lad that has lost his Dad over here, why not give him a share of your home life. Later in life you would have something to look back to, for memories can be more tangible than dreams. In his youth you would find comfort and faithful gratitude.*
>
> *Ken, this wicked world needs good men, so, for the sake of those that are still square shooters, don't do anything rash. If you cannot find rest and peace out your way, come for a while my*

way. Juliette and I will always welcome you as a brother. We both have known the agony of a long wait and the dread of a forced parting in this world. When I was scared in Italy it was not from the fear of stopping a bullet, but from the fear of leaving Juliette stranded. We would therefore understand your sorrow and help you rebuild your life along the lines of other ambitions.

All this, Ken, comes from the bottom of my heart . . . I will finish now by wishing you God's help and guidance, for there are problems that are above human reasoning.

God bless you,
John

Gardiner poured into his letter every reason he knew for living, but there was one simple, fundamental argument he did not even try to propose. It is an almost universal rule that the first consolation offered to someone who has lost a love is that there will be someone else, that there are other fish in the sea, but there is no mention in Gardiner's letter of Ken ever finding another woman. He knew he could suggest that Ken rebuild his life around his parents, some father-less child or his close friends, but he could not spend a year in Italy with Ken without understanding that building his life around anyone but Margaret was unthinkable for him.

Believing that, by the time his letter reached Canada, Ken would be back in Moose Jaw, Gardiner sent it to 923 Alder Avenue. It was only when my grandparents read it, which they did before receiving Eccleston's letter, that they began to realize that what had happened to Ken had not been an accident. Gardiner's comments were clearly in response to a letter from Ken, and it was easy to see what kind of letter it was. My grandmother wrote to him at once begging him to tell her anything Ken might have divulged to him. "I feel sure," she said, "that he gave you the picture and confided in you, so you probably know more about it than we do. It was no doubt the last letter written, we did not hear from him after he got out there. If you can tell us anything will you please do so? We would like to know anything you can pass along."

This request created a terrible dilemma for Gardiner. My grandmother had ended her letter—as she did all her letters that year—"a heartbroken mother," and he knew how desperately the Calders needed to understand why their son died. On the other hand, he had learned how profound a parent's grief could be when his brother Austin was killed in action in 1943, and he recognized that the details of Ken's final conversations with Margaret were so unpleasant and his last thoughts so bitter and disillusioned that they would only intensify the pain. "Christ!" Gardiner said years later. "You can't give a letter like that to a woman who has just lost her son after five and a half years of war. I would not have wanted *my* parents to read that cry of total despair." And so, instead of sending the letter, he gave them a muted paraphrasing of what Ken had written.

Gardiner's decision was made less difficult by the fact that he had already sent a copy of Ken's letter to my father, who had begun his own investigation almost as soon as he had been told of his brother's death. Earle, then at Camp Shilo, wrote to Gardiner on July 15, the day after he attended the Court of Inquiry, pointing out that his parents did not then know the real cause of Ken's death. Gardiner replied that "Ken was such a genuine friend of mine that I cannot yet make myself believe that the Civvy St. meeting that we had talked about so much will not come." And, with some brief explanation, he attached a copy of the letter.

Earle seems to have shared Gardiner's view that his parents could only be further hurt by reading the letter; certainly there is no evidence that they ever saw it. When he sent a copy to the Department of National Defence, in an attempt to have Ken's gratuities paid to the Calders rather than to Margaret, he asked that they not be told of his correspondence.

Ken's letter to Gardiner and his notes to the Vancouver Chief of Police and to Margaret are remarkable for their reason and coherence.

They are not, as might be expected, the disjointed observations of a deranged mind or the ramblings of a man who has drunk himself into incoherence. They are the well-organized, carefully considered thoughts of someone who has looked at his situation and sees only one course of action. We may disagree with his conclusion, and deeply regret its outcome, but it was not the product of an irrational mind.

What then was it a product of?

There can be no doubt that Ken returned from Europe suffering from some form of battle fatigue. As Bill McAndrew has demonstrated, the Italian campaign caused the highest number of mental breakdowns in Canadian soldiers in the Second World War. Many of these men became battlefield casualties, were identified and were treated. Many exhibited the symptoms of what is now called post-traumatic stress disorder: nightmares, sleep problems, depression, hysteria, severe anxiety, phobias and dissociations. Many more had less obvious symptoms and were never identified.

The truth is that every man or woman who was in combat during the war suffered some form of disorder. When the heroic American GI Audie Murphy was asked how combat soldiers survive having been in a war, he replied: "I don't think they ever do." Citing this remark in *Doing Battle,* Paul Fussell reveals that it was several years after demobilization that he finally regained his emotional balance, and that he has never lost certain instinctive reactions, such as jumping to the alert at the machine-gun sound of a jackhammer in the street. Similarly, Ron MacFarlane told me that a year after the war he dove onto the grass in a Toronto park at the sound of a car backfiring; and other veterans shocked their families by hitting the dirt at the sight of a low-flying aircraft or becoming traumatized by an unexpected clap of thunder. As a boy in the 1950s, I can remember our family watching a fireworks display at the Saskatoon Exhibition and having to leave before it finished because a World War II veteran who was with us could not endure the explosions. Less dramatic but no less eloquent were the actions of thousands of returned soldiers who would simply get up and leave the room whenever the conversation turned to the war.

In his note to Margaret, Ken said that he was "awfully tired now, can't fight any more." If this suggests a long-term exhaustion, then he was suffering from a condition common to returning soldiers. When Jack Leddy came back from serving as a medical officer in the Second World War, the hospital administrators "found it difficult to understand our deep fatigue, our mental and physical exhaustion." So deeply seated was this fatigue that when he visited his wife, he was almost too exhausted to talk or listen. "I lacked concentration," he said. "I couldn't work at anything for very long. I would try to read but I would feel the need to sleep after an hour . . . I felt weak most of the time." As a result of this fatigue he failed his medical fellowship exam in January 1945 and then again in March. It took two years away from the battlefield before he was able to pass.

Another non-combatant, the painter Alex Colville, who was in his early twenties when he went overseas as a war artist for the last two years of the fighting, recently described the cumulative exhaustion to journalist Sarah Milroy. "The one thing one doesn't know about war," he said, "is how tired you are. Too tired to really run. Too tired, at times, even to be afraid." For him the ending of Steven Spielberg's film *Saving Private Ryan* is particularly significant: the hero, played by Tom Hanks, simply "becomes so tired that he dies. He sort of dies by being unable to carry on."

If Jack Leddy's hospital administrators could not identify the mental and physical exhaustion of the returning veterans, the average Canadian civilian was able to recognize it even less. Four months before the end of the war, Angus Mowat wrote to his son Farley about a speech he had given to the women's section of the Canadian Club. "It had never occurred to most of them," he said, "that a soldier can be wounded or deeply damaged by anything except bullets and shells and that sort of thing . . . What they don't know about is the burning out process, and nobody, not our gabby retired generals, nor our great medical minds, nor, certainly, the politicians and their mouthpieces the press and radio, is telling them." Such internal wounding was not discussed by public figures, claimed Angus, because it would make war less acceptable to those who were needed at the front. Five months after he wrote this, when the revelry of VE day had died down and the soldiers were returning by the thousands, battle fatigue was no more obvious to Canadian civilians. The war was over, people were anxious to get on with their lives, and veterans were expected to pick up where they had left off in 1939.

For Angus Mowat there was a "burning out" that was much deeper and more debilitating than mere exhaustion. Writing to Farley early in the war, he warned him against losing his will to live in the face of battlefield hardships and horror:

> *The most unfortunate people after the last war were not those who were wounded physically, but those who had had their feet knocked out from under them spiritually and never regained them. The beer parlours and the gutters are still full of them, poor bastards, and nobody understands. Or so few that it doesn't matter.*
>
> *Your job, and I mean your duty to yourself, is to continue that little spark of something or other that's in you inviolate from war . . . The danger of losing it grows as time goes on. A wearing-down process. I have seen it in half a dozen fellows I knew intimately. The two most striking cases were Lawrence and Davis, both of my company in the old Fourth Battalion. Both had had four years of it. Both were simply worn out, spiritually. And both committed suicide. I don't mean that they shot them-selves, but they went out and let the Germans do it because there was nothing left alive of the spark within them. They didn't even know what was the matter with them and there wasn't anybody to tell them because we were all too inexperienced to*

*see. If you can guard against that burning out you will be
greatly blessed.*

I believe that Ken had much of the spark burned out of him in Italy
and Holland, and that he would not have killed himself at any other
time in his life. As his Italian campaign diary reveals, he grew increasingly exhausted, ill and dispirited with each day of mud, shelling and
casualties. Like Mowat and so many other men serving in such conditions, his anger with the zombies who refused to volunteer for battle,
the government that refused to send them over, and the civilians who
did not understand what the men were enduring made him discouraged and disillusioned. The cynicism bred in Paul Fussell in the killing
fields of France in the last year of the war left him with a fundamental
scepticism that set the tone for his distinguished academic career and
his personal life. Ken's discouragement made him count all the more
heavily on a renewed relationship with Margaret as something to cling
to, something he thought positive and durable. It also rendered him
terribly vulnerable when the relationship turned out to be something
very different.

Ken returned from Europe physically and spiritually exhausted. In
Moose Jaw he found few people, including his own brother, who had
the slightest understanding of what he had seen and endured.
Anything he told the Lions Club about the war was news to them.
And as he looked around Moose Jaw, he must have noticed how life
had continued without him, how men his age had prospered,
advanced and been promoted. The Creamery had generously offered
him his old job, but that would have been going back, as if nearly six
years counted for nothing. Opening his own sporting goods store,
where he could use the managerial skills developed overseas, would
have been a step forward, if Margaret had saved the money he sent her
for a down payment.

If Ken had felt detached from life in Moose Jaw, it still held his
family, old and trusted friends like Henry Evans, and fellow servicemen

from the Seventy-seventh Battery. Vancouver, an unfamiliar city in which he was a stranger, had none of these supports. It was now Margaret's terrain, and it was there that she had chosen to confront him with her infidelity and fight him for a divorce. And it was a contest in which his particular battle skills were irrelevant. Had Margaret broken the news to Ken in Moose Jaw, where he had supportive friends and relatives, he would probably have survived the crisis. Had she written of it to him in Europe, where he had the sustaining friendships of John Gardiner and others in his unit, he is unlikely to have killed himself. In Vancouver he had no one; the chance meeting with Jack Eccleston, while showing the restorative value of a sympathetic ear, came too late to save him.

But even this is an oversimplification of Ken's state of mind at the end. How, for example, does one interpret Jack Eccleston's comment, made twice in his letter, that Ken was especially concerned that Margaret go to Moose Jaw to tell his mother why she wanted a divorce? Does my grandmother's remark to Gardiner that "Ken and I were very close, always pals, he was . . . always thoughtful of Mother" have darker implications, that his thoughts had always been too much of his mother? If she had indeed been instrumental in Ken's decision to marry Margaret, as one of his cousins has suggested, and if he could not bear to return to Moose Jaw to be judged by her as having failed in his marriage, the irony is cruel. And the word "grief" no longer has the power to convey what my grandmother must have endured in her final years.

It may be, too, that Ken concluded he had not met another standard. As an army officer for nearly a decade, he was expected to solve problems, and he had succeeded in that both in training exercises in Britain and in action in Italy and Holland. He had commanded large numbers of men in difficult situations, and he had become accustomed to being respected and obeyed. He had not been taught how to cope with failure; lack of success on the battlefield was unacceptable and often drew a reprimand from senior officers. Now, on a battlefield of a much different sort, he had lost, and he did not know how to walk away from his defeat.

By that last night in Vancouver, all Ken really understood was military life and military men. In his last letter to Gardiner he wrote that he took Margaret's disclosure of her infidelity "like a good soldier," and he scribbled on the *Reader's Digest* article about self-sacrifice in combat that such men were "the only people who count." And when he had sealed the door and windows in the kitchenette and turned on the gas, he awaited the end wearing his artillery officer's uniform. A bitter statement to the world about what men in uniform were coming home to, one last proud display that he was one of those "only people," or had he come to believe that it would have been better had he died in the Liri Valley or in the push through the Gothic line?

And what of Ken's service pistol, found among his belongings in Vancouver and returned to Moose Jaw by the Chief of Police? It is not customary for a Canadian Army officer to take his firearm with him on a month's leave, and it would have been easy for him to leave it securely in his family home. And what of Ken's comment to the Chief that "I don't want to stretch a rope for murder so I'm getting out the easy way," with its oddly Shakespearian image of wanting to avoid "a future existence with maggots in my brain"?

The inescapable conclusion, it seems to me, is that Ken went to Vancouver with enough doubts about Margaret that in a dark corner of his mind was the thought that he might need to use the pistol. In the end, of course, he was not the sort of man to commit murder, even in the face of betrayal, so he turned the violence against himself in order to end his pain. And so that no suspicion should fall on Margaret and Story, he left his letter for the Chief of Police.

The pistol was sent to my father in Moose Jaw.

CHAPTER FOURTEEN

"This I'll promise you: I am going to see Dr. Story. I am going to beat him with my bare hands within an inch of his life."

If Ken did not have it in him to strike back at his wife and her lover, my father certainly did. "I have a violent nature," he wrote John Gardiner three months after Ken's death. "This simply means that to me violence is necessary in order to have peace within myself. I suppose Ken has told you that I hold many championships with pistol and rifle. He was an expert himself. His temper was even, however, but mine is not."

However much Earle wanted to exact what he considered justice with his fists or his firearms, he realized that such violence would simply bring further pain to his parents. "I am now the only son of heartbroken parents. Yet I long to do something about it." When they were children, he explained to Gardiner, he was always protective of his younger brother, subtly insinuating himself into Ken's quarrels with neighbourhood bullies. "I do not suppose that he ever realized that, when I appeared and discovered what was going on, I deliberately engineered things so that the fight became mine, not his."

Nothing is more indelibly etched in Earle's letter to Gardiner than his anguish at having been powerless to protect Ken in this last fight. "I can never realize why he left no letter for me," he wrote. Perhaps, he conjectured, Ken deliberately avoided writing him so as to impel him to inflict retribution on those responsible for the tragedy. "Did he think that by [writing] he would sidetrack me? *Or* did he think that by sending no letter he would send me on a trail that would leave me relentless?"

Thus, for Earle, a letter of explanation from Ken would have "sidetracked" him; that is, the matter would have been settled and there would have been some emotional closure. As it was, his brother's silence left the matter open and unresolved, with Earle needing to do something to find the "peace within myself."

Within days of Ken's death, Earle had moved to make what was left of the fight his own. When Margaret was in Moose Jaw for the funeral, he told Gardiner, he conducted his own "cross examination" of her. She admitted, he said, that she had not prepared one meal during the week that Ken was with her. Her husband had turned thirty-four several days after he arrived in Vancouver, but his first birthday back in Canada was one without celebration. As well, claimed Earle, Margaret admitted having given Ken six bottles of whisky during the week, repeatedly admonishing him "not to do anything foolish." Her reiteration of "remember your promise not to take your own life," he suggested to Gardiner, constituted "murder by psychology" by a highly skilled nurse and doctor.

Determined to prevent Margaret's benefiting from his brother's death, Earle wrote to the Department of National Defence to ask that she be denied Ken's war service gratuity, the lump sum payment to armed services personnel for days served during the war. Having been told that, in special cases, the mother could be awarded the gratuity of a deceased soldier instead of the wife, he argued that his parents were more deserving than Margaret. She had, he said, Ken's entire savings from five and a half years, in addition to seven hundred dollars from the sale of his car. Most importantly, her affair with Boyd Story disqualified her from benefiting financially from his death. As evidence, he attached copies of Ken's notes to the Commissioner of Police and Margaret, his annotation on the *Reader's Digest* page, his letter to Gardiner, and Eccleston's letter to my grandmother. If, after reviewing this evidence, the Department of National Defence proceeded to award the gratuity to Margaret, Earle added rather ominously, "I will then be compelled to obtain satisfaction by my own means."

The truth is, of course, that Earle had no means of obtaining "satisfaction" outside of committing criminal violence, and he never knew whether the Dependents' Allowance Board had acted upon any of his allegations. Within a couple of years he was beyond being satisfied by anything. In the twenty-eight months after Ken's death he began a rapid psychological and physical degeneration that would eventually lead to his being confined in a mental hospital for the last eleven years of his life. Triggered by the suicide of his brother, his decline is graphically documented in four places: the letter he wrote to John Gardiner three months after the event, his army personnel file, his Winnipeg General Hospital file and his Selkirk Hospital for Mental Diseases file.

The emotional and psychological impact of Ken's death on Earle is apparent on every page of the letter to Gardiner. He begins by telling him that "I cannot help but feel that you will consider this a letter from the dead" and goes on to remark that "Ken died July 6th. I have been a nervous wreck ever since. I still do not know what to do." Before mailing it, he reread his letter and provided his own critique in a postscript: "I know that you will think this letter is from a crank, but really I can't even suggest that I am anywhere in my right mind."

Earle's letter may not be the expression of a crank, but it is certainly tortured and desperate. Ironically, Ken's letter to Gardiner, written within hours of taking his own life, is well organized, logical and articulate—despairing and pained, yes, but calm and controlled. By contrast, Earle's is disorganized, confused and full of rationalization. It is repetitive, disjointed and marked by misspellings and fragments of words.

Two days after writing Gardiner, Earle was examined by a board of medical officers at the army base in Barriefield, Ontario. Though the immediate reason for the examination was reported as a recurrence of chronic dermatitis of the scalp and eyebrows, he told one officer that "I have no complaints except that I am in a state of nervous tension." This tension, he said, began "about 6 July, 1945 following the suicide of [my] brother Captain K.A. Calder." After an interview with Earle, the psychiatric examiner concluded that "conversation shows that there was no sign of nervous tension until family trouble about July, 1945. Today he is a bit tense, talkative."

Several months later, in January 1946, Earle was recommended for a transfer to Military District No. 12 in Regina. While commenting that his general impression was favourable, the commanding officer there described him as "a strange personality. Appears capable. Is very willing, but extremely self-contained and reticent."

In Earle's army personnel file, nearly two hundred pages long, these comments are remarkable because they are almost the only reservations expressed about him. In fact, his military record up to Ken's death was exemplary. As I was growing up, I knew nothing of this, and when I opened his file in 1997 there were a number of surprises awaiting me.

First there were the personal details that began to turn a shadowy figure into a flesh-and-blood person. He had completed his entire grade eleven year in Moose Jaw but did not write the examinations. Illness, I wonder? Or some youthful intransigence? It does not say. Despite having completed only grade ten, he is described as having an excellent command of English and a rudimentary knowledge of French and German, surely not common expertise for a young Saskatchewan man in the thirties.

Earle's love of fishing and hunting and his many trophies for target shooting were familiar facts. But I never knew that he played the piano, swam regularly, collected stamps and edited a stamp collecting column for the Moose Jaw *Times-Herald*. Nor that he did "an exceptional amount of reading" and enjoyed doing research into a variety of topics. As I read this material, I began to find myself thinking that this was a man of interesting parts, one whose company, as adults at least, I might have grown to enjoy. And given my own love of fishing and hunting, my youthful passion for stamp collecting, my lifelong habit of swimming, and my career of reading and research, could I actually be a chip of this old block?

The summary of Earle's employment prior to his enlisting in September 1940, on the other hand, seems to confirm my mother's description of him as a man who lacked drive and discipline. After dropping out of high school, he took dairy courses with the Caulder Creamery in Moose Jaw but worked for the Creamery for less than two years. For the next five years he worked at Fred Cooper's shoe repair shop, and then he was a sales clerk at the Moose Jaw Hardware for four years. From 1938 to 1940 he was what he termed a "self-employed salesman for various products such as washing machines, radios, and sporting goods." A few months before his enlistment he stopped freelancing and began to work as a sales clerk at Security Lumber.

Even this record, Earle's own version told to an army interviewer, seems to have been an embellishment. According to the *Henderson Directory* for Moose Jaw, following his employment with the Creamery, he took a position—very likely as a travelling salesman—with an enterprise with the Monty Pythonish name Indestructible Neckware Company. This was apparently followed by a short spell with French's Dry Cleaners. In all, it seems he had at least seven jobs in eleven years. Ken, meanwhile, had remained with the Creamery and risen to foreman during that period.

According to his personnel file, Earle enlisted in the militia in 1925. Like Ken he was underage, and he too joined the King's Own Rifles of Canada. Before long, though, their military paths diverged. While Ken transferred to the Seventy-seventh Battery, an artillery unit, in 1927, Earle remained with the KORC until 1934. In 1937 he also joined the Seventy-seventh, and he was there when the war broke out.

I have often wondered why my father did not follow Ken, enlist in the Canadian Active Service Force and volunteer for overseas duty. They had joined the militia together as boys, and he was as attracted to the military ethos as Ken. At twenty-nine he was not too old for active service, he was married but without children, and there was no promising career to be put on hold. Had he come to view cynically the calls to fight for the Old Country? Did he think the young men who chose to fight for King and Country were mugs?

But Earle's choice was not as easy as that of his younger brother. Ken had risen to the rank of captain in the Seventy-seventh Battery, and even though, on joining the active service, he dropped to lieutenant, he would still go to Britain as a commissioned officer. Earle, on the other hand, was not an officer, so he would have to enlist as a gunner, the artillery equivalent of a private. Surrounded by nineteen-year-old recruits, he would seem like an old man. Moreover, if he remained to train in the Seventy-seventh, one of the officers commanding him would be his younger brother. He may well have had too much pride and been too accustomed to his role as the dominant brother to be able to accept this secondary position.

Throughout the winter of 1939–40, when little was happening on the battlefields of Europe, Earle was conducting his own phony war, working in the lumberyard. In April 1940 he rejoined the KORC, and in September he was granted a transfer to an active force training corps in Regina. Over the next three years he took a number of courses—in the Theory of Instruction, Platoon Weapons and Battle First Aid—and was promoted to sergeant. In August 1943 he was sent to the Officers' Training Corps at Brockville, and in November he got his commission as a second lieutenant. A month later he was promoted to lieutenant. He was made acting captain in April 1945 and captain in November of that year. Along the way he took further courses in Chemical Warfare and Demolitions and Mines.

Earle may have been slower than Ken in joining the active service, but his rise through the ranks from private to captain was a considerable achievement. And, remarkably for a man who had seemed unambitious and directionless before the war, his evaluations and performance reviews were consistently glowing. Today, in the age of freedom of information, when every officer knows that his comments may be seen by the subject, an ombudsman or lawyers, such positive reviews are common. During the Second World War, by contrast, evaluations were written *about* people rather than *for* people, and the times required that they be candid and sometimes brutally frank. Thus, many an aging veteran nostalgically reviewing his own personnel file today has left the National Archives indignant at discovering the derogatory remarks made about him by an officer fifty years earlier. In Earle's case, however, there is almost nothing but commendations.

Earle's recommendation for officer training in June 1943, for example, refers to

> a superior degree of learning ability, excellent mechanical knowledge, good in arithmetic and an excellent command of English. He appears to have considerable initiative, enterprise, interest and enthusiasm for his work and this to such an extent that he is considered as potential officer material of a very high calibre. With his ability, experience, and qualifications he should make an excellent officer in the Infantry.

A month later the commanding officer in Regina described Earle as "a most capable instructor. He has a high learning capacity and possesses leadership and initiative, smart appearance, and is capable of handling any situation with resource and energy." In Chilliwack in July 1943 he was said to be "energetic and sincere," someone who "takes a great pride in his achievements."

As a commissioned officer Earle continued to receive excellent evaluations. In January 1944 he was characterized as "a smartly turned out, capable-looking officer of brisk, alert personality. Has self-confidence and is ambitious. Appears reliable and well balanced . . . Good character. He will be an able and conscientious officer." At the Canadian Small Arms School four months later he was rated as "very good" in knowledge of work, capacity for work, attention to detail, verbal and written expression, desire for knowledge, and personality. In his theory examination he received 91 percent. And at Shilo Camp as late as April 1945 he was reported to be "reliable and hard-working. A well-qualified, conscientious and valuable training officer."

When I first opened Earle's personnel file in 1997, I was certainly not expecting to find such an exemplary record. Given what little I knew about his character and behaviour, I would not have been surprised to read a litany of comments about laziness, lack of discipline, insubordination and unreliability. I found myself feeling a sense of pride in his accomplishments, as I had at the age of thirteen when he was demonstrating jiu-jitsu moves to us in Moose Jaw.

It was a strange and novel sensation, at the age of fifty-six, to feel pride in my father. After all, only a dozen years earlier, when I was asked for biographical details for my entry in the *Canadian Who's Who,* I had omitted any reference to him. Kenneth, the scrupulous historian, had recorded his paternity in his entry, but I, like a sullen teenager, acted as if I had never had a father. If I had achieved anything to warrant being in the book, I thought, none of the credit should go to him. In fact, looking back, I realize that throughout my life I have only ever acknowledged my father when legally required to.

And now I was suspicious of this new sensation and wondered if I deserved to feel it. Can you feel pride for a man whose only real connection to you is biological, who seems to have done nothing after conception to nurture or support you? Did being Earle Calder's son— and not someone else's—make any positive difference? Was what I was feeling really just some pride in the family name, the same pleasure one feels on learning that an ancestor was a renowned woodsman or prize-winning sculptor? I don't know the answers to these questions; I only know that I felt a disconcerting pride on reading that Earle Calder was a highly regarded officer.

But I was not wrong to be surprised at Earle's success in the army. Few people who knew him in Moose Jaw in the thirties would have expected it. And many might have wondered how such a transformation could have occurred.

The answer is, of course, hardly new: wartime—particularly the profound upheavals of the two world wars—dramatically transforms a nation's life and often the lives of individual men and women. National mobilization, even in countries far from the battlefields, changes the rules and demands different things of the citizenry. Qualities in a man that in peacetime may be anti-social or destructive can be the very elements that make him a good spy or a good soldier. In Elizabeth Bowen's fine novel *The Heat of the Day*, Robert Harrison is a shadowy, secretive, devious man. An insignificant figure in peacetime, he becomes the perfect counter-intelligence agent in Second World War London, rising in prominence and power. George Patton's warrior mentality made him one of the Allies' most valued generals, but it was not a quality that would have served him in peacetime.

Earle would not have joined the army, nor is it likely to have wanted him, if Canada had not been at war. Once he was in the active service, military regulations undoubtedly imposed a discipline on him that he was never able to apply to himself in civilian life. Having accepted that discipline and become an officer, he was then able to order other men around, an appealing situation to someone who had always enjoyed exerting his will over others. Always seeing himself as a man's man, he must have relished teaching young men self-defence, small-arms firing and demolition removal.

Whatever the reasons, Earle flourished in the army as he had never done before, but behind this success always lay the uncertainty of civilian life. In an occupational history form he filled out in 1942, he indicated that the lumberyard had not promised him a job after the war nor did he wish to return to it. In a review by an Officers Classification Board in January 1944, the question "Is civilian employment available for purposes of rehabilitation?" was answered "Indefinite," and his situation was summarized: "Lieut. Calder was a sales clerk prior to entering Army. No promise of re-employment and his plans are indefinite."

Earle had advised the board that he wanted to remain in uniform and proceed overseas, but by this time the army realized that junior infantry officers should be young men. It had not considered his age when it sent him on officer training, and now it concluded that, though he was "a competent, well trained officer with some years of instructional experience, he is too old for overseas service in commissioned rank." He "should and could have gone forward in the ranks long ago." Although he had begun his active service too late to be sent to Europe, he was too experienced and capable not to be used, so he was attached to the Home War Establishment for the duration of the war.

In May 1945, as Ken was on his way home from Holland, Earle volunteered to serve in the war in the Pacific, which looked to be going on for at least another year. On August 4 he was placed on a list of alternate candidates to serve in the Pacific Force should any appointed officers not take up their positions. But within a week the bombs on Hiroshima and Nagasaki erased the need for any further Canadian forces to fight the Japanese. Still determined to stay in the army, he applied in November to serve in the Interim Force, but he was rejected because he was over-age at a time when the army had an abundance of young officers returning from action in Europe. Thus, despite his efforts, he was demobilized in March 1946.

In Regina on March 21, Earle was given the customary employment counselling interview provided to servicemen returning to civilian life. His own Statement of Future Plans was only slightly more specific than his earlier "indefinite" prospects: "I am going to try finding a job as a salesman." With this vagueness, however, seems to have been some bravado, if the counsellor's buoyant evaluation is anything to go by:

> This is a neat, alert and confident officer of 36 who has no definite job arranged but intends to seek employment as a salesman and has made several promising contacts in the fields of life insurance and automobile sales. This appears to be the most appropriate field for him because all of his pre-war employment was along those lines, he "made a good living" out of it and likes the work.

Capt. Calder is a friendly, jovial and vivacious man who has been variously described as having "excellent command of English," having "initiative and enterprise," being a very good organizer and a first class instructor, and having good leadership ability. His rise from the rank of Pte. to that of Capt. and employments in administrative positions both as a non-commissioned and commissioned officer prove that he is aggressive, ambitious and has a high degree of responsibility. These factors together with his previous experiences in the sales field indicate that he should be quite successful in work which requires a pleasant and friendly disposition, energy, initiative and ability to meet people. He would probably succeed as a field man for a loan company, as auto or life insurance salesman or in other allied fields.

A great many parents of teenaged boys will recognize the dynamics at work in Earle's approach to this employment interview. Tell the parent/counsellor what he or she wants to hear and get him or her off your back: I'm really anxious to work; I've got a couple of hot leads; Mr. Smith says I can have a job in his shop whenever I want; I know I can handle it big time; stop worrying, folks. And in this case the counsellor seems to have accepted Earle's own exaggerated version of his pre-war sales success.

Much of the employment evaluation is based more soundly on Earle's undeniably positive military record. The ambition, discipline and sense of responsibility that he discovered in the army and that allowed him to rise through the ranks were indeed qualities which could have led to success on Civvy Street. Many Canadian servicemen—John Gardiner and Ronald MacFarlane among them—used the skills that had been developed and honed in uniform to fashion successful post-war careers. One might reasonably have assumed that Earle would at least have coped with civilian life, and perhaps thrived.

Behind the confident façade presented to the counsellor, however, was a deeply troubled man. Though he still gave his home address as 168 Hochelaga Street, he would never live there again. Armed with the proof of his adultery in Kingston the previous September, my mother had already begun divorce proceedings. Within two months her case would be heard, he would become estranged from his parents because of their support of her, and he would be advised by the sheriff to leave Moose Jaw. Very quickly, then, he lost his wife, children, parents, and the only job in which he had ever been truly successful. Departing Moose Jaw meant leaving his hometown and any supportive friends he might have there to go to a city, Winnipeg, where he knew few people.

Looming darkly over all of these problems was, of course, Ken's suicide. There had been no closure on the helplessness and rage he felt on hearing that his brother—without seeking his aid—had taken his own life. How could there be? His conviction that Ken, by his silence, had charged him to seek revenge left him with a duty that could never be fulfilled, and the "peace within myself" that he sought would remain forever elusive. Moreover, now that he needed a confidant, a trusted sibling to whom he could unburden himself, there was no one. His wife and parents might turn against him, but his brother and fellow soldier would have remained loyal.

Adrift in civilian life, isolated and haunted, Earle fell on hard times with remarkable swiftness. On being demobilized, he had been given a rehabilitation grant, a clothing allowance and a service gratuity of $502.50, around $5,000 in today's currency. Eight months later, on the day before Christmas, he was applying to the Department of Veterans Affairs for financial assistance. He had been employed for only four months with a grain company in Domain, Manitoba, and had to leave, he said, because the grain dust was affecting his health. He was then out of work and living in the Salvation Army hostel in Winnipeg.

Earle was awarded an out-of-work allowance of $50 a month for ten months, though his personnel file indicates he was still receiving some sort of payment from the DVA as late as December 1949. The last entry in his file is an order from the Directorate of Army Personnel in 1953 striking him from the Reserve Officers List. The Department of National Defence had been unable to locate him to ask if he wished to be placed on the Supplementary Reserve List. To the department, his last known address was 168 Hochelaga Street, where he had not lived for seven years.

Had Earle gone on to live out his days in some Winnipeg rooming house, regaling his barroom buddies with his tales of service life, and perhaps showing up at the local Legion every Remembrance Day proudly wearing his Canadian Volunteer Service Medal and his War Medal 1939–45, I would never have known how he ended his days. But, as I discovered in late 1997, whatever the personal demons he fought in the years following the war, the battle was neither quiet nor private; it was public and well documented. Recalling the letter of inquiry that Uncle Art had received from a psychiatrist in Selkirk, Manitoba, I played a hunch and wrote to the Hospital for Mental Diseases. Earle, they replied, had indeed been a patient there—a long-term resident—and there was a lengthy file on him.

If Earle's army personnel file is a record of accomplishment, the Selkirk file is emphatically one of deterioration and collapse. In June 1960, it said, he was examined by the psychiatric department of the Winnipeg General Hospital and diagnosed as having Korsakoff's Syndrome caused by chronic alcohol addiction. Suffering from severe memory loss, he could not recall how he had arrived at the hospital. He could say only that he had worked for Western Messenger Transfer, a moving company, for five or six years, followed by some casual labour, "and the next thing he knew he was in hospital." He did remember drinking a half-bottle of whisky a day ever since the end of the war (in later interviews he claimed to have drunk a 26-ounce bottle a day).

The Selkirk file does not state what led to Earle's examination at the Winnipeg General, but it suggests that he had become a public nuisance: "Patient apparently got along well till he got involved with alcohol and about 1958 began to show a deterioration with loss of memory, poor judgement, and eventually required supervision." The records of the Winnipeg General, however, reveal that he had become, if not a public nuisance, certainly a very troubled and angry man well before 1958.

In July 1948, according to his hospital case notes, he was slugged from behind in a holdup and left unconscious in the street. The following June, he got into a street fight, suffered a number of facial blows that blackened both eyes and broke his nose, and was knocked unconscious. This left him dazed and amnesic, but bystanders later told him that he had got up off the street and fought very hard until he was stabbed in the shoulder. Three months after this beating, he was admitted to the Winnipeg General suffering from severe headaches, some paralysis of his arms and legs, and loss of memory. He had ended the war, he told the examining physician then, with "nervous upset and anxiety fatigue." He was, he said, discharged from the army in 1946 as being sound and healthy but suffered nervous anxiety for a year after that. Since then he had worked variously at a grain elevator, a hardware store, a coal company, a department store and a car wash.

In the decade following this beating, Earle seems to have sunk deeper into the rough and semi-criminal life of the mean streets. By the time he was treated for ulcerating lesions at the Winnipeg General in November 1957, his address had become "Rupert Street Jail" and his occupation was listed as "prisoner." He was, noted a doctor on that occasion, "wanted by City Police on discharge." When he was brought to the hospital by police in April 1960, he was comatose, having drunk himself into unconsciousness, and it was at this point that officials concluded he could not be released onto the streets again.

On the recommendation of the psychiatrists at the Winnipeg General, Earle was admitted to Princess Elizabeth Hospital, where he remained until February 1961. There he was termed "tractable" and not in need of mental hospitalization, so he was sent to a convalescent home for five months. Here, reported the supervisor, he "hangs around street corners, picks up cigarette butts and empty bottles. Very childish, begs cigarettes. Quarrelsome with patients and staff. Wanders off, never in for meals or medication. I don't think a nursing home is the place for him; he should be under supervision."

Despite the supervisor's recommendation, Earle was sent to the Nightingale Nursing Home as a City of Winnipeg welfare case, where he remained for nearly two years, until he became too unruly for its staff to handle. An agitated director of nursing services wrote to the psychopathic department of the Winnipeg General on April 2, 1963, that "I have had the choice between two responsibilities this morning—that of accompanying Earle Calder to your Department or staying here to quieten the feeling of fear and apprehension that prevails in this Nursing Home because of Earle's violent outbursts of temper during the past few days." At times, said the director, Earle could be congenial and co-operative, and "his conversation can appear quite normal, witty and full of Biblical and Shakespearian quotations." On the whole, though, "he has always resented any infraction upon what he feels should be his private way of life." The greatest difficulty—and the cause of the immediate crisis—was his antagonism toward the senile patients who shared his room.

As Earle later explained it to a Selkirk psychiatrist, the two old men would frequently defecate and urinate on the floor. They were quite capable of going all the way down to the kitchen if they were hungry, he said, but not able to go two doors along the hall to the bathroom. He threatened to "clean the clock of the man urinating beside his bed," he said, and he once tried to rub the nose of one of them in the feces, which caused "a wild situation" in his dormitory. Finally, he had pushed an eighty-year-old man down a flight of three steps, and this led to the director's plea for help.

The Psychiatric Institute, at the Winnipeg General, examined Earle and confirmed that he had severe memory loss as well as confabulation, no insight and poor judgment. He was designated a "mentally incompetent person" whose affairs were turned over to a committee of his estate assigned by the government of Manitoba; and by a provincial Government Order of Commitment in April 1963 he was confined to the Selkirk Hospital. His "estate" when he arrived there consisted of two certificates of military qualification, one Officer Training Centre certificate and a Pilot pocket watch. The years of alcoholic haze, hard times and street life had left him only his military record and his father's watch, taken from Kenneth and given to him at my grandfather's funeral in 1954.

The severe amnesia that is a prominent element in Korsakoff's Syndrome makes it difficult to be certain about the source—or sources—of Earle's mental breakdown. But his file is not devoid of references to his family and his past life. Interestingly, given his estrangement from his parents, he claimed to have come from a "perfect model home," and his speech, according to one observer, was inevitably interspersed with the remark "My mother always said . . ." There was no history of alcoholism or mental disorders in his family, he declared, but—and this is repeated a number of times in his file— he did have a brother who committed suicide.

In the midst of the ruins of his life and of what was left of his mind, Earle clung to the successes of his days in uniform. According to one psychiatrist, "he took considerable time reminiscing about what an excellent soldier he was in the last war, rising from private to captain, how well he was thought of then and after discharge. A considerable amount of this was probably bragging." Bragging, yes, and exaggeration when he referred to returning from overseas and when he claimed to have been a major. "He is," concluded one interviewer, "certainly living in his past."

Earle spent the rest of his life—another eleven and a half years— in the Selkirk Hospital for Mental Diseases. For the first three or four years, several friends took him to their homes for a few days at Christmas or Thanksgiving, but soon he became too difficult for them to handle. At the hospital he was initially uncooperative, sarcastic and hostile toward other patients. "If you wanta get miserable about it, I can take it," he liked to tell the attendants. When he concluded that the hospital's behaviour modification program was ridiculous, he went nine meals without eating to prove his point. To their suggestions that he do some work, he countered that he was an ice cream maker and they did not have anything in his line. Reason in madness? I wonder.

By April 1967, Earle's condition had deteriorated so precipitously that he had to be transferred to the infirmary, where he remained until his death. With each year he became increasingly withdrawn, confused, asocial and uncommunicative. He began to disrobe and walk around the ward naked, to urinate on the floor and to wander away from the hospital grounds when unsupervised. For the last five years of his life he was confined to a geriatric chair, mute and doubly incontinent. Needing help to dress and prompting to eat, he often sat with his head resting on the chair table or lay in bed in a fetal position. In a cruel irony, the man who had always tried to control everyone else's life had lost all control over his own.

On the day in 1967 when my father was transferred—permanently, as it turned out—to the infirmary, I turned twenty-six. It was the time when Kenneth and I were deciding whether to respond to the inquiry made to my uncle by one of the hospital psychiatrists. Had we gone to Selkirk, I now realize, we would have found a man who was then described as "a mechanical doll whose batteries have run down": slow to respond, frequently mute, with little memory left and no awareness of time. More likely than not we would have found him in his customary position, sleeping with his head resting on the sitting-room table.

Who can say what reaction our visit would have elicited from Earle? Indifference? Interest? Anger? Regret? Would he have even known who we were? In any case, the Selkirk file suggests that his mind had by then deteriorated to the point that there could be no retrieval. As for Kenneth and me, relatively inexperienced young men who would have gone to the hospital with curiosity and apprehension, such a meeting would have been deeply disturbing.

If Ken had lived, would Earle have avoided the mental hospital? Who can say? His marriage would still have collapsed, and he would still have had to confront the uncertainties of civilian life. He might still have drunk to excess, but perhaps not in the pain-numbing, self-destructive way he did in the years following Ken's death. At least one large wound would not have needed cauterizing.

When Earle died at the age of sixty-four in the early morning of December 28, 1974, the Selkirk Hospital informed Clarence Allen, one of his remaining friends from his Winnipeg days. Someone contacted the Last Post Fund, an organization that pays for the funeral expenses of servicemen who "die in straitened circumstances, friend-less or without means of obtaining a dignified funeral." He was buried in Selkirk after a brief ceremony in the harsh cold of a Manitoba winter.

On a much more benign afternoon in August 1998, Kenneth and I drove north from Winnipeg and, in a corner of St. Clements Cemetery, found Earle's grave. Like Ken's, it was marked by the stan-dard Canadian military headstone, and on it was engraved: "Earl F. Calder, Capt. C[anadian] I[nfantry] C[orps]." His name was misspelled, but chiselled into the stone was his best self, the man he had grown into being during the war years.

It would be dishonest to say that Kenneth and I were profoundly moved at finally seeing where our father lay. This was not, after all, a once-in-a-lifetime pilgrimage to some Italian hillside or French or Belgian graveyard where a beloved father, brother or son rests among his fallen comrades. But we did feel a sense of completion, as if one last puzzle piece in our family history had been fitted into place.

I find myself now, though, thinking of that solitary grave in a cemetery of strangers, and of that little grouping of Calders hundreds of miles away in the family plot in Rosedale Cemetery,

Moose Jaw. It does not seem right that he should not be with them, one soldier lying beside another, another lost son returned home. But perhaps it is sadly appropriate. And in any case, what is to be done? The dead are dead and it cannot matter to them. It is only in the living that the rifts can be closed. And so my *Who's Who* entry now contains the name of Earle Fenwick Calder. And Kenneth has a picture of him on his study wall—not as large as Ken's, but nonetheless among the family photographs.

CHAPTER FIFTEEN

Though it has taken me a long time to recognize its enduring effects on my brother and me—and my father—I was always aware that Ken's suicide had profoundly transformed the lives of the Calder family. What I could not know, and did not learn until recently, was that his death had torn apart another family, one of the most prominent in British Columbia.

Among Boyd Story's four siblings was his sister Evelyn, born two years before him. A bright and strong-minded young woman, she won a scholarship to McGill University College in Vancouver, where she not only excelled academically but also became a leader in student politics. Through these activities she became friends with an equally strong-minded young man, Sherwood Lett, then at the beginning of what would become a brilliant career in law, the military and the public life of Vancouver.

Born in Ontario in 1895, Lett enrolled in McGill University College when his father, a Methodist minister, moved the family to Vancouver in 1912. Affable and gregarious, he was soon prominent in student politics and societies: class president, a member of the executive of the Literary and Debating Society and of the Men's Athletic Association, and president of the Alma Mater Society. As well, he was the leader of the Sunday school orchestra at his father's church.

Soon after the Great War began in 1914, McGill University College created an Officers' Training Corps, and Lett joined immediately. By taking additional courses, he earned a commission as a lieutenant in the militia, and in December 1916 he joined the regular army with the 121st Battalion ("Western Irish"), based in New Westminster. The Western Irish went overseas in August 1916, and a year later Lett got to the western front when he volunteered to be signal officer for the Forty-sixth Battalion, a unit originating in southern Saskatchewan.

When Lett joined the Forty-sixth, it was fighting just west of Vimy Ridge, and over the next year he saw action at the Ypres salient and the battle to take Passchendaele Ridge. In July 1918 he was appointed adjutant of the Forty-sixth, and several weeks later he so distinguished himself at the Battle of Amiens that he was awarded the Military Cross for "conspicuous gallantry and devotion to duty." The citation said, "He worked unceasingly and showed great ability throughout."

Lett returned to civilian life when the Forty-sixth Battalion was demobilized in Moose Jaw in June 1919. As the city acclaimed its returning heroes, he marched with the men up Main Street, up North Hill and into the Exhibition Grounds. Among the four thousand cheering, flag-waving children assembled there who saw the smartly turned out and decorated young adjutant lead the troops into the Grounds was the eight-year-old Ken Calder. Though both would serve in the next war, their paths never again crossed. In death, however, Ken would present Lett with one of the most difficult personal crises of his life.

In 1919, of course, neither man nor boy expected to be fighting another war in Europe in twenty years. Lett returned to Vancouver to begin his career in law, though his articling was interrupted when he won a Rhodes Scholarship and earned a BA from Oxford. Upon being admitted to the British Columbia bar in 1922, he joined Davis, Pugh, Davis, Hossie, and Ralston, one of the largest and most distinguished law firms in Vancouver. There his affability and diplomatic skills soon made him one of the firm's most effective corporate lawyers.

Lett's devotion to his career did not prevent him from exercising what he considered his public and private duties. In the two decades after the Great War he served on the advisory board to the Salvation

Army, was president of the Canadian Club and the Canadian Institute of International Affairs, and was a member of the Institute of Pacific Relations, the Japan Society, the board of directors of the Career Institute and the senate of UBC.

If Lett's community spirit was unusually strong, his loyalty to his family was even stronger. His father had died when Sherwood was nineteen, and in the years after the war he found himself the self-appointed guardian of five single women: his mother and four sisters, one of whom was a widow with three young children. He not only supported them financially but became the authority to whom they would turn, the kind adviser and wise consultant who kept the family bonds strong. As one niece told Lett's biographer, "Another facet of the gifts [Sherwood and Evelyn] gave to the family was arranging events when the family gathered together. They had many family parties—at holiday times, for special events, for visiting relatives, etc. so that, as children, we were acquainted with all the Lett family and the Story side of the family too."

Lett was proud of his service in the Great War and maintained a close contact with the military throughout the twenties and thirties. On his return from Oxford, he joined the Irish Fusiliers of Canada as its adjutant and was soon promoted to major. By 1929 he was second-in-command, and in 1933, as lieutenant-colonel, he was appointed to command the battalion. In May 1940, when the phony war ended and German forces began to overrun Norway, Belgium, the Netherlands and France, Lett accepted an invitation to become brigade major of the Sixth Canadian Infantry Brigade in the Second Canadian Infantry Division. In December 1941 he assumed command of the South Saskatchewan Regiment, where he won the loyalty of the prairie boys with his fair-mindedness and attention to the unit's well-being. Three months later he was made brigadier and appointed to command the Fourth Canadian Infantry Brigade.

Five months after he assumed command of the Fourth Brigade, Lett was leading it in the disastrous and bloody landing at Dieppe. In the savage barrage of artillery fire and gunfire directed at his landing craft, he was hit by shrapnel and the bone in his upper right arm was shattered. Through the pain of this wound, Lett continued to try to radio situation reports to his superiors, and for this he was awarded the Distinguished Service Order. Once back in England, it was clear that his injury would require extensive treatment, so he was sent back to Vancouver.

Lett returned to the war in February 1944, and several weeks after the D-Day assault on June 6, 1944, he was commanding the Fourth Brigade in Normandy. In July, while in a forward position assessing the battle situation, he was again wounded, though this time less seriously, by shrapnel in the leg. For his actions in this campaign he was made a Commander of the Order of the British Empire.

On his recovery from this second wound, Lett could have returned to lead the Fourth Brigade, but he felt, as he said, that he "could quite honourably afford to let some of the others take a crack at it now." Moreover, he believed that he owed it to his law partners to return and take up his share of the growing practice. Most important, he was convinced that his families—both the immediate and the extended one—had been without his guidance long enough.

Lett was out of uniform and back practising corporate law in Vancouver in July 1945. By then the Letts were aware that Boyd's marriage was in difficulty and that he was seeing a great deal of his nurse, Margaret Bruce. So far as they had been led to believe, her engagement to an artillery officer serving in Europe was over and she and Boyd would likely marry when his divorce came through. There would be some reconfiguration of relationships, but there would be no reason not to welcome the pair into the warmth and closeness of the extended family over which Sherwood and Evelyn presided.

Ken's death changed all that. When Sherwood heard that Ken had killed himself over Margaret's affair with Boyd, he told Evelyn: "I don't care whether he's your brother. That couple will never enter our house again." He had never met Ken, but he had commanded young men like him through the horrors of Dieppe and the mud and blood of Normandy. Ken was not one of his boys, but he had fought for his country and did not deserve such a betrayal. Torn between his patriarchal concern for family unity and his officer's sympathy for a returned man, his loyalty lay ultimately with the serviceman. In Mrs. Lett's words, "My husband felt very keenly—was protective of his men. He declared: 'This has happened to too many.'"

Boyd and Margaret were married a year after Ken's death, but Sherwood held firm to his edict. The Lett and Story families would gather for anniversary and birthday celebrations, and for Christmas and Thanksgiving dinners, but Margaret and Boyd were never invited. "It was," recalled Mrs. Lett, "a very serious time for our family."

This familial breach lasted seven years. Then the suicide of a member of the Story clan shocked the Letts and led Evelyn to conclude that the rift caused by Sherwood's decree had prevented them from being fully alert to the stresses being endured by members of their extended family. So, as she later recalled, "I took on the Brigadier and said: 'Our family is falling apart. This has got to stop!'" Sherwood relented, and Boyd and Margaret were welcomed back into the fold, though ironically, the couple were able to enjoy this reconciliation for only three years before Boyd died of heart failure.

Sherwood Lett himself died in 1964, but not before he enhanced his reputation as a judicious and politic man. In 1951 he was named chancellor of UBC, and three years later he went to Vietnam as leader of the Canadian contingent sitting on the international commission overseeing the truce between the North Vietnamese and the French negotiated at the Geneva conference. In 1963 he was made chief justice of the Supreme Court of British Columbia.

Evelyn Lett remained in Vancouver until her death at 102 years of age in 1999. A remarkable public figure in her own right, she continued to be an active contributor to her community, supporting the university and at the age of eighty chairing a campaign to raise funds to convert a heritage house into a centre for the elderly. She seems never to have seen herself as elderly, playing bridge once a week in her hundredth year and saying: "There are many things I'll do, but I'll never open with a club bid." At 101 she travelled to Ottawa to receive the Order of Canada.

It was this Evelyn Lett whom I met in 1997. Through Boyd Story's obituary in the *Vancouver Sun,* I had learned that he had had two sons, one of whom, David, I was able to locate in Coquitlam. With some trepidation, given the shared history of our families, I wrote to him in the fall of 1996 and explained my project. One evening several weeks later, he called, curious about how I had located him but not at all hostile to my asking questions about his father's life. In the course of our conversation he mentioned that his Aunt Evelyn, who was 100, would know more about the circumstances of Margaret's affair and Ken's death than he did—David was in the navy at the time of Ken's suicide—and he thought she would be willing to talk to me. He would speak to her about it.

Not long after this conversation I received a letter from Mrs. Lett outlining the story of Sherwood's reaction to the affair and the suicide, and in a subsequent telephone conversation she agreed to see me if I came to Vancouver. Thus, one rainy afternoon the following February, David picked up my wife and me at the Sylvia Hotel to take us to his aunt's penthouse on West Fifteenth Avenue.

In the car on the way, we got to know a little about David. Once a football player, he was athletic like his father and looked younger than his seventy years. He confessed that it still pained him to recall his parents' divorce and the breakup of the family home, which he clearly blamed on Margaret. She was, he said, "a sluttish woman" who, not content with having "caught" his father, had twice made passes at him. He had not attended their wedding, which in any case was at the registry office, and after Boyd's death he had seen little of Margaret.

Whenever David spoke of Evelyn, it was with respect and, it seemed to me, awe; and we did not have to be in her presence long to realize that she was still the vigorous matriarch of a large family—the kind of woman of whom a grandson would later say: "You didn't usually cross her. You didn't trifle with Nana." As we stepped out of the elevator directly into her comfortable suite, with its spectacular view of the Vancouver skyline and the mountains to the north, we were greeted by a diminutive but elegant woman who looked much younger than her hundred years.

As two young women—maids or cleaners—busied themselves in the kitchen, we sat down to talk in the living room. Professional curiosity made me cast my eyes over the pile of books beside Mrs. Lett's chair, and it was clear that she was *au courant* with contemporary Canadian history and literature. She was nearly finished Ondaatje's *The English Patient,* she said, and didn't I agree that parts of it were obscure? I did. More obvious than the books, though, were the pictures of her offspring—two daughters, seven grandchildren and seven great-grandchildren—arrayed on the mantel and on tables throughout the room. Most, if not all, of the figures had been cut individually out of the photographs and pasted on upright cardboard backing, so that they stood like members of a tribe around an icon.

David began the conversation with directness: "Well, you must have a lot of questions for us." Over the next few hours, Mrs. Lett and David attempted to provide answers to our queries, speaking openly about Boyd and Margaret, and of what little they knew—or had been led to believe—about Ken. Both said that Margaret had saved Boyd from severe alcoholism, but in many other ways each seemed to be remembering a different woman. David did not find her attractive, while his aunt thought she was "an all-Canadian girl": dark, with good features, brown eyes and straight teeth. Unlike David, Mrs. Lett had maintained some contact with Margaret after Boyd's death, and on Margaret's own death she arranged for her ashes to be placed beside Boyd's in the family plot in Ocean View Cemetery.

If David had repeated his claim that Margaret had tried to seduce him, the attractive teenage son of her husband, I think Mrs. Lett would have been shocked. But perhaps I am being naive. I did have the feeling that, though she was interested in my inquiries and generously prepared to collaborate, she knew more than she felt it appropriate to tell me and was playing her cards carefully. Perhaps the shrewd bridge player was finessing me with a sanitized picture of Margaret, one that made that particular part of her family's history seem less troublesome.

In any case, as our conversation wound down in the late afternoon, Mrs. Lett turned to her nephew and declared: "David, I think we should have a drink before the Calders leave." David dutifully poured the drinks and sat down, and before I knew it, Mrs. Lett had raised her glass and said: "To the Calders!" I was so flabbergasted that I was temporarily speechless. After a moment I attempted an appropriate response: "To the Storys . . . and . . . er . . . to the Letts!"

What I had witnessed was not another bridge ploy but the healing gesture of a matriarch who had grown wise over her long life. I think she sensed that a fifty-five-year-old man turning over the stones of the far distant past as I had been doing was seeking some kind of closure. Her brother had been an important element of a painful part of that past, but her gesture was not apologetic. It seemed to say: Wrongs were done in the past and pain resulted. It's all right—and perhaps necessary—to recognize that, but the past is gone and we are here. We all—two families—suffered from the human frailty that led to the events of that July in 1945.

At least that is how Mrs. Lett's toast struck me. And as we walked out of her apartment into the Vancouver rain that afternoon, I felt a kind of buoyancy. Some of the ghosts had been silenced.

CHAPTER SIXTEEN

In Holland in the summer of 1945, after John Gardiner had sent his cable and his letter to Ken to plead with him not to take his own life, there was nothing more he could do for his friend. He could only wait in his battery's camp near Utrecht—wait and wonder. Even had my grandparents then been aware of his efforts to reach Ken, they would not have known where to send a cable.

Two weeks after he opened Ken's letter, John was back at the Second LAA Battery headquarters, to check on his mail, when the sergeant said: "Say, Lieutenant Gardiner, that day you came in and were upset by one of your letters—was it from Captain Calder? I thought the handwriting looked familiar, and I should have recognized that it was the captain's." Gardiner replied that, yes, the letter had come from Ken. "Then I think I should tell you," continued the sergeant, "a couple of days ago one of the Moose Jaw boys got a letter from his aunt back home, and she told him that she had been to Captain Calder's funeral the day before."

So he really had done it, Gardiner thought. He had feared the worst, but it was still hard to comprehend that it had actually happened. Only weeks earlier they had sat having a beer in Holland, talking about getting together when they were both back on Civvy Street, and now Ken was no more. Together they had endured the cold and mud at Ortona and Rimini, they had survived the shelling, the bombing, the land mines and the machine guns from the Adriatic to the Liri Valley and back, and they had withstood jaundice, malaria and any number of other hazards. Ken had always said he was lucky, and he

233

had come through the war with barely a scratch. Together they had kept alive their dreams of picking up the pieces back in Canada, dreams that had been their shield against resignation and despair through the long months of fighting.

Now, one dream had proven to be an illusion; Ken was dead, and Gardiner could not help thinking about his own future. Ken had written so warmly of Juliette's unmistakable love of him that he wondered now whether, in those desolate last days in Vancouver, the contrast between Juliette's ardent fidelity and Margaret's cold rejection had contributed to Ken's devastation. And he told himself, too, that his friend, even in such pain, would not have burdened him with so pessimistic a vision—"9 out of 10 returned men are coming back to the same thing"—if he had not been sure of Juliette's loyalty to him.

In 1939, when war had broken out and Gardiner had returned to St-Lambert from California, where he had been a tour guide for fifty-five visiting Australians, Juliette said: "Let's go for a walk. There are some things I want to discuss." As soon as they were alone, she asked him if he intended to enlist. When he replied that he planned to join the local artillery battery, she said, "I knew you would. And we have to talk about it. I won't marry you when we don't know where you'll be going and we don't know how long you'll be away. We don't know what that kind of separation will do to us, what kind of companionship or consolation you might find yourself seeking over there. Really, we don't know whether we can remain faithful to each other in such circumstances. I can't marry you when things are like that. But I'll wait for you. The only condition is that if one of us gets involved with someone else, he or she must tell the other so that no one goes on for several years thinking that everything is fine."

If it had been up to Gardiner, he and Juliette would have been married immediately. He had known her, the daughter of a St-Lambert pharmacist, for a number of years, and he was sure of his love for her, but he knew that she was right. So he accepted her conditions. Moreover, he decided to send a substantial portion of his monthly cheque to her to put into a savings account so that on his return they would have enough money to make a down payment on a house. Government regulations prohibited soldiers assigning any of their pay to anybody not related to them—a rule designed to prevent soldiers being exploited by unscrupulous women—so Gardiner had the funds sent to his mother. On the last day of each month throughout the war, Juliette dined at his parents' home, and at the end of the evening Mrs. Gardiner would hand the cheque to her.

Ken, too, regularly sent a portion of his pay to Margaret, but the two men were looked upon as strange fellows for doing so. One day curiosity got the better of a member of the Second LAA and he asked Gardiner: "Hey, you never gamble with the boys. You don't chase the signoras. God, you only drink forty-five-cent rotgut wine. What do you do with your money?"

"I send it to my girlfriend," he replied. "A hundred and eighteen dollars every month."

"Jeez, John," said the soldier. "What if she takes off with your bundle?"

"Well," replied Gardiner, "if she's only interested in the money, she can take it right now and I'll be better off without her. She doesn't need to skin me for another two years."

The soldier left shaking his head, told the rest of the troop what he had learned, and before long Juliette was known throughout the battery as "Gardiner's $118-dollar-a-month girlfriend."

For her part, Juliette seems to have been remarkably secure and sure of herself. She was certain that she would not be unfaithful in John's absence, but, aware that circumstances might make a man wayward, she was prepared to forgo the legal guarantees of a marriage contract. At the same time, while recognizing the possibility that John might stray, she seems to have been sure of him as well. Once, during the Italian campaign, he teased her by writing about two things for which Italy was most famous: good wine and full-breasted women. "Here I am in Italy," he announced. "Forty thousand bottles on one side of me and forty thousand tits on the other. What should I do?" Many women would have been offended and disconcerted by such a remark, but Juliette merely replied by the next post: "Get drunk, you fool!"

Throughout the war Juliette had worked as a telephone operator in St-Lambert, and as she had promised, she had waited for him. Now, as the Dutch summer wore on, he was restless and anxious to get back to her. But who could know when that might be? When the Fifth LAA Battery farewell dance was held in the town of De Bilt on August 28, the program listed the significant dates in the battery's history—from mobilization in August 1940 to the end of hostilities in May—but beside "Farewell to Holland" and "Hello Canada" there were only question marks in bold type.

Though Gardiner chafed at the boredom and the waiting, the months in Holland gave him and his fellow soldiers a chance to become adjusted to peacetime, a period of decompression between the killing and Civvy Street. The army had taken them all—farm boys, university students, trappers and mechanics—and turned them into hardened soldiers, and now, without much help, they had to learn how to be civilians again. Ken had had six weeks to try to adjust his vision from the desolation of a devastated and starving Holland to the comfortable and complacent streets of Moose Jaw, and only a week longer to attempt to cope with his wife's infidelity. Gardiner had nearly five months to adapt to peacetime and prepare himself for life back in Canada.

The waiting was made more tolerable by the presence of Roger Jean-Marie, who, like Gardiner, had been transferred to the Fifth LAA Battery so that he could be returned to Montreal. Roger had spent the war in the Fifty-fourth Battery, and it was there that he achieved an unusual kind of distinction in the last month of fighting. On April 17, when the battery was making a sortie north of Apeldoorn to flush out remaining pockets of German resistance, he was doing reconnaissance ahead of his men on a motorcycle. As he approached the small village of Vaassen from the southwest, everything was quiet, and, being curious, he rode confidently into the central square. Unknown to him, the Germans were still in the far side of the village and were retreating from it into the countryside to the east.

Roger had not been in the square for more than a few minutes when villagers began emerging from houses and crowding around and cheering him and his motorcycle. Before long, the mayor of the little community came out of the village hall, looking very official and carrying a document of some sort. "You are the liberator of Vaassen," exclaimed the mayor in broken English. "You must sign this." Roger looked at the document, but it was all in Dutch and he became nervous when he could not understand a word of it. What might he be putting his name to on behalf of the Canadian First Army? Or, for that matter, the Government of Canada? But he overcame his unease and signed the paper, and this became the signal for more noisy celebration. The document, he later learned, declared that he was the man who had brought freedom to the village.

In the Fifty-fourth, Roger was teased about being "the liberator of Vaassen," but it was never a joke to the people of the village. In the decades after the war they twice invited him and his wife, Mariette, back for reunions, and some villagers travelled to see him at his home in Dixville. When he returned at the time of the momentous fiftieth anniversary celebrations in 1995, the people of Vaassen wanted to recreate their day of liberation with Roger again riding a motorcycle into the village. At the age of seventy-seven, he thought that would be unwise and so he politely declined, but he was delighted when the Dutch government issued a commemorative stamp showing him with a military motorcycle on the outskirts of Vaassen.

Roger and Gardiner had crossed the Atlantic together back in 1943, and finally, in the last week of September 1945, they left the Netherlands together when they boarded the *Nieue Amsterdam,* two of the 9,000 men crammed on a ship built to carry 1,800. They arrived in Montreal on October 1 and went their separate ways—Roger to

Dixville and Gardiner to St-Lambert. Three days later, Gardiner and Juliette were married. When her father asked Gardiner how he expected to be able to provide a home and support a wife, Gardiner pointed out that the $118-a-month cheques that he had sent Juliette every month had grown to $6,000 in the bank, more than enough to pay for a decent house.

The newlyweds had a two-week honeymoon in the eastern United States, and immediately on their return Gardiner enrolled in Hautes Études Commerciales, a school of the Université de Montréal. The dean of his college urged him to wait a year because registering so late would almost certainly mean he would do badly and thus lose the funding to which he was entitled under the Veterans Rehabilitation Act. Gardiner replied: "I don't have a year to lose. I need to start now."

Gardiner's return to the university classroom did not begin well when, on his first day in his economics course, the professor looked at him and then at his class list, and said, "Oh, yes, you're the guy who had the all-expenses-paid holiday in Italy paid for by His Majesty's Government."

"Yes, I am," Gardiner replied. "So that sonsofbitches like you would be free to say whatever you like."

On a less inflammatory occasion, he was arguing a point with a professor and, as the discussion became increasingly intense, the class began to howl with laughter. Thinking that the students were laughing at some fault in his reasoning, he became exasperated until one of them tugged at his shirt sleeve and explained: "John, we don't use that kind of language in the classroom." Like many veterans, he discovered that five years of barracks profanity was not easily jettisoned.

University enrolments had been low during the war years, but in 1946 the flood of veterans wanting to make up for lost time meant they doubled. Across the country, universities scrambled to find class-room space—often moving army huts and air force hangars onto campuses, where they frequently remained for decades. Many of the hastily recruited instructors were younger than the veterans they were teaching, and when they looked across the lectern at their classes they saw toughened men who had experienced a kind of hell they could only imagine.

In many ways, though, these students were the best the instructors would ever have. Like Gardiner, most were fiercely motivated, and if the army had taught them anything, it had taught them discipline. The younger students might drift casually from high school to university, pushed by ambitious parents or peer pressure or curiosity, but the veterans were there with a purpose. They pursued their studies with such zeal that some universities designed courses so that a year's work could be done in four months, while others allowed veterans to compact two years of study into one.

Ron MacFarlane had not gone beyond grade eleven when he enlisted in 1939, and when he was demobilized six years later he did not know what he wanted to do or what he was capable of doing. An army psychologist advised him that "if you're prepared to work, you can do anything you want to do," and a cousin suggested he study law. MacFarlane was not sure about law, but when an army counsellor told him to forget about it because he had not finished high school and would need a university degree, he was provoked. "OK," he replied. "That's what I'll do." He went back to high school, took two years in one, got into Osgoode Hall because he had achieved first-class honours in grade thirteen, and graduated with a degree in law. He went on to practise for years in Ontario and eventually became a provincial court judge.

Gardiner, because he was determined to return to university in the autumn of 1945, was ahead of the great rush of veterans, and thus he was looked on—and, indeed, saw himself at thirty years of age—as an old man. In the weeks leading up to the Christmas examinations, when study groups were forming, students found reasons to avoid working with this odd figure with the colourful language. By the finals in April, however, everybody wanted to be part of his group, and Juliette had to get used to making ham sandwiches and providing beer night after night for half a dozen intense crammers.

When he convocated at the end of the academic year, Gardiner was awarded the Governor General's Medal for being the top student. He had actually earned the second highest marks, but the faculty decided he was the most deserving of the award. He was the only veteran in the 1946 graduating class of Hautes Études Commerciales.

Gardiner had hit Canadian soil and Civvy Street at full speed, marrying and completing his degree in eight months, and now he wasted no time in getting a job. Indeed, he wrote his last examination on a Friday afternoon and on Monday morning he was a railway worker. His father's company, the Canadian National Railway, was looking for executive material, and it had learned that junior officers who had been successful in the armed services made excellent candidates. Moreover, unlike many of the young men based in Montreal, Gardiner was prepared to move anywhere the CNR placed him.

There was some urgency in Gardiner's finding a job since Juliette was pregnant; their daughter Suzanne was born the following September. In the decade that followed, she would be joined by three boys: Austin, Paul and Phillip. In the meantime, the family moved first to Winnipeg, where John was responsible for freight sales in western Canada, then back to Montreal, then to Toronto and again back to Montreal. Along the way, John became a vice-president of the CNR.

Wherever he went, Gardiner took with him the memory of Ken Calder, and wherever he went, he took his friend's last letter. On the trip back across the Atlantic on the *Nieue Amsterdam,* he had carried it in the breast pocket of his shirt, unwilling to entrust it even to his duffel bag. Back home, whether in St-Lambert, Winnipeg or Toronto, he kept it securely in a drawer in his bedroom, stashed under a pile of his shirts. Across the country, in the bedroom drawers, closet shelves and trunks of thousands of ex-servicemen, were German Lugers, Italian Berettas, bayonets and commando knives, trophies smuggled home to remind the victors of their battles. Gardiner had brought no such souvenirs with him; his relic was a letter, words entrusted to him, words he was compelled to preserve.

For a number of years the letter lay in the bedroom drawer, its presence known only to Gardiner and Juliette. Then one day, when Suzanne was ten or twelve years old, she had finished ironing her father's shirts and was putting them back in his drawer when she spotted the old envelope addressed in faded ink to his army address. Of course, as all young people will do, she read it. Though she did not fully understand the implications of it, she knew it spoke of serious issues, and so she showed it to her mother and asked if it belonged in the shirt drawer. "Oh, yes," replied Juliette. "That's the letter from your father's friend." Suzanne put the envelope back and did not mention it to her father.

Nothing was said of Ken's letter until a few years later, when Suzanne was in her early teens and beginning to date. Like many teenagers, if she went out with a boy who seemed inappropriate or came home a bit late from a movie, she had to face her father's reproaches. On one such occasion an exasperated Gardiner went into the bedroom, came back with the letter and waved it at her, saying: "You're too young to know what you're doing. You're too young to know what love really is. You don't know what it could lead to, but *I* do! Read this! You'll see that if you fall in love with the wrong person, you can ruin your life." Gardiner did not produce the letter after this episode, but from time to time he referred to Ken Calder's tragedy when he wanted to caution Suzanne about matters of the heart.

Few teenagers can have faced such heavy artillery in their inevitable coming-of-age battles with their parents, and it would not have been surprising had Suzanne developed a deep distrust of relationships. But set against the grim story of Ken's experience with Margaret was the example of her own parents' loyalty and love of each other, a contrast that Gardiner himself recognized. In the decades following the war he was often struck by how differently his and Ken's lives had turned out. Ken married before going overseas in the hope of finding security, and he returned to infidelity; Juliette refused to marry Gardiner when he enlisted, but she waited for him throughout the war. Both men regularly sent money home to build a future; Juliette faithfully put her monthly sum in the bank so that they were able to buy a house, while Margaret saved nothing that Ken sent and so his dream of having a sporting goods store turned to ashes. Ken ended up dying on the floor of a gas-filled kitchen in Vancouver, while Gardiner built a successful career and had a close and happy family life.

As the Gardiner boys grew into their teens, they too heard about the suicide of their father's army friend; as Suzanne observed recently, "we grew up with the story of Ken Calder." And, she added, "the only other army officer Dad ever spoke of with such respect was Paul Triquet, the Van Doos captain who won the Victoria Cross for his actions at Casa Berardi, outside Ortona."

As adults, though, the Gardiner children suggested to their father that he should throw "that old letter" away. Ken's suicide had happened a long time ago, and it did not matter any more. There was no longer any point in hanging on to the letter.

"I can't do that," Gardiner replied. "Don't you understand? He paid me the highest compliment anybody can be given when he wrote to me—and only me. In those years over there, he met thousands of guys, and why the hell would he pick me? Because he knew that I would *understand*! No other friend in my life has treated me that way, with such trust. Our friendship was very deep."

Perhaps no friend could match Ken's gesture of trust, preserved on several sheets of paper in an old envelope, but there still was Roger. His bond with Gardiner, born in a shouting match at Sherbrooke and nurtured during their time overseas, remained alive through Christmas greetings when they did not see each other for twenty years after the war. Then, in the late 1970s, John took early retirement when Juliette had a heart attack and he realized that she needed him to be at home more. They knew they would spend their remaining years in Quebec, but where?

Roger and Mariette lived at Dixville, from where he was able to oversee the running of his family's newspaper at Coaticook, three and a half miles away. They persuaded the Gardiners that this quiet village, nestled in scenic forests and hills, would make an excellent retirement site, and so, in 1977, John and Juliette built a house along the river there. They had been attracted to the pastoral beauty of the area, but at heart it was John's friendship for his wartime pal that drew them there. "Roger is much closer to me," he once said, "than any two brothers of mine combined."

For nearly two decades the Gardiners enjoyed their retirement in Dixville, watching their children's careers flourish. Suzanne became a teacher of English as a second language at Collège Édouard-Montpetit in Longueuil, a suburb of Montreal; Austin a gynecologist practising in Indiana; Paul an economist with Union Gas in Chatham, Ontario; and Phillip, a chartered accountant, the Country Managing Partner for Ernst & Young in Caracas, Venezuela.

Then, in a three-year span in the 1990s, John lost the two people closest to him, Juliette in 1994 and Roger in 1997. At a family dinner—Roger and Mariette having become part of the "family"—following Juliette's funeral, he spoke at length about her and their enduring relationship, and he challenged their children to do so as well. It was here that he quoted Ken's description of her as he had seen her in the Montreal railway yards that day in 1945. And to paraphrase John's own question about why Ken chose him to receive his last letter, one might ask why, out of the hundreds of people who had known Juliette well and been charmed by her over the many decades, John chose the forty-nine-year-old words of a dead friend. Did they carry some special authority for him? Was Ken some kind of measuring stick, to be applied not only to teenage relationships but to more profound commitments? Was John, at a critical point in his life, honouring a man who had honoured him so deeply in the midst of his own crisis?

Two years later, John opened his morning newspaper to read of the Somalia Inquiry and of another Ken Calder under fire. An Ottawa bureaucrat of any other name would have been only mildly interesting, if that, but this one caught his attention. The name was the same, he thought, but the odds were heavily in favour of its being no more than coincidence. Still, he had to do something. So he wrote his letter to my brother, and we all met in Ottawa on that June weekend in 1996.

∽

In the months following our meeting, we kept in touch. John would remember something he had not told us, and phone, and for an hour or more on a Sunday evening we would hear more about Ken and him. We must have listened with earnest attention and asked many questions, because he once observed to Roger that "I've always known the meaning of the word 'orphans,' but I never really understood it until I met these two men." I was surprised when John told us about this remark, never having considered Kenneth and myself parentless, but I suppose our eagerness to learn as much as we could about the uncle and the father who disappeared from our lives so early made us, even in our fifties, resemble orphans.

It was not surprising, then, that John's attitude toward us became avuncular and that we saw more of him. And a new generation of Calders began to know the Gardiners. In the autumn following our meeting in Ottawa, my brother, Kenneth, his wife, Odile, and their son, Robert, accepted John's invitation to visit him in Coaticook, where he was then living. His daughter, Suzanne, made the trip down from St-Lambert and one of her brothers, Paul, and his wife drove for thirteen hours from their home in Ontario to met this nephew of Ken Calder. The following May, Kenneth and I spent a weekend with John in Coaticook, talked ourselves into exhaustion on the first day, and dined with Roger and Mariette on the second. Roger was, as John had described him, a "little bear" of a man, and the table in the elegant French restaurant—kept open that evening specially for us—rang with familiar stories of their wartime escapades recounted again. The men's affection for each other was touching.

Only two months after that meeting, Roger died suddenly of a heart attack. He was mourned in Vaassen, where a village official wrote of its "liberator" that in this "little village of the Netherlands he will always live in our hearts and never be forgotten." John was devastated by the loss of Roger, who had become an even more important anchor in his life after Juliette's death, and in attempting to console Mariette—and himself—he reached once more into his wartime memories. Roger, he noted, had nearly died when he was torpedoed and left floating in the Mediterranean without a life jacket in July 1943. Fifty-four years later, his family and friends were in a sea of grief, said John, and needed to find their own life preservers.

John kept in touch with Kenneth and me after Roger's death, but sometime in 2001 we noticed that his telephone calls had become less frequent; then they stopped altogether. We contacted Suzanne and arranged to travel together to see her father in Coaticook in February. The little French restaurant that had been warmed by such affection five years before was now dark and lifeless, so we bought some very good wine and the fixings for what Suzanne turned into a splendid meal at John's apartment. Kenneth and I were not there long before we learned to our dismay that John's silence was the result of a decline in his short-term memory: he had difficulty recognizing us. But as the wine flowed at the dinner table and the conversation turned once more to Italy in 1944, the tales began to be told so animatedly again—stories of an eccentric major, of military absurdity, of men who survived the battles and those who perished, and of the women who waited for them and those who moved on.

At the end of the evening, Kenneth and I left the apartment feeling that a window had opened six years earlier, and that we had been extraordinarily lucky to have been then given such a vivid picture of the distant past. Before our departure the next morning, we met John and Suzanne for breakfast in a little restaurant in Coaticook, but this time the conversation was not of war and the remote past but of the more commonplace present. Then, as we were preparing to leave,

John announced that, before we hit the road, he had something to say on behalf of Suzanne and himself. Then, with absolute clarity and purpose, he said: "I'd like to thank you both for travelling so far to see me. And after all of these years, we can be happy that the horrible thing that happened to Ken, a tragedy which we have all shared, has in the end brought our two families together in friendship. Ken and I never did meet on Civvy Street, but here *we,* his friends and relatives, are." As I shook his hand outside the restaurant, I wondered what Ken would think if he knew how much of him had been kept alive by this most loyal of friends.

CHAPTER SEVENTEEN

And what of Margaret?

The sole named beneficiary in Ken's service will, made out three days before Ken left for overseas, Margaret was awarded his estate, which she reported to the Department of National Defence as consisting of $301.52 in his two bank accounts and $243.35 in their joint account in Vancouver. Of the thousands of dollars Ken had sent to be saved for a home and a business, she made no mention. As the widow of a serviceman she was entitled to a pension, but she hoped to marry Boyd Story and, knowing that this would immediately make her ineligible, did not bother applying for it.

The war service gratuity, however, was a different matter, and Margaret applied for Ken's on December 3, 1945. Though the gratuity was normally paid to the person who had been receiving the deceased soldier's dependents' allowance, entitlement to it was not automatic, and though he never knew it, Earle's letter about the matter sent up a red flag in the Department of National Defence. This led to some extraordinary discussions there about how Ken's gratuity should be disposed.

Concerned by the material revealing Margaret's infidelity, the Department of Pensions referred it to Brigadier R.J. Orde, the Judge Advocate General, the highest-ranking legal counsel in the Department of National Defence. He advised that, under certain circumstances, the minister of defence was permitted to designate the recipient of the war service gratuity. If the facts did not permit the minister to exercise his discretion, he stated, a submission to the Governor-in-Council would

be warranted in light of "the special circumstances disclosed herein"—
that is, Margaret's infidelity.

When it was determined that the Governor-in-Council did not in
fact have the authority to change the beneficiary—in this case, desig-
nating my grandmother—the Judge Advocate General recommended
an extraordinary course of action. "This," said Brigadier Orde, "would
be to have a special Act of Parliament passed to cover only this case.
This special Act would of course be put forward as a private Bill either
by the Minister of National Defence or the Minister of Veterans
Affairs." To assist the Dependents' Allowance Board, he provided two
draft bills, one that provided for payment of the gratuity to my grandmother and the other that simply denied it to Margaret.

In the end, the deputy minister of veterans affairs declined to put
the matter before Parliament, and Margaret was awarded Ken's gratuity. Before this, however, the Dependents' Allowance Board had determined that she had not been entitled to the dependents' allowance
payments she had received from October 1943 onward. It cited two
reasons: her move to Vancouver on that date indicated that she was
self-supporting and thus not in need of a financial subsidy, and her
subsequent prolonged affair with Boyd Story disqualified her on moral
grounds. "By her own admission," it said, "the officer's wife had disen-
titled herself to Dependents' Allowance." She in fact owed the
Government of Canada $1,417.07 in overpayments.

It seems astonishing now that a government agency would make
such moral judgments and contemplate the extreme step of putting
the matter before Parliament. In exercising this kind of moral discretion, however, the Dependents' Allowance Board was merely following
a common practice of the time. In a letter to the executive director of
the Montreal Council of Social Agencies in 1942, the chairman of the
Board, R.O.G. Bennett, explained that "in the main, the Board
considers a woman morally unworthy to receive an allowance who has
had a child by a man other than her husband, or who is closely associated or living with a man in her husband's absence." In one case, a

woman with four children was cut off entirely from an allowance by the Board because she was living in a "domestic relationship" with another man. It was general practice in Canadian welfare legislation, Bennett continued, "to demand fidelity on the part of the wife in receipt of public funds." Even in the mothers' allowance regulations, where in most cases the mother was a widow, the procedure was to declare her ineligible if she had "irregular relations with a man."

Based in part on these moral grounds, the Dependents' Allowance Board sought to recover the allowance paid to Margaret by deducting it from the gratuity. The wheels of bureaucracy grind slowly, however, and in July 1947 the Board learned to its dismay that the gratuity had already been paid to Margaret. There was nothing further it could do. The case was closed.

By this point Margaret had moved on. Marian's divorce from Boyd had been granted in 1946, and he and Margaret were married in a quiet ceremony at the registry office, without any relatives present and without any announcement in the newspapers. Marian remained with the boys in the family home in Point Grey, and Margaret and Boyd lived for a year in a house in the Shaughnessy area before settling into an apartment on Fir Street, just off Granville. Neither residence was more than six blocks from the building in which Ken had killed himself. Margaret might have moved on from Ken's suicide, but she did not move far from it.

My grandparents never saw Margaret again after she returned to Vancouver following the Court of Inquiry in July 1945 and their subsequent discovery of the details of Ken's last days with her. Neither she nor they wished to have anything to do with each other, but since the Department of Veterans Affairs was required in the first instance to consult a serviceman's widow, the Calders had to deal indirectly with Margaret over several matters very important to them. In June 1948 my grandmother wrote to the department to ask why no military headstone had been erected over his grave even though it was three years since his death and she had filled out the proper forms more than a year earlier. Apparently, the department had been sending letters to Margaret, who had done nothing about them. Following my grandmother's urging, the headstone was put in place.

In October 1949 an official of the Moose Jaw branch of the Canadian Legion wrote to Veterans Affairs on behalf of the Calders to request that it ask Margaret to forward Ken's war service medals to them. "As Calder's wife has remarried and does not appear to have any interest in the medals," he argued, "it is recommended that Ken's medals be forwarded to the mother." Several months later, Margaret sent the six medals—the Canadian Volunteer Service Medal, the 1939–1945 Star, the Italy Star, the France–Germany Star, the Defence Medal and the War Medal—to Moose Jaw. Along with them she sent her Memorial Cross, the medal awarded to the widows and mothers of servicemen killed during the war. My grandmother, who like Margaret had been sent hers several months after Ken's death, wore it proudly on every November 11 for the rest of her life. To this day Margaret's remains untouched in its case.

For nine years after they were married, Boyd continued his practice from his office on Alma Street and, because of the financial strain of his divorce, Margaret worked as his nurse. Boyd had been distressed by Sherwood Lett's exclusion of them from the family gatherings and was delighted when the banishment ended in 1952, but this reconciliation was to last only three years. On September 10, 1955, Boyd celebrated his fifty-seventh birthday by playing a round of golf, and in the evening he and Margaret babysat his son David's young children. After a nightcap with David and his wife, they returned to their apartment, and an hour later Boyd, his heart weakened by his childhood diphtheria, was dead of cardiac arrest. Margaret suddenly—and in her mind for the first time—was a widow.

Margaret was only forty-three when Boyd died, but she never remarried. She stayed in Vancouver for the rest of her life, but it does not seem that she was ever truly settled. She continued to work until her mid-sixties, but her nursing career never fulfilled the promise she had shown as a student at the Moose Jaw General. She had a series of jobs: at a Tuberculosis Control Centre for two years, for a trio of physicians for another two, at Woodward's department store for nine years, at Pearson Hospital for four years and finally at Blenheim Lodge for another four. It is perhaps not unusual for a nurse to change jobs so often, but during this time she also moved frequently—and, it would seem, restlessly—living in five apartments in less than a decade.

For eight years Margaret remained in the apartment she had shared with Boyd. In 1963 she moved to a house on Matthews Avenue, and the following year she rented an apartment on Twelfth Avenue, two blocks from Shaughnessy Lodge, the Tenth Avenue building in which Ken killed himself. Twelve months later she moved yet again, this time to an apartment at 1125 Tenth Avenue, just a block and a half down from Shaughnessy Lodge. She remained there for four years but in 1969 moved to 1240 Tenth Avenue, a mere three doors away from the Lodge. She lived here for nine years before moving to her final residence in a complex several miles away.

How does one account for this remarkable behaviour? Many people, when they have experienced the violent death—particularly the suicide—of a loved one, are compelled to move to another city to avoid painful reminders. Others who wish to remain in the city feel that they must at least move to another part of it, and will ever after avoid that neighbourhood where the trauma occurred. From the time of Ken's death until her final home in retirement, however, Margaret never lived more than eight blocks from the scene of his suicide, and indeed seemed to be drawn back to it.

When I asked her sister, Lillian, about the matter, she explained that these apartments were close to Margaret's work and that she liked living in that part of Vancouver. If this is true, she must have been remarkably insensitive to Ken's distress and oblivious to any responsibility she might have had for his death. For thirteen years she could not have left her apartment without seeing the building where she had endured that dreadful week trying to persuade him that their marriage was over, and to which she returned one afternoon to find him dying in her kitchen. Only someone who was thoroughly indifferent to what went on there could ever see it as just another neighbourhood building. But then Margaret seems to have been indifferent to Ken, particularly after his death. When the town where she grew up, Tuxford, Saskatchewan, produced a local history book in 1981 and each family in the community was invited to provide its history, a paragraph describing her education and nursing career concluded simply: "Margaret married Dr. Boyd Story and lives in Vancouver." Ken Calder, it would seem, had never been part of her life. And he would not be remembered in her obituary in 1987.

But perhaps indifference is too simple an explanation for Margaret's return to the shadows of Shaughnessy Lodge. Perhaps she was driven by its opposite: compulsion. When she moved back onto Tenth Avenue, Boyd had been dead for ten years and Ken for twenty. Could it be that memory had by then contracted time, shrinking the years between their deaths, and that from this new perspective she was now conducting her own court of inquiry into the events of that week in 1945? Had memory and time—and experience—fashioned for her a new and perhaps more complicated scenario of what actually occurred then?

If this were a novel by Dostoevsky or Conrad, Margaret would have been drawn, inevitably and inexorably, back to the scene of . . . of what, exactly? Crime? Trauma? Tragedy? Haunted by guilt, she would have been compelled to find atonement in some ritual such as the daily witnessing of the site of the suffering. Or she would have been moved by defiance, by the determination to prove her guiltlessness by regularly and repeatedly walking by Shaughnessy Lodge, each outing a little trial by fire.

But this is not a novel. If it were, we would know a great deal more about Margaret. Instead, she flits through these pages like a ghost, leaving a trail but not often being clearly seen, of all the central figures in this story the one whom I understand the least. If I have been able to discover the richer dust concealed in memory about Ken, Earle,

John Gardiner, Roger Jean-Marie, Boyd Story, Sherwood Lett and the others, I have failed with Margaret. But this failure has not been for lack of trying.

On her death on July 3, 1987, Margaret was survived by two siblings: a brother, Lloyd, in Montreal and her sister, Lillian, in Moose Jaw. In the earliest stage of my research, in the late summer of 1996, I wrote a short letter to each to let them know I was writing a book about Ken and that I would like to talk to them about his marriage to Margaret. I was particularly interested, I said, in what they might be able to tell me about why they married so suddenly in 1939 and what Margaret's life had been like after Ken's death. I also placed a request for information in the Moose Jaw *Times-Herald* and was interviewed about the project on the CBC radio station heard throughout Saskatchewan. Nevertheless, I received no reply from Lloyd or Lillian.

For the next year I went about gathering information from various sources: John Gardiner, Evelyn Lett and David Story, Ronald MacFarlane, Ken's cousins Jack Fenwick, Phyllis Burton and George Fenwick, Lena Vail, the National Archives and other institutional records. Then, in August 1997, I wrote again to Lillian, but this time a much longer letter detailing the many questions that had arisen from my conversations with those who knew Margaret. Why, I asked again, did she marry Ken so suddenly before he left for Britain? Did she really come to consider that her marriage to him was not truly a marriage? Did she, as she told Ken at the end, have several affairs before meeting Story? Had her family been affected in some way by Ken's death, as the Gardiner and Lett/Story families had been? Why had Margaret returned to live so close to the place where he had killed himself?

For six weeks nothing happened. Then one evening in late September the telephone rang and it was Lillian: she had received my letter and wanted to talk about it. She would be passing through Saskatoon on the Friday afternoon before Thanksgiving weekend and she could come to my house. With her would be her husband, Melvin, and her daughter, Peggy, and her husband, Dr. Art Quinney, who lived in Edmonton. Quickly guessing that Holly would be working that afternoon, I said I would be alone.

A year earlier, as I had begun to learn about Margaret's family, the name Peggy McGillivray stuck out as if I should know it. Then I remembered that, when Kenneth and I were doing our undergraduate degrees at the University of Saskatchewan, Peggy McGillivray was one of our fellow students: bright, attractive and energetically involved in a multitude of student activities. She very likely sat in some of the same classes we did, and our paths must have crossed. At the time neither Kenneth nor I were aware that the three of us were in any way connected, however distantly, by the uncle who bore his name and the aunt who gave Peggy hers. I suspect that she did not know about it either, and looking back, I could not help wondering what would have happened if, like characters in a Thomas Hardy or Emily Brontë novel, they had begun dating, a second-generation Ken and Margaret unaware of the tragedy of the first.

Hoping to break the ice—or at least put a bit of a crack in it—at the end of my telephone conversation with Lillian, I mentioned that Peggy had been a student at the university at the same time as my brother and me. As a conversational gambit, however, this comment fell flat. It was clear that Lillian was not into small talk—at least with me—and the tone seemed to be set for our meeting.

As the day approached, it turned out that Holly was not needed at work, so I asked her to sit in on the meeting. In my interviews with Evelyn Lett, David Story and others, she had proven to have a good eye for detail and an ability to ask shrewd questions that I might have overlooked. I came to appreciate being able to balance my responses with a sensible second opinion, especially one formed from a female perspective. And realistically, since I did not think it judicious to ask Lillian if I could tape the conversation, I wanted to have someone else in the room to confirm for me what was said.

When we greeted our visitors at the door, Lillian seemed surprised to see Holly and commented, "I thought you said she wouldn't be here." Holly went about making tea and putting out some cookies and biscuits, while the rest of us sat down in the living room and began to talk. Attractive, well dressed and, despite her grey hair, looking younger than her eighty or so years, Lillian sat on the sofa straight-backed, with a certain dignity and a touch of formality.

It soon became clear that Lillian did not want to be there, that she had come only because she had been advised that she should talk to me or was driven to it by the assertions in my letter. It was obvious that she was burning with cold anger. She had received my first letter, she said, and, alerted by a friend, had heard me on the CBC, but she assumed I was writing a book only about Ken and so she did not bother to reply. After reading my second letter, though, she wanted to know "why you are digging up all this dirt and why you are assuming all these things." Everything about Margaret I had suggested in my letter was wrong. Who could have told me those things?

I explained that some of them had come from interviews with people who had known Margaret and Ken, some had come from Ken's last letter to Gardiner and Jack Eccleston's to my grandparents, and some from Ken's personnel file. Each presented one version of the past, I said, and if she had a different interpretation of events, I would very much like to hear it.

Truth—or something like the truth—does not reside in one memory or one testimony but in the aggregation of many memories and many testimonies, and I was eager to be told an alternate version of Margaret, one that would balance the largely negative one that had emerged for me. How might things have looked to a woman who hastily married a soldier about to leave for overseas; who lived apart from him, in an entirely different world, for five and a half years; who fell in love with another man; who married this man after her husband's suicide and lost him a decade later, and who lived out the rest of her life alone?

But as the conversation unfolded that afternoon, it became clear that I was not going to get that alternate reading of Margaret. Instead,

Lillian declared that everything I had written was wrong. Ken and Margaret were married in Moose Jaw, not Regina, as I had claimed, and the nine-month delay in announcing the wedding was not the result of any need to keep the marriage a secret. Ken killed himself, not because of Margaret's infidelity, but because he came home to learn that the only job he could have was as a driver for the Co-op Creamery. Boyd had not been an alcoholic, and the estrangement with the Letts had not resulted from Ken's suicide but from Boyd being the first member of that family to be divorced. Earle, rather than being angry with Margaret, was very supportive of her in the months following Ken's death.

During the conversation Lillian's husband said very little, but both Peggy and Art, more relaxed than the rest of us, amiably tried to defuse the tension and offer what they knew. Peggy had not known of Ken's existence until sometime in her teens, but she remembered that Margaret was fastidious, someone who liked her surroundings to be arranged and orderly—"the only woman I knew who would wear an apron over an apron," said Art. They had once taken her camping, which she found too disordered an experience to enjoy, and Peggy regularly visited her in Vancouver. There was, they said, nothing particularly unusual about her.

Having essentially listened for an hour or so, I began to ask some of the harder questions. Did Lillian know why Margaret married Ken so suddenly? No, she replied, she did not. What was Margaret's life like in the decades after Ken's death? Margaret and Boyd were very happy, replied Lillian; in fact, Margaret was "a happy person" for the rest of her life. Had Margaret ever talked about Ken in those years? Yes, she had, but she could not remember what she had said. Did Ken's death have an effect on her family, as it had altered the family life of the Letts, the Gardiners and the Calders? No, said Lillian, the Bruce family had not been affected in any way. Of course, she added, any suicide is unfortunate, but the Bruces never really considered Ken and Margaret to be married. They had only eight days together after the wedding, and we needed to remember that on some of these days one or both of them would have been working.

By this point I had grown frustrated at the little I was learning and angry at the apparently nonchalant attitude toward Ken's suicide. Lillian might be distressed by my "digging up all this dirt" about her deceased sister, but damn it, my grandparents had spent the final years of their lives grieving for a lost son. I was not expecting an apology for Margaret's role in his death, but some sort of acknowledgement of her part in what had been such a grievous event would have provided a modest form of closure. Now I just wanted the interview over with, but we were in my home and I could hardly ask Lillian and her family to leave. So I gave up asking questions, went silent and let Holly carry on the conversation.

It was at this point that Lillian said something that shed some light on the matter. "You know," she said, "after Ken died, your grand-mother spread stories about Margaret around Moose Jaw." And I understood then, I think, why Lillian so resented my probing into the past and why she could never co-operate with my research. My grand-mother was a strong-willed woman who did not wear her emotions on her sleeve, and even in her grief she is unlikely to have told anyone but her closest friends about the circumstances of Ken's death. Her sister Macy, on the other hand, had a sharp and outspoken tongue, and she loved to gossip. Moose Jaw was a small enough city in those post-war years that some version of her comments may well have found its way to the Bruce family. Moreover, the city's middle-class community was cohesive enough that the paths of two families like the Calders and the Bruces would inevitably have crossed from time to time—some even attended the same church—and those encounters must have been awkward. Two provinces away in Vancouver, Margaret was spared any discomfort, but the rest of the Bruce family, including the younger sister who spent the rest of her life in Moose Jaw, were not. Indeed, before he died, Ken's cousin Jack Fenwick told me that he always felt a strain whenever he came into contact with a member of Margaret's family—even though he did not return from overseas until after Ken's death.

Death and the passage of time, of course, had washed away most of that tension, and the rest had been buried in memory and in archives as the younger generation—that of Kenneth and myself, and of Peggy and her sister—got on with our lives and careers. What I was seeing in Lillian was the last survivor of whatever form of discomfort had come out of the breach created between two families, and now I was digging up those memories buried so long ago. Ken and his tragedy had come alive for me as I uncovered more and more of the past, and I wanted Margaret to come alive in the same way. In the end, I guess, it was less painful for me to breathe life back into a distressing story than it was for Lillian to go back in memory and revisit it.

And, so, what of Margaret?

Can one blame her for not being in Moose Jaw, waiting for Ken's return and the resumption of the marriage to a man she had not seen for five and a half years? Many women did wait years for their men, but, as novelist Joan Barfoot explains, the odds against love surviving such an extended separation were high:

> Imagine this: two people . . . are apart for four dangerous years. They don't know at the moment of separation that that's how long it will be before they see each other again. But for four years they will live on different continents. Their daily jobs, circles of friends, conversations, comforts, deprivations, ambitions, disappointments—all their individual circumstances— will be utterly different. For four years they cannot embrace, or even hear each other's voices. How does love survive this?

Of course, for thousands of couples during the Second World War, love did not survive. "Dear John" or "Dear Jane" letters were common as months stretched into years, and many marriages fell apart shortly after servicemen returned to their wives and to civilian life. Even when marriages survived the lengthy separations, the intimacy was often lost and never recaptured. Couples were reunited, had children and got on with their lives in the post-war boom, but without the emotional closeness and understanding they had enjoyed before the war.

The experience of Fred and Norah Egener, about whom Barfoot was writing, was very different. Fred went overseas with the Canadian Army in June 1941 and did not return until the summer of 1945. Then, said Norah later, "when we were reunited physically and spiritually, it was as if our time apart had never existed. It was as if I'd seen him yesterday . . . Our marriage not only survived the four-year separation, it was eternally enriched." Why did the Egeners' relationship endure—and even become enriched—when that of so many other men and women dissolved? In part the answer lies in their marriage being solidly grounded when Fred left: they had known each other for nearly a decade, had been married for five years, had a two-year-old son and were expecting another child. But a selection of their wartime correspondence, edited by Barfoot and published as *A Time Apart: Letters of Love and War,* reveals that it was really their letters, the only form of communication left to wartime couples, that kept their familiarity, understanding and commitment alive.

Over four years the Egeners wrote hundreds of letters, many of them ten to twenty pages long, as if, said Norah, "we were writing a daily journal expressing our most intimate thoughts, aspirations, fears, anger, joy and love." She wrote of the daily events of the household, of the doings of the children—their growth and development, especially of the daughter Fred had never seen—of their friends and relatives, and of the life of her community. Fred described, in as much detail as censorship allowed, his life in England, Italy and Holland, attempting, as Barfoot says, to let his wife see his experiences through his eyes. In this way they were able vicariously to experience something of what the other was doing and thinking, and to sense the subtle changes in his or her attitude and outlook. And in a testament to the power of language, of the written word, they came together again in 1945 as if they had seen each other the day before.

The written word was not able to preserve whatever love Ken and Margaret swore to each other on their wedding day in 1939, perhaps because there was never enough to build on. Though, like the Egeners, they had known each other for a decade or so, their relationship deepened only two months before their marriage, and they had only five days and nights together before enduring an even longer separation than the Egeners'. They had not set up a household, had children or built up a bank of shared experiences on which they could draw as a meeting point in their correspondence. Not grounded in such a reserve of common memory, their letters must increasingly have described a world and daily life unfamiliar to each other.

Then too, not everyone is a comfortable and accomplished correspondent. Fred and Norah had been university students and learned to express themselves in a descriptive and nuanced language, but neither Ken, the creamery foreman, nor Margaret, the nurse, were accustomed to writing lengthy and evocative letters. Despite not having gone beyond grade ten, Ken became a capable correspondent during the war, but of course writing to one's parents and other relatives is much different from writing to one's spouse; Ken's natural reticence and emotional self-containment meant that his letters to Margaret may not have been as expressive as she would have liked. We will never know what that correspondence was like, but if his dedication to writing to his parents and relatives is any indication, he at least wrote faithfully to Margaret throughout the war. Her letters to him no longer exist, but we do know that she ceased to write Ken often or warmly.

Given these circumstances, it is hardly surprising that Ken and Margaret's relationship did not survive their separation or that she fell in love with someone else. Her affair with a man in Moose Jaw in the early years of the war, which she revealed to Ken in those last days in Vancouver, is hardly defensible. But as Ken's absence stretched to four and then five years, a large piece of the average person's lifetime, it is understandable that she would be unable to remain faithful to him.

What is much less forgivable is the manner in which she dealt with her estrangement from Ken. If she knew, a year or so after he left, that their marriage had been a mistake, she should have written him about it while he was still in Britain, and not yet on the battlefield, where such letters often made servicemen reckless and suicidal. She was, after all, thirty years of age, a mature woman, a senior operating-room nurse accustomed to making hard decisions and dealing with people in difficult circumstances. Instead, she seems to have ignored the problem, perhaps hoping that the war would eventually solve it for her.

But Ken, as he was fond of saying, seemed to be born under a lucky star, and the war ended without resolving Margaret's dilemma: Ken was returning and he wanted her to meet him in Moose Jaw. Had she gone there, familiar ground for him, where he had family and friends to sustain him, she could have confronted him with the painful truth that she wanted out of their marriage. As distressing as this would have been, he is unlikely to have killed himself in that milieu.

Instead, Margaret made Ken come to her, to a city in which he was a stranger, and to an apartment she had undoubtedly been sharing with her lover. For three days she remained cold and distant, and then, when she had finally gathered her nerve to tell him that she had been unfaithful and was leaving him, she had *her* support, Boyd Story, close at hand. Ken must have felt that he was in alien territory and, when talking to the two of them, that he was the problem, the enemy, they needed to eliminate. For five and a half years he had survived the best efforts of known enemies, those wearing German uniforms; he had not expected to face enemies back in Canada, and when he found them in his own home, he could fight no longer.

EPILOGUE

Few experiences can be more moving than walking through a battle-field cemetery—Vimy, say, or Passchendaele, Ypres, Dieppe, Hong Kong, Ortona or any of the hundreds of others scattered throughout the arenas of war. At Cassino, on the edge of the Liri Valley, one has a choice of burial grounds. High up on the slope of Monte Cassino, near the monastery, is the Polish cemetery and the graves of 1,100 men who, as the inscription on the memorial says, gave their bodies to the soil of Italy and their hearts to Poland. Seven miles away, on a hillside, a statue of grieving parents sits at the entrance to the German ceme-tery, where nearly 20,025 *soldaten,* brought there from all over south-ern Italy, are buried three deep. In the Commonwealth War Cemetery on the outskirts of Cassino, the second-largest World War II graveyard in Italy, are interred 4,265 British, Indian, New Zealand and Canadian soldiers.

Not many visitors to a battlefield cemetery are prepared for their first look at the row upon row of grave markers, and the response is almost always the nearly visceral one perfectly described by Canadian infantry-man Stan Scislowski: "A sigh, almost a sob escapes me, and I find it hard to hold back the tears." Most linger much longer than they had intended, caught by the poignancy of so many dead and most of them so young: here a nineteen-year-old infantryman from Trenton, there an eighteen-year-old gunner from Penticton, and between them a twenty-year-old medical orderly from Winnipeg. And once in a while one of the "old men," killed in his tank or his trench at the age of twenty-eight. Then, perhaps most touching of all, are the headstones that say simply "A Soldier of the Second World War: A Canadian Regiment."

Visitors feel a compulsion to read all the inscriptions; one cannot help thinking that each of the fallen deserves this tribute, and it is dismaying to realize that many of them have lain there unseen by their families and loved ones, for whom a pilgrimage of several thousands of miles has been financially impossible or emotionally daunting. But visitors can pause before only so many headstones before they have to leave. There is a limit to how much they can take in, and the sheer numbers begin to blunt their perception: amid the legions of dead buried in an Italian field, it is easy to lose sight of the individual man lying beneath the markers. Easy, that is, until, on a headstone in the Canadian cemetery outside Ortona, one is arrested by the words of a mother—or perhaps a father or a wife—that say "To the world he was only one / But to me he was the world."

The men are buried in such numbers in these cemeteries because, following a practice established in the First World War, fallen British Commonwealth soldiers were interred in the war zone in which they died. It was both difficult and impractical to ship so many bodies back to Canada, but the War Graves Commission also believed that they should lie among the comrades with whom they had formed very strong bonds. Many of the men had lived apart from their country, their community and their family for years; and so it is perhaps appropriate that they rest with those with whom they fought. Thus, walking through these cemeteries today, one sees their youth, senses their comradeship, and mourns the loss of the lives they could have had and what they could have become. It is harder to remember that these men, now never to be demobilized, were not always soldiers, that before they donned a uniform they were somebody else, each one someone's world. And that when they died, someone else's world changed forever.

In many ways, the deaths of those young men lying in the cemeteries become more grievous when one knows the worlds from which they came, and there is no more striking way to situate them than to examine the wartime newspapers of any Canadian town or city. In the early years the news is of recruitment, conditions in Britain, training schemes and soldiers' boredom. Beginning in late July 1943, following the invasion of Sicily, one begins to notice a grim change to the page devoted to local, community news: across the top, photographs start to appear—in the beginning two perhaps, then three, and then possibly a half-dozen, portraits of servicemen from the surrounding area who have been killed in action. And this is what one sees in each day's issue for almost the next two years. In another time these young men's photographs would have celebrated the winning of a football championship, a scholarship or an award; here, they mark the end of such possibilities.

Each of these young men was somebody's son, brother, father, uncle, husband, fiancé, lover or best friend. Among them were somebody's favourite student, the best hope for another hockey title or possibly a town's first university graduate. Some had been destined to take over the farm, join their father in the family business, or carve out a career envisaged in the sweat and sacrifice of their parents. Some would simply have gone back to the construction crew, the warehouse or the fishing fleet; and in time they would have married, built a home, had children and grown old. Each of these young men, had they come back safe and whole, would have changed the shape of their family and the life of their community, not just in the post-war years but for several generations.

If, on the day before John Gardiner's letter arrived in Ottawa, someone had asked me how my uncle's death had affected three generations of my family, I would have had a simple reply. I would have said that, at the best of times, the sudden and unforeseen removal of one member of a family changes its shape and dynamics forever. When that family is fragmenting, as the Calders were at the end of the war, that removal has an even more devastating effect. Had Ken not killed himself, had he returned to Moose Jaw—or gone elsewhere—and started anew, he would surely have been a bridge between his brother and the parents from whom he was estranged. Given the deeply embedded strains in Earle's relationship with his mother, whose convictions governed the Calder home, Ken might never have effected much of a reconciliation, but he would undoubtedly have been a mediator and a line of communication.

I would have said, too, that in whatever way Ken might have rebuilt his life, it is inconceivable that he would not have taken an interest in his two young nephews and become a sort of surrogate father. When I think of the men I saw at the last reunion of his old unit, the Second LAA, in Yorkton, I wonder what he would be like had he too been one of this band of survivors—now old and infirm, but intensely proud—and what he would have been like had Kenneth and I known him through the years of our childhood and adulthood. Who can say what that handsome young man in the military uniform would have become over a long life, and what he would have meant to us?

What is certain is that Ken would have become our link to our father. It is hard to believe that he would not have reported on our doings to Earle, perhaps even forcing his accounts on a reluctant listener, and he might have arranged some meetings. Whether this would have been a good thing for us is certainly debatable, but, indisputably, our lives would have taken a different course.

It is now seven years since John Gardiner's unexpected appearance shone a new light into hidden corners of Calder family history, and I have come to realize that my answer would have been too simple. Sifting through old documents and probing fading memories, and the re-examination of my life and that of my brother that this process demanded, has made me recognize that the effects of Ken's suicide were far more complex and subtle than I had imagined.

First, if Ken had lived, it is unlikely that my father would have spent his final years in a mental hospital. In the first months following the war, Earle was facing several acute dislocations: his marriage was collapsing; he was, after five years of accomplishment in the army, having to confront once again the uncertainties of civilian life and of his own abilities; and he was becoming an exile from his own community. More vulnerable than he had ever been in his life, he needed the supportive bond the Calder boys once shared.

What Earle got instead was Ken's suicide, and as his hospital files make plain, his brother's despairing act triggered in him a more prolonged, but ultimately no less complete, self-destruction. He had begun to drink heavily during the war years, but nothing like the pain-numbing, memory-obliterating way that he did following Ken's death. He had always, as his cousin said, "been handy with his fists," but the speed with which he became a street brawler in Winnipeg suggests a man not only angry with life but inviting it to strike him down. That Ken would kill himself without seeking his brother's help seemed to leave a wound in Earle that could be cauterized by only the most extreme assaults on his being.

It is likely, too, that Ken's death was partly responsible for the severe and irreparable breach that developed between Earle and his parents eight months later, when Mother filed for divorce. The Calders were churchgoing people for whom infidelity would have been morally repugnant at any time; in the intensity of their grief over one son killing himself because of his wife's adultery, they must have been especially unwilling to forgive the faithlessness of the other one. Thus, even in an age when adultery and divorce were, like suicide, causes of public humiliation, the Calders sided with their daughter-in-law rather than with their own son, supporting her throughout the divorce proceedings.

In the months following Ken's death and Earle's departure, the relationship between the Calders and Mother deepened, and for the rest of their lives they treated her as a daughter, perhaps the daughter they had once hoped to have and had lost in infancy. When Kenneth and I were growing up, we, like most children, thought that the pattern of our family life was normal and that such a close connection between Mother and our paternal grandparents was commonplace. I recognize now that an attachment of such depth was, if not unique, certainly unusual. Even in the present age of much easier and more frequent divorces, when couples often part merely because their interests and outlooks diverge, it is not unusual for parents to become distanced or completely estranged from their former son-in-law or daughter-in-law. In 1946, when most divorces entailed more severe ruptures, it would not have been surprising if the ties between Mother and Earle's parents had become strained and broken.

Of course, we were all that was left of the family that Ida and Lorin Calder had begun with such promise in 1907; and of the four younger people they had around them in Moose Jaw in the fall of 1939—Ken, Earle, Margaret and Mother—only Mother remained. And they came to recognize that, though her education had been limited and she had not won any medals, she was steady, courageous, determined and loyal. It was obvious to them that she would raise their grandsons according to the values by which they lived—hard work, responsibility and thrift—and by which they had tried, with mixed success, to raise their own sons. There must have been times, in those years when Kenneth and I were sent to visit them in Moose Jaw, that they looked in on us, settled for the night in the same bed in the same room that had been Earle's and Ken's, and were struck by a sense of life repeating itself. And perhaps a sense that life would be better for us, their shattered hopes for their sons realized in us. This may be what lay behind a remark, still vivid in our memories, that Grandma Calder made sometime during the Korean War. "I hope," she said firmly, one hot August afternoon as we walked down Alder Avenue, "that you boys never have to go and fight in a war."

Mother could not have failed to see that we were filling a great void in our grandparents' lives, but it would still have been easy for us to have become detached from them. Had she remarried when we were still young boys, there is a good chance we would have become assimilated into our stepfather's family and perhaps now even bear a different name. Moving to Saskatoon, when I was seven and Kenneth was four, and living across the lane from our affluent cousins, the Scharfs, might well have weakened the links to Moose Jaw and eroded our Calder identity. But Mother worked very hard to prevent that from happening.

Mother had grown up with a deep respect for the past and especially for family history. She was proud of her own family's roots in Queenston Heights, the Talbot Settlement, and the forests and lakes of Ontario's Muskoka country; and she knew that, living with her, we boys would be bound to absorb the Remey lore. But it was much less certain that we would grow up with as strong an identification with the Calders. Our grandparents were approaching seventy years of age, and in the absence of Ken and Earle there would soon be no Calders left to enrich, invigorate and re-create the connection by their living presence.

And so, until their deaths in the mid-1950s, Mother made sure that our grandparents were very much part of our lives. On the morning of my first day of school in Moose Jaw in 1947, I was driven across town so that Ida and Lorin could witness their grandson, decked out in new clothes and clutching a fresh, crisp scribbler, taking the first of his many steps toward adulthood. In August of the next year they were allowed to take me on an extended motor trip to visit Grandpa Calder's American relatives spread out in the northwestern United States, and memories of family gatherings still linger—a picnic with Ken and Earle's cousin Grace in Fargo, and a corn roast on a farm in Iowa. Then there were those half-dozen years when, as soon as school was out, I was put on the bus to Moose Jaw to spend the summer rediscovering Alder Avenue, my friend George McCarthy, my comic book collection and the artifacts of my grandparents' home. Kenneth was considered too young for more than shorter stays, but he got there often, and we shared the bedroom that had become ours. On dark nights, when the lights were switched off, we would look apprehensively toward the attic door, which opened into the room, and pull the blankets over our heads to shield us from whatever spectres lay in the dark beyond. We were, of course, too young to know that, if there were ghosts in the house, they were benign though troubled spirits, and that no blanket could keep them from becoming part of us.

The visits to Alder Avenue ceased with Grandma Calder's death in the spring of 1956. The house was put up for sale and, with a friend's help, Mother disposed of the contents. To our lasting regret, the letters that Ken had written to his parents throughout the war disappeared, but Mother kept anything recognizably part of the Calder family history. Thus, an old trunk in our basement in Saskatoon was filled with letters, photographs, war souvenirs, shooting medals and military decorations, and such ornaments as the little nickel-plated artillery-piece lighter and the Windsor Castle oak wall plaques that we knew so well in our grandparents' home. Indeed, Mother seems to have saved everything associated with Ken, but stored in the trunk too were numerous pictures of Earle, some that she had not discarded after their divorce and some that she had found in a box at Alder Avenue. Unwilling to have his likeness on a wall in our home, she must have known that the time would inevitably come when his sons would want—or need—or be ready—to open that trunk and examine the past.

A few years after Grandma Calder's death, when Kenneth was in his early teens, he took a step toward opening that trunk. Looking through a living-room cabinet one afternoon when Mother was at work, he came across a leatherette case under some photo albums, untied it, and found the letters related to Ken's suicide from Captain Eccleston and John Gardiner to Grandma Calder. And just as Suzanne Gardiner would be compelled to read Ken's last letter when she came across it in her father's shirt drawer several years later, Kenneth had to see what lay in these pages. Since we had not yet been told the circumstances of Ken's death, he could make only a youthful guess at what the letters meant, but he knew that these scraps of paper were fragments of a larger narrative of profound importance to us.

Perhaps a historian was born that afternoon. Kenneth came to realize that it was not only these letters that documented a past—our past—but all the relics that Mother had preserved from the Calder home. Each carried a meaning that might be deciphered, some surrendering their significance easily and others remaining enigmas, the import of which one could only guess at. Kenneth became determined that such relics, all that we had left of the Calders—especially of our uncle and our father—must be preserved. And in hanging that picture of Uncle Ken on his bedroom wall, he began the process of constructing a Calder family history, of putting a face where there had been a void—or at least a mystery.

In the years that followed, Kenneth became the family historian, guarding the papers and artifacts; and he began a long process of searching for our origins. Even as a high school student he knew he wanted to be a historian, to move beyond learning about our particular circumstances to uncover aspects of the larger public past and make meaning out of them. And so the boy who wanted to know more about those two men shrouded in mystery became the man who would write about the foreign policy of imperial Germany and about the aspirations of central European nationalities during the First World War. Despite devoting his career to policy at the Department of National Defence, he has essentially always been a historian, devoting much of his spare time to reading history voraciously and compiling a massive family history. In his coming retirement he will haunt public record offices and other archives from New Hampshire to Ontario to Scotland, poring over old documents and papers so that he can better understand the people and the historical forces that brought us to where and who we are today. And in that rich past, what most attracts him is the Calders.

And what of me? I have devoted a career to teaching and writing about English literature, but my interest there has always been in literary history rather than literary criticism. Indeed, I have often thought that I should have followed my undergraduate instincts and pursued history rather than literature. Few things in my professional life have given me as much pleasure as sitting in a special collections room of a library in London, New Haven or Austin, and sifting through a writer's letters, government memoranda or old photographs in order to reconstruct what might have been the life and personality behind the books we read.

Struck by our eagerness to know all he could tell us about Ken, John Gardiner called us "orphans," and in a way he was right. Even in our mid-fifties we were still looking for the uncle and the father who had disappeared from our lives so many years earlier; and to find them—to feel that we were truly Calders—we had to become historians. In the end, perhaps the orphan and the historian are driven by the same urge: to uncover and make meaningful the past preserved in documents, files, reports or memoranda, and in the ephemeral, elusive memories of the surviving witnesses to that past; or in the letters, diaries, souvenirs and photographs—preserved in dusty attics, in old trunks or under shirts in dresser drawers—in which those who have long ago left us still live.